THE BUREAU OF
THE BUDGET

PERCIVAL FLACK BRUNDAGE

Foreword by Robert P. Mayo

The budget of the United States affects the lives of Americans and other nationals all over the world. The job of juggling it belongs to the Bureau of the Budget (BOB), a relatively small and, in the view of the author, seriously understaffed federal agency, created in 1921 as part of the Executive Office of the President. Not only does the BOB work on three budgets—last year's, this year's, and next year's—at the same time, it also supervises and evaluates the management of the multitudinous programs, both civilian and military, on which the nation annually spends many billions of dollars.

How is it all accomplished? In this book, former Budget Director Brundage gives a clear account of the complex operations of the Bureau. He explains the budgetary process, using actual figures and cases to demonstrate the changes a national budget undergoes from its original formulation in the separate agencies and departments, through the offices and divisions of the Bureau, to the White House, and then into and out of Congress. He gives the reader a new understanding of the many difficult considerations that must go into balancing revenues against needs, weighing priorities, and analyzing the comparative values of alternative programs. In the course of discussing the defense, natural-resources, agriculture, health, education, welfare, housing, commerce, transportation, space, and interna-

tional-affairs budgets, the author gives a broad picture of the whole U.S. Government at work. (In his Preface, Mr. Brundage asserts that "you can learn more about the government of the United States by working in the Bureau of the Budget for six months than by spending six years in almost any other branch.")

The chapter on management function describes the supervisory control that the Bureau is charged with maintaining over all government programs and explains how the planning-programing-budgeting system is used as a tool in this activity. The Bureau's relationships with Congress, with state and local governments, and with the public are the subject of another interesting chapter. In conclusion, the author analyzes budget figures, trends, and opportunities for the future and recommends courses of action he believes should be followed in the years immediately ahead.

THE AUTHOR: Percival Flack Brundage spent forty years as a certified public accountant before he was asked by President Dwight D. Eisenhower to join the Bureau of the Budget. He served in the Bureau for four years, two of them as Director (1956–58). A former senior partner of Price, Waterhouse and Company, he continues to be active in a number of organizations, including the National Bureau of Economic Research, the Atlantic Council of the United States, the International Movement for Atlantic Union, and Project HOPE.

The design used on the front of the jacket is adapted from the seal of the Executive Office of the President, of which the Bureau of the Budget is a part.

PRAEGER PUBLISHERS
New York • Washington • London

THE BUREAU

OF THE BUDGET

BUDGET

Percival Flack Brundage

E PLURIBUS UNUM

Praeger Library of U.S. Government
Departments and Agencies

PRAEGER LIBRARY OF U.S. GOVERNMENT
DEPARTMENTS AND AGENCIES

The Bureau of
the Budget

PRAEGER LIBRARY OF U.S. GOVERNMENT DEPARTMENTS AND AGENCIES

Consulting Editors

ERNEST S. GRIFFITH

Former University Professor and Dean Emeritus, School of International Service, American University; former Director, Legislative Reference Service, Library of Congress; and author of *The American System of Government* and *The Modern Government in Action*

HUGH LANGDON ELSBREE

Former Chairman, Department of Political Science, Dartmouth College; former Managing Editor, *American Political Science Review*; former Director, Legislative Reference Service, Library of Congress

The Bureau of the Budget

Percival Flack Brundage

FOREWORD BY
ROBERT P. MAYO

PRAEGER PUBLISHERS
New York · Washington · London

PRAEGER PUBLISHERS
111 Fourth Avenue, New York, N.Y. 10003, U.S.A.
5, Cromwell Place, London S.W.7, England

Published in the United States of America in 1970
by Praeger Publishers, Inc.

Library of Congress Catalog Card Number: 72–83330

This book is No. 20 in the series
Praeger Library of U.S. Government Departments and Agencies

Printed in the United States of America

To Amittai Brundage,
who, for many years,
has been my help and inspiration

Foreword

by ROBERT P. MAYO

Director of the Bureau of the Budget

The Bureau of the Budget was established by the Budget and Accounting Act of 1921 as part of the Treasury Department. It was intended from the very first to be a staff agency to help the President carry out his responsibilities for effective public management. Yet, it was not until 1939 that the Bureau became the nucleus of the newly created Executive Office of the President and became truly independent of any cabinet department.

Percival F. Brundage was the twelfth Director to serve the President. He is remembered fondly by his many friends at the Bureau as a gentleman of great courtliness and generosity, who was wise in the ways of raising the *esprit* of the staff to new heights.

Percy Brundage contributed significantly to the development of the federal budget system. Coming to government after a distinguished career with Price, Waterhouse and

Company, he was uniquely qualified to come to grips with the inadequacy of government accounting systems in yielding the kind of information necessary for effective management.

The story of the recommendations of the second Hoover Commission is chronicled in Chapter II of this book. What the book does not tell is the part Percy Brundage played in the implementation of those recommendations. He was not only deeply involved in the effort to pass appropriate legislation, he was also responsible for establishing the Office of Accounting within the Bureau of the Budget to take the lead in an accelerated program for improving the accounting function throughout the government. The foundations that were laid during his tenure as Director still shape the Bureau's efforts in financial management.

It is typical of the author to remain modest about his part in this chapter of the Bureau's continuing efforts to help the President meet the problems of managing an increasingly complex government. He is a true personal friend of mine and a true friend of good financial management.

Preface

To some people, accounting and budgeting are dull and dry subjects. To me, they are quite the opposite. They are the bones and structure of life. They are vital and exciting. You can learn more about the government of the United States by working in the Bureau of the Budget for six months than by spending six years in almost any other branch of the government.

After forty years in the practice of public accounting, in which budgeting and management services as well as auditing were an important part, I had the good fortune to spend four stimulating years at this center of the federal government. Every government agency has to ask for money annually and explain why it is needed. To analyze, to question, to synchronize, and to justify these demands is one of the major responsibilities of the Bureau. But there is much else, besides, as I shall point out.

To begin with, there is the philosophy—of budgeting and of government. President Dwight D. Eisenhower, to whom I had the honor to report when I was Budget Director, sum-

med up what I believe should be the nation's budget philosophy in his farewell address January 17, 1961:

> Each proposal must be weighed in the light of a broader considera-
> tion: the need to maintain balance in and among national pro-
> grams—balance between the private and the public economy, balance
> between cost and hoped-for advantage—balance between the clearly
> necessary and the comfortably desirable; balance between our essen-
> tial requirements as a nation and the duties imposed by the nation
> upon the individual; balance between actions of the moment and the
> national welfare of the future. Good judgment seeks balance and
> progress; lack of it eventually finds imbalance and frustration.

The budget of the United States is much more than a
report on and plan for the operations of government for
specific periods. It is a reflection of the Administration's philosophy and goals, limited by the resources at its disposal.

One of the most important and difficult budgeting problems is to find the funds to start new programs as the need
arises; both the Bureau and Congress are frequently criticized
for failure to meet new or developing needs. However, it is
equally important and difficult to reduce or terminate the
older programs that have become less necessary but have in
the meantime created vested interests that, for political reasons, are not easy to disregard.

It will be readily apparent to readers of this book that the
Director of the Bureau of the Budget must, like the President, take a broader view of priorities than that held by the
man who heads a specialized department or agency. One of
my successors at the Bureau, who served a different Administration, spoke of the reasons for this difference in a lecture at
Harvard. His "Reflections on Spending," later issued in pamphlet form by the Brookings Institution, of which he is now
president, are quoted here, in part, with his permission:

> Consider the official who directs the day-to-day operations of even a

broadly defined program; let us call him the bureau chief. He directs the work of large numbers of people, he disposes of large sums of money, he deals every day with weighty, intricate, and delicate problems. He has probably spent most of his adult years in the highly specialized activity over which he now presides. He lives at the center of a special world inhabited by persons and groups in the private sector who stand to gain or lose by what he does, certain members of Congress who have a special interest in his actions, and a specialized press to which he is a figure of central importance. The approbation which is most meaningful to him is likely to be the approbation of the other inhabitants of this special world. The rest of the federal government may seem vague and remote, and the President will loom as a distant and shadowy figure who will, in any event, be succeeded by someone else in a few years.

It would be unreasonable to expect this official to see his program in the Presidential perspective. The President wants him to be a zealot about his mission, to pursue the goals of his program with skill, enthusiasm, and dedication. To ask him at the same time to be Olympian about his role and his claim on resources—to see in a detached way that he is a part of a hive in which many other bees have missions of equal or greater urgency—is to ask him to embrace a combination of incompatible attitudes. There are few Olympian zealots. One has to live with the knowledge that where you stand depends on where you sit.

Director Kermit Gordon's grasp of the problems of budget management—admirable as they were, and are—was outmatched on at least one occasion by another writer. When Kermit Gordon resigned from his post to go to Brookings, Mrs. Gordon wrote him an open letter on budgetary matters that quickly became a Washington classic. It read:

> Since I have so little confidence in my own capabilities as a financial manager, I decided to take as my model the Federal Budget, and I have managed our finances in exact conformity to its sound principles. If they are good enough for Uncle Sam, they are certainly good enough for the Gordons.

So I am here to tell you that we, too, will have a deficit this year; that the deficit will be less than last year's; and that last year's was less than the year before. Moreover, with continued prudent management *and* a strong revenue situation, I look forward to a balanced budget in 1968. Our debt continues to decline—as a percentage of gross national product, that is.

I remember your telling me how pleased Wilbur Mills was when you made these same statements to him, so I am sure you will be equally pleased with my report. I also remember your saying to me once that the family budget should be easier to manage than the Federal budget because I don't have to contend with the likes of the American Legion and the Rivers and Harbors Congress. Well, I can hardly wait to introduce you to the children's dentist. And just wait till you meet the plumber.

There is one little trick that I stumbled on all by myself. I asked you one time where the CIA appeared in the annual budget. You wouldn't exactly answer, but I got the impression that the CIA figures were included under other headings so that no one could tell exactly how much money they got. I've been doing *that* for years, and it works just fine. See under "Stamps."

The current Director of the Bureau of the Budget, Robert P. Mayo, and his assistants and the very capable staff of the Bureau have been most cooperative and helpful in supplying material for this book and in taking time to explain recent changes and policy decisions. They and former members of the staff have also made criticisms and suggestions on the manuscript. I wish to express my great appreciation and indebtedness to them—particularly to Percy Rappaport, former assistant director of the Bureau of the Budget; Roger W. Jones, assistant director of the Bureau of the Budget; Raymond T. Bowman, assistant director for Statistical Policy; Samuel M. Cohn, assistant director for Budget Review, Dwight A. Ink, assistant director for Executive Management; Wilfred H. Rommel, assistant director for Legislative Reference; and Jack W. Carlson, assistant director for Program Evaluation. Also, Carl W. Tiller and Frank W. Krause, of the Office of Budget Review; the Office of Executive Management's Charles F. Parker, assistant director for Program and Administration; Fred E. Levy, assistant director for Legislation, Reorganization Plans, and Executive Orders; and William J. Armstrong, director of the Financial Management Staff; William Pfleger, Jr., director of the General Government Management Division; Carl H. Schwartz, Jr., director of the Natural Resources Programs Division; Mark W. Alger, deputy director of the Human Resources Division; Mrs. Velma N. Baldwin, director of Administration; and Ruth Fine, librarian, and her staff.

The consulting editors of the Praeger Library of Government Departments and Agencies, Ernest S. Griffith and Hugh Langdon Elsbree, have made numerous constructive suggestions, and Mrs. Lois Decker O'Neill, Praeger's Washington editor, has helped put the manuscript into readable form. Despite their efforts, there may be some lapses into "governmentese," and I must confess that certain technicalities in budgeting and accounting are hard to erase. It is also difficult to describe the budget process as of any particular date. Changes are continually taking place and contemplated. My description in these pages is based on my knowledge of the procedures in effect under President Eisenhower and my observation of the indicated differences under Presidents John F. Kennedy, Lyndon B. Johnson, and Richard M. Nixon.

PERCIVAL F. BRUNDAGE

Washington, D.C.
October 15, 1969

Contents

A section of photographs follows p. 92.

List of Charts and Tables

The Bureau of
the Budget

I

The U.S. Budget, 1780-1930

The budget of the U.S. Government is larger than that published by any other government. Its importance has grown with the nation and the greater centralization of power in the nation's capital, until today it affects the lives of people the world over with its variety of programs, both domestic and foreign.

The budget history of the United States can be divided into four general periods. From 1780 to 1921, the different departments and branches of the federal government prepared their financial requests separately, each setting forth its own needs. These requests were assembled in the Treasury Department and presented to Congress without comment or revision.

With the passage of the Budget and Accounting Act of 1921, the preparation of the budget and certain management duties became the responsibility of the Bureau of the Budget, as a separate branch of the Treasury but directly under the President, who was required to present the annual budget as a whole to Congress. During the next decade, a relatively small Bureau staff systematized the preparation and presentation of the budget, provided leadership, and controlled expenditures, with annual budget surpluses through fiscal 1930.

The third period, from the beginning of the Great Depression through 1939, was one of experimentation and budget deficits. The Bureau staff remained small, numbering about forty, but new philosophies about budgeting were being developed and many more responsibilities were being assigned to the Bureau.

Finally, under the Reorganization Act of 1939, the Executive Office of the President was established and its duties were defined by executive order, with the Bureau of the Budget as a part of the Executive Office responsible only to the President (under Reorganization Plan I). With the additional responsibilities assigned to the Bureau, its staff grew rapidly to a total during World War II of more than six hundred, and it was relied upon more and more by the President. Its importance and influence were diminished slightly by working arrangements that prevailed under President John F. Kennedy, but its ascendancy has since been restored.

Today, the Bureau of the Budget is considered by many to be the single most important part of the Executive Office of the President. One of its principal duties is, of course, the preparation of the annual budget of the United States. A number of other important duties, some statutory, some under the direction or delegated authority of the President, include responsibilities for the initiation of suggestions for improved management policies and procedures within the executive branch, the consolidation and control of government statistical services, the coordination of executive-branch positions on proposed legislation, and the preparation of executive orders and reorganization plans. The Bureau even has responsibility for such seemingly minor matters as travel and expense allowances, personnel restrictions, and car pools for the rest of the government.

Beginning with Hamilton

In the early years of the nation's existence, the central government under the Articles of Confederation did not have sufficient power to raise necessary revenues. In April, 1789, George Washington, shortly after becoming President under the new Constitution, submitted to the House of Representatives a plan for revenue-raising import duties. This was approved, and, in July, a customs system was adopted. Soon thereafter, the Act of September 2, 1789, clearly based upon English law and procedure, established the Treasury Department and made it the duty of the Secretary "to prepare and report estimates of the public revenue and the public expenditures."

Alexander Hamilton was appointed the first Secretary of the Treasury. In his "First Report on the Public Credit" (January, 1790), he stated that "an adequate provision for the support of the public credit is a matter of high importance to the honor and prosperity of the United States." Hamilton was broad-minded. He advocated a balanced budget, but he also pointed out that where "the national debt is properly funded, and an object of established confidence, it answers most of the purposes of money."

Total revenues for the first fiscal period 1789-91 were $4.4 million, with a surplus over expenditures of $150,000; during this period, interest payments amounted to half the current expenditures. The population of the country at that time was under 4 million and the economy was predominantly one of agriculture and trading.

During the growing years of the young nation, practically all the Presidents and members of Congress believed that economy in public as well as private spending was a virtue and that public debt was an obligation to be feared and paid off as soon as possible, like a church mortgage. In spite of the costs incurred by the Louisiana Purchase and the War of 1812, the public debt was extinguished in 1837, during the second term of Andrew Jackson. Customs duties still provided the principal revenues; internal revenue taxes were imposed during the War of 1812 but repealed a few years afterward. In these years, the policy of the government with respect to the use and disposition of public lands was very important and frequently discussed, with the proceeds of sales often appropriated for internal improvements.

The Act of Congress of May 10, 1800, is worth noting for its interest from a budget point of view. It imposed on the Secretary of the Treasury the duty of preparing and laying before Congress at the commencement of every session a report

> on the subject of finance, containing estimates of the public revenues and public expenditures, and plans for improving and increasing the revenues, from time to time, for the purpose of giving information to Congress in adopting modes of raising the money requisite to meeting the public expenditures.

There is no evidence that this procedure was ever followed out, and—partly because of the jealousy and hostility between the legislative and executive branches—later statutes modified the requirement, until the Act of July 7, 1884, stipulated only that all estimates of appropriations and deficiencies "shall be transmitted to the Congress through the Secretary of the Treasury and in no other manner."

During the first 110 years of the nation's existence, up to the beginning of the present century, the total receipts of the federal government, mostly customs revenues, amounted to only $15 billion, its expenditures to a little over $16 billion, with a national debt on June 30, 1899, of $1.4 billion. The average annual expenditures, including the cost of four wars, were, therefore, under $150 million a year. Except for the

War of 1812, practically all the expenditures were made within the country. The average annual expenditure during the last two decades of the nineteenth century was around $300 million in 1900 dollars.

Throughout this period, Congress remained insistent on maintaining its responsibility as the sole authority for expenditures. In his book *The Spending Power* (New Haven, Conn.: Yale University Press, 1943), Lucius Wilmerding, Jr., referred to an example of an unauthorized, unbudgeted expenditure by President Abraham Lincoln, who, at the beginning of his Administration,

> authorized and directed the Secretary of the Treasury to advance, without requiring security, $2,000,000 of public money to John A. Dix, George Opdyke, and Richard M. Blatchford of New York, to be used by them in meeting such requisitions as should be directly consequent upon the military and naval measures necessary for the defense and support of the Government. For this action there was no warrant whatever in law but by taking it and other actions like it Lincoln conceived himself to have saved the Government from overthrow. His justification was that he had acted under a law higher than the statutes.

The First Budgetary Review

The first thorough review of the whole budgetary process was made by the Commission on Economy and Efficiency, appointed by President William Howard Taft in 1911.* Its report, entitled "The Need for a National Budget," was transmitted to the Senate and House of Representatives by the President on June 27, 1912, with the statement that he approved the recommendations and asked for the enactment of

*The members of the Commission were Frederick A. Cleveland, Chairman, and Frank J. Goodnow, William F. Willoughby, Walter W. Warnick, and Merritt O. Chance.

"the legislation necessary to put them into effect." It is a comprehensive document and an important milestone in the history of budgeting and fiscal policy—both in the philosophy expressed and in the recommendations made. The President's message stated:

> Notwithstanding the magnitude and complexity of the business which is each year conducted by the executive branch and financed by the Congress, and the vital relation which each governmental activity bears to the welfare of the people, there is at present no provision for reporting revenues, expenditures, and estimates for appropriations in such manner that the Executive, before submitting estimates, and each Member of Congress, and the people, after estimates have been submitted, may know what has been done by the Government or what the Government proposes to do.

Six recommendations of the Commission were endorsed by the President. The first was that the President, as the head of the executive branch of the government, should submit a budget to Congress each year, not later than the first Monday after the beginning of the regular session.

The second recommendation spelled out what the budget was to contain: (1) a budgetary message, setting forth in brief the significance of the proposals; (2) a summary financial statement setting forth the national financial condition, together with a statement of the condition of appropriations and other data pertaining to the "general fund" as well as to the other funds of the government, an account of revenues and expenditures for the last completed fiscal year, and a statement showing the effect of past financial policy as well as budget proposals on the general-fund surplus; (3) a summary of expenditures, classified by objects, setting forth the contracting and purchasing relations of the government; (4) summaries of estimates, setting forth the estimated revenues compared with actual revenues for a period of years and the estimated expenditures compared with actual expenditures for a period of years; and, finally, (5) a summary of changes in law, setting forth what legislation should be enacted in order to enable the administration to transact public business with greater economy and efficiency.

The third and fourth recommendations were that each department and "independent establishment" submit detailed annual accounts to the Treasury and Congress and that the Secretary of the Treasury submit to the Congress detailed reports "supporting the Executive conclusions and recommendations." The last two recommendations were that detailed accounts should be kept and reports submitted by each department so that the President could recommend to Congress for its consideration desirable changes in appropriation bills "in order that the Government may do work and accomplish results with economy and efficiency and as will definitely fix responsibility for failure so to exercise such discretion."

The Commission in its report recognized that the recommendations required "a complete reversal of procedure by the government," whereby the executive branch would submit a statement to the legislature giving "its account of stewardship as well as its proposals for the future" and presenting "in summary form the facts necessary to shape the policy of the government as well as to provide financial support." This statement would "serve the purposes of a prospectus."

William F. Willoughby, a member of the Taft Commission and later director of the Institute for Government Research, predecessor of the Brookings Institution, wrote extensively about this period. In *The National Budget System* (Baltimore, Md.: The Johns Hopkins Press, 1927), he recalled that "disclosure of the President's intention to prepare a budget roused Congress to action to defend itself in the constant struggle with the Executive over the powers of the Government." In one of the appropriation acts, a provision was inserted that the expenditure estimates must be presented "only in the form and at the time now required by law, and in no other form and at no other time."

In the elections of November, 1912, President Taft was defeated and lost his power as leader of the Republican Party. The Commission report, however, had focused attention on the need for a radical revision of the budget system. The Chamber of Commerce of the United States held a referendum among all its members about the proposed new budget system, with a majority in favor. In 1916, both political parties incorporated planks in their platforms supporting it. That same year, the Institute for Government Research was formed; its chief efforts for several years went to drafting legislation and securing support for a properly devised budget system.

Pressures for Reform

By June 30, 1916, the national debt had been reduced to $1.2 billion, but, with the entry of the United States into World War I in 1917, expenditures rose precipitously. Income and excess profit taxes were introduced, but, with expenditures of $18 billion in fiscal 1919, the national debt rose to $25.5 billion.

The expansion of federal activities and the sharp increase in the public debt made the need for budget reform more urgent. It became clear that the presentation to Congress through the Treasury by different agencies of requests unrelated to each other or to the total of all amounts recommended was quite inadequate, even though the authorizations had to be handled through the substantive committees of Congress.

James W. Good, chairman of the House Appropriations Committee in 1919, introduced a resolution calling for the appointment of a select committee on the budget to study the problem and report to the House of Representatives. His proposal was adopted on July 31, 1919, and he was made chairman of the temporary committee. Extensive hearings were held, and a bill was introduced and passed overwhelmingly by the House. By then, the Senate was too busy with its consideration of the Treaty of Versailles to take any action, but President Woodrow Wilson called for the adoption of a budget system in his annual message to Congress on December 2, 1919. Meanwhile, Senator Medill McCormick had also become interested in the subject and had secured the passage of a resolution forming a Senate select committee, of which he was made chairman. He held hearings at which the testimony of two witnesses is of particular interest.

On behalf of the American Institute of Accountants, Francis Oakey advocated the position of a "Secretary of Administration," under the President, who

> should be charged with the duty, first, of investigating the work requirements of the various departments, bureaus, offices, commissions, boards, etc., that come under the executive branch . . . looking into their needs and their plans, and their means and facilities for carrying out those plans, consulting with these departments, bureaus, or commission heads, after they have submitted their estimates, to determine whether the estimates are justified, and if not, to try to come to some agreement with the various departments as to how they should be changed before submitted.

Nicholas Murray Butler, president of Columbia University, testified:

> My point of view, Senator, is that the introduction of a properly formulated national budget is not an end in itself, but a means, and a very important means, to improving the whole administrative organi-

zation of the National Government. . . . It is almost universally referred to as a means of saving money; but even if under a budget
system not a single dollar was saved, there would be every possible
assurance that every dollar was wisely expended.

The Senate passed a revised bill somewhat different from
the House bill on May 1, 1920, and it was referred to conference. The House bill provided for the creation of a budget
bureau directly under the President, while the Senate bill
provided for an enlarged office of the Secretary of the Treasury somewhat like the British Chancellor of the Exchequer,
with an internal bureau responsible for the preparation of the
budget. A compromise bill was passed and sent to the President on May 29, 1920.

Much to the surprise of Congress, the bill was returned by
President Wilson on June 4, 1920, without his approval. One
of its provisions, for a comptroller general independent of the
administrative branch and beyond the power of removal by
the President, represented, Wilson felt, an unconstitutional
limitation upon his power.

Not until a new Congress met on April 11, 1921, were the
two original bills reintroduced—the Good bill in the House
and the McCormick bill in the Senate. Each was passed, another conference committee was promptly appointed, and
agreement was finally reached on May 25, 1921, on legislation substantially like the House bill except that the director
of the budget and his assistant or deputy would be appointed
by the President and would work under his orders but would
be located within the Treasury Department. It still called for
a comptroller general, to be appointed by the President but
removable only by joint resolution of Congress; President
Wilson's objection had not been removed. However, the bill
was passed by both houses, and President Warren G. Harding
signed it on June 10, 1921.

The Act of 1921

The Budget and Accounting Act of 1921 is the basic legislation for today's Bureau of the Budget. (See Appendix B.) It provides for "a national budget system and an independent audit of Government Accounts" and under Section 201 of Title II, states that:

> The President shall transmit to Congress on the first day of each regular session the Budget, which shall set forth in summary and in detail the estimates of the expenditures, appropriations, and receipts for the ensuing fiscal year and for the last completed fiscal year.

Section 202 provides that, if the estimated receipts for the ensuing fiscal year and cash balances are insufficient to cover the estimated expenditures, "the President in the Budget shall make recommendations to Congress for new taxes, loans, or other appropriate action to meet the estimated deficiency." In Section 203, provision is made for supplemental or deficiency estimates with the requirement of a statement of the reasons therefor. Section 206 contains the following severe restriction:

> No estimate or request for an appropriation and no request for an increase in an item of any such estimate or request, and no recommendation as to how the revenue needs of the Government should be met, shall be submitted to Congress or any committee thereof by any officer or employee of any department or establishment, unless at the request of either House of Congress.

Section 209 is particularly interesting as dealing with the new management responsibilities of the Bureau:

> The Bureau, when directed by the President, shall make a detailed study of the departments and establishments for the purpose of

enabling the President to determine what changes (with a view of securing greater economy and efficiency in the conduct of the public service) should be made in (1) the existing organization, activities, and methods of business of such departments or establishments, (2) the appropriations therefor, (3) the assignment of particular activities to particular services, or (4) the regrouping of services. The results of such study shall be embodied in a report or reports to the President, who may transmit to Congress such report or reports or any part thereof with his recommendations on the matters covered thereby.

The basic philosophy of the Budget and Accounting Act of 1921 was grounded on the President himself assuming responsibility for proposing the budget to Congress, thus eliminating the concept of departmental self-determination, but with Congress retaining the right to dispose of the proposals as it wishes. This budget was to be the financial expression of the government's policies and program for the ensuing fiscal year, including recommendations for new legislation and the activities of government corporations. The budgetary process was designed to reduce duplication, waste, and inefficiency both within and between agencies through a coordinated over-all review on behalf of the President, and it was intended also to promote better administrative management as well as fiscal planning and control. It should be noted, however, that Congress had no intention of weakening its authority over appropriations; House Committee Report 362, Sixty-sixth Congress, First Session, stated on page 7:

It will doubtless be claimed by some that this is an Executive budget and that the duty of making appropriations is a legislative rather than Executive prerogative. The plan outlined does provide for an Executive initiation of the budget, but the President's responsibility ends when he has prepared the budget and transmitted it to Congress. To that extent and to that extent alone does the plan provide for an Executive budget, but the proposed law does not change in the slightest degree the duty of Congress to make the minutest examination of the budget and to adopt the budget only to the extent that it is found to be economical. If the estimates contained in the President's budget are too large, it will be the duty of Congress to reduce them. If in the opinion of Congress the estimates of expenditures are not sufficient, it will be within the power of Congress to increase them.

General Charles G. Dawes was the first Director of the Bureau of the Budget. He was appointed by President Harding on June 21, 1921. A very forceful officer, he expressed his objectives in a statement issued at that time:

> As Chief of Supply Procurement in the American Expeditionary Forces, under a general plan whose principles were established by General Pershing, I superimposed in France, under his direction, a system of business coordination over the decentralized services of the Army. It was because of this experience that I felt justified in assuming an analogous task under President Harding to inaugurate a system of coordinating business control over the various departments and independent establishments of government which, for one hundred and thirty-two years, have been almost completely decentralized.

General Dawes was fortunate in that, when he was appointed, Andrew W. Mellon was Secretary of the Treasury. Mellon was not only a recognized genius in fiscal matters but also a considerate and humble associate. In his first report to the Cabinet, Dawes noted:

> I am glad to say that the Secretary of the Treasury walked upstairs to my office—one of his subordinate bureau chiefs—because he regarded it as necessary in connection with a call from me for information needed by the President of the United States. That will be an historic walk in the annals of the Budget Bureau.

In a long report to the President six months later, December 5, 1921, Director Dawes set forth his understanding of the Bureau's responsibilities, including the following comments:

> There is a tendency on the part of many to assume that the Bureau of the Budget is established primarily for the sake of reducing expenses. The Bureau of the Budget is designed, through its facilities for securing information, to be in a position to give impartial advice to the President and to Congress in all matters regarding the proper business functioning of government. Because at the time of the establishment of the Budget Bureau there was a great necessity existing for the reduction of governmental expenses, and since under the old decentralized system of governmental business great extravagance existed, the activities of the bureau which became most prominent were those where it acted as an agent for the imposition of Executive pressure in forcing down expenditures where not in contravention of congressional mandate and efficiency. This is but one function of the Budget Bureau.
>
> It must be as willing to advise an increase in appropriations where the same is clearly in the interest of governmental efficiency and true economy as it is to advise reductions in expenses, which at the present time are so necessary. It is only by this method, under which it gives an impartial business judgment as to the necessity for expenditures and the functioning of government, that it can, in the long run, maintain its proper influence with the Executive and with Congress and justify its existence.

Director Dawes left the impress of his personality on the operations of government, especially the organization and duties of the Bureau. It should be mentioned that he made the earliest use of the Bureau for clearing legislation. He wanted to see all agency proposals and agency reports on proposals referred by Congress that might, in the words of Budget Circular 49, December 18, 1921, "create a charge upon the Public Treasury or commit the Government to obligations which would later require appropriations to meet them."

Although he considered Bureau clearance essential to enforcing the provisions of Section 206 of the 1921 Act previously quoted, Dawes did very little toward carrying out the Bureau's management responsibilities under Section 209 of that act. This inaction may have been due to the existence at the time of the Bureau of Efficiency, which had had its origin in the Taft Commission on Economy and Efficiency. After Wilson became President, the Civil Service Commission had carried the Taft effort along by establishing its own Division of Efficiency, which Congress had recognized in the Appropriation Act of 1916. Then, on February 28, 1916, as a part of the Urgent Deficiency Appropriation Act, the Division of Efficiency had been made an independent body called the Bureau of Efficiency. Its duties were to establish and maintain a system of efficiency ratings for the classified service, investigate the personnel needs of the agencies, and investigate duplication of statistical work in the government. It seems to have been generally understood that, with the enactment of the 1921 Act, the Bureau of Efficiency would be consolidated with the Bureau of the Budget. An amendment to this effect was adopted by the Senate but lost in conference. Director Dawes apparently decided not to undertake administrative studies under Section 209, in order to avoid possible duplication of work by the two bureaus.* Public Law 428, passed March 3, 1933, abolished the Bureau of Efficiency. Its records were transferred to the Bureau of the Budget.

When he accepted President Harding's appointment, General Dawes had stipulated that he would serve for one year only. He stuck to his word and resigned at the end of fiscal 1922. His successor was General Herbert M. Lord, chief finance officer of the Army, who had worked closely with him

---

*The Bureau of Efficiency made a number of management studies over the years but received a lot of criticism and not much encouragement. In the unpublished "Statement of Work of the Bureau of Efficiency 1914-32," prepared by its chief, Herbert D. Brown and addressed to the Chairman of the House Appropriations Committee, February 6, 1933, considerable savings were reported but not substantiated.

in organizing the Bureau and followed his policies from 1922 to 1929. Colonel J. Clawson Roop, also a Dawes collaborator, became the third Director and strengthened but did not enlarge the Bureau's position. His term extended until 1933.

The 1920's were years of expansion and optimism. A deficit of $13.4 billion in fiscal 1919, which included terminating the war and "bringing the boys home," was followed by eleven successive years of surpluses. This was a period of business prosperity and frugal administration, during which it was again considered sound fiscal policy to maintain a balanced budget and reduce the national debt during peace time—even after the stock-market crash in October, 1929.

The Bureau of the Budget had been created but had only begun to function in its modern sense. Developments early in the 1930's marked another turning point for it and for the nation.

II

Depression, War,
and War's Aftermath

The decade of the 1930's marked an important change in the viewpoint of all three branches of the federal government, starting with the executive and then extending to the legislative and judicial branches. The Bureau of the Budget was one of the first agencies to be affected.

With the beginning of the Great Depression in fiscal 1931, federal receipts dropped by $900 million or 23 per cent, while expenditures increased by $250 million—resulting in the first deficit since 1919 and the first of sixteen annual deficits in a row. In fiscal 1932, receipts dropped even more drastically, over $1 billion, and expenditures increased by $1 billion to $4,659 million, or more than twice the receipts.

In the 1932 political campaign, Franklin Delano Roosevelt advocated reductions in government expenditures and, after his inauguration in 1933, proposed further retrenchments and a 15 per cent reduction in the compensation of federal employees. Later in the year 1933, President Roosevelt shifted his position and started on the New Deal recovery program, with an attempted differentiation between the regular services of government—to be reduced to a minimum—and the emergency public expenditures that he deemed necessary. At the same time, economists and business leaders were exploring more thoroughly the reasons for business cycles, and important new philosophies of government and budgeting were being developed.

The Emergence of New Concepts

Wesley C. Mitchell of the National Bureau of Economic Research, established in the 1920's, had been engaged in a thoroughgoing study of business cycles and how to control or mitigate them. As early as 1923, Mitchell had published a paper, "The Problem of Controlling Business Cycles," in which he stated that "the time for effective action is the time when industrial activity is approaching the elastic limit set by full use of existing plant and when further expansion will be primarily a speculative boom." He also wrote that "it is desirable to raise discount rates in future periods of expansion, whenever signs appear that production is nearing its limit," and he urged long-range planning for public works. This, he said, "required a campaign of public education." Arthur F. Burns (later chairman of the Council of Economic Advisers, 1953-56 and now Counsellor to the President) had joined the staff of the National Bureau in 1930 and was working with Mitchell on his studies of business cycles. They collaborated on a number of papers and books on this subject, which were of great interest to the Budget Bureau. Simon Kuznets, also on the research staff of the National Bureau for many years, published *Seasonal Variations in Industry and Trade* (New York: Columbia University Press, 1933) and was working on his monumental studies of national income and capital formation, which were to have an important influence on economic and budget policy, both in and outside government.

When the Roosevelt Administration's substantial emergency loan expenditures began, stocks of all kinds—particularly agricultural products—stood at a very high level. John Maynard Keynes, the English economist, in *The General Theory of Employment, Interest, and Money* (New York: Harcourt, Brace & World, 1936), pointed out:

> The New Deal partly consisted in a strenuous attempt to reduce these stocks—by curtailment of current output and in all sorts of ways. The reduction of stocks to a normal level was a necessary process—a phase which had to be endured. But so long as it lasted, namely, about two years, it constituted a substantial offset to the loan expenditures which were being incurred in other directions. Only when it had been completed was the way prepared for substantial recovery.

President Roosevelt found that public-works programs cannot be expanded easily and rapidly at will, just as later Presidents have found that authorized expansions cannot be terminated rapidly when no longer required; public-works expenditures can be planned in advance, but they cannot be turned on and off like a water tap. The increase in expenditures for fiscal 1934 was only slightly over $2 billion above 1933, a third of what the President had estimated it would be in January, 1934, or, as Lewis H. Kimmel noted in *Federal Budget and Fiscal Policy, 1789-1958* (Washington, D.C.: Brookings Institution, 1959): "closer to the original 1934 estimate submitted by President Hoover than to the revised figure announced one year later by the new administration."

Lewis W. Douglas became Budget Director on March 7, 1933. He was forceful in presenting his views but resigned a year and a half later. Although he made no announcement of his reasons, the press attributed his resignation to a disagreement with the President about the need for economy. He went on to become ambassador to Great Britain (as had one of his predecessors, General Dawes). Daniel W. Bell, who had served in the U.S. Treasury in various capacities for twenty-three years, succeeded Douglas. Bell was thoroughly familiar with budgetary practices and fiscal policy, which was what the President wanted in order to carry out his plans. However, the new policies for economic recovery were not easy to work out.

Harold D. Smith, who in turn became Bell's successor as Budget Director, wrote later, in *The Management of Your Government* (New York: Whittlesey House, 1945):

> The contribution made by public works to recovery was large, but it was not decisive. Federal expenditures for new construction, including work relief construction, during 1933-38 averaged 1.6 billion dollars a year ... yet the increase in Federal expenditure was almost entirely offset by a sharp contraction of state and local expenditures for construction, a contraction necessitated by severe declines in revenue, unfavorable bondmarket conditions, and lack of reserves. Since the need for public works in many communities had been met in the building boom of the 1920's, state and local governments could make these curtailments without immediate reduction of essential public services. Private construction expenditures were also greatly curtailed; over this period the shrinkage averaged more than 6 billion dollars a year.

The increase in taxes combined with government pump-priming resulted in increasing budget receipts, from $1,997 million in fiscal 1933 to $3,015 million in 1934 and $3,706 million in 1935, while expenditures went up from $4,598 million in fiscal 1933 to $6,645 million in 1934 and $6,497 million in 1935. The national debt doubled in five years, reaching $32.8 billion by June 30, 1935. (Expenditures had exceeded $6 billion only three times before fiscal 1934. In 1918, they were $12.6 billion with a deficit of $9 billion; in 1919, $18.4 billion with a deficit of $13 billion; and in 1920, $6.3 billion with a surplus of $291 million. Since fiscal 1934, expenditures have exceeded $6 billion every year.)

All kinds of new agencies were established to reduce unemployment and stimulate business. The conception of the welfare state became established in the United States and abroad, although it was by no means generally accepted by Americans, running contrary as it did to the basic philosophy of their adventuresome forebears. The place of individual initiative, the local administrations, and the county, state, and national governments became, and still are, controversial subjects in politics and economics as well as in barbershop conversation.

In 1933, the budgetary functions of the Bureau were increased by the issuance of an executive order giving it authority to make quarterly apportionments. This authority had previously been exercised by department heads. In 1936, the Bureau was given the duty of assisting the President in the consideration, clearance, and preparation of executive orders and proclamations. Another function was added in 1937, by the liquidation of the National Emergency Council and the transfer to the Bureau of the Council's authority to examine nonfiscal legislation for conformity with the general program of the President.

The Brownlow Recommendations and the Reorganization Act of 1939

Then came the most important changes in the national budget procedures, and the organization of the executive branch of the government, since the Budget and Accounting Act of 1921. They were made as the result of a report by the President's Committee on Administrative Management, consisting of Chairman Louis Brownlow, Charles E. Merriam, and Luther Gulick. Their report was submitted to President Roosevelt on January 8, 1937, and he summarized it in a special message to Congress on January 12, 1937, as follows.

To bring our administrative management up to date, the Committee presents an integrated five-point program, which you will find set out in its report. It includes these major recommendations:

1. Expand the White House staff so that the President may have a sufficient group of able assistants in his own office to keep him in closer and easier touch with the widespread affairs of administration, and to make the speedier clearance of the knowledge needed for Executive decision.

2. Strengthen and develop the managerial agencies of the Government, particularly those dealing with the budget and efficiency research, with personnel and with planning, as management-arms of the Chief Executive.

3. Extend the merit system upward, outward, and downward to cover practically all non-policy-determining posts; reorganize the civil-service system as a part of management under a single, responsible administrator, and create a citizen board to serve as the watch-dog of the merit system; and increase the salaries of key posts throughout the service so that the Government may attract and hold in a career service men and women of ability and character.

4. Overhaul the 100 independent agencies, administrations, authorities, boards, and commissions, and place them by Executive order within one or the other of the following 12 major Executive departments: State, Treasury, War, Justice, Post Office, Navy, Conservation, Agriculture, Commerce, Labor, Social Welfare, and Public Works; and place upon the Executive continuing responsibility for the maintenance of effective organization.

5. Establish accountability of the Executive to the Congress by providing a genuine independent postaudit of all fiscal transactions by an auditor general, and restore to the Executive complete responsibility for accounts and current transactions.

Roosevelt added:

As you will see, this program rests solidly upon the Constitution and upon the American way of doing things. There is nothing in it which is revolutionary, as every element is drawn from our own experience either in government or large-scale business.

I endorse this program and feel confident that it will commend itself to you also with your knowledge of government, and to the vast majority of the citizens of the country who want and believe in efficient self-government.

The Bureau's staff at this time still consisted of approximately forty employees. It was plain that the Brownlow Committee proposals, if enacted, would mean a tremendous expansion. They were thoroughly discussed in Congress and the executive branch for two years and finally incorporated in the Reorganization Act of 1939, which, after many amendments to the House and Senate bills and conference adjustments, was approved on April 3, 1939.

The most important provisions of the Reorganization Act of 1939 related to reorganization plans. Title I, Part I, Section 4, provided:

Whenever the President, after investigation, finds that—

(a) The transfer of the whole or any part of any agency or the functions thereof to the jurisdiction and control of any other agency; or

(b) The consolidation of the functions vested in any agency; or

(c) The abolition of the whole or any part of any agency . . . is necessary to accomplish one or more of the purposes of Section 1 (a), he shall

(d) Prepare a reorganization plan for the making of the transfers, consolidations, and abolitions, as to which he has made findings and which he includes in the plan.

Each plan was required to show in detail the records, property, and number of personnel affected and the unexpended balances of appropriations to be transferred. It was then to be submitted simultaneously to both houses of Congress when it was in session, and the President was to state "that such transfer, consolidation or abolition is necessary" and to indicate the expected savings in expenditures. After a reorganization plan was submitted to Congress by the President, it automatically became effective in ten days unless disapproved by a majority of both houses of Congress.

The history of the development of Presidential authority to reorganize executive agencies and their functions is sufficiently important to review briefly at this point, inasmuch as reorganization plans became a principal responsibility of the Bureau of the Budget.

The Overman Act, a World War I statute, authorized the President to redistribute functions among executive agencies by regulation or order and specifically empowered him to utilize, coordinate, or consolidate any executive or administrative commissions, bureaus, agencies, offices, or officers and to transfer any duties or powers from one department, commission, bureau, agency, office, or officer to another. The power granted to the President under this Act was limited to matters relating to the conduct of the war and was available only until six months after the war's termination. Numerous orders were issued by the President under the Overman Act, fifteen before the armistice.

The Act of June 30, 1932, empowered the President to effect reorganizations by executive order. However, reorganization plans that were submitted were disapproved by the House of Representatives on January 19, 1933, and this Act was subsequently amended by the Act of March 3, 1933, and the Act of March 20, 1933, which prescribed standards to guide the President and terminated the provision for the Congress to disapprove an executive order or part thereof (except by legislation regularly enacted). Numerous reorganizations were effected under the authority of these acts.

The next step was the Reorganization Act of 1939, under which five reorganization plans were transmitted to Congress.* All became effective. The first plan under the Act established the Executive Office of the President, made the Bureau of the Budget a part of the Executive Office, and transferred to the Bureau the functions of the Central Statistical Board and the Central Statistical Committee.

New Duties and Expansion for the Bureau

President Roosevelt, by Executive Order 8248 on September 8, 1939, defined the functions of the divisions of the newly established Executive Office of the President and assigned the following duties to the Bureau of the Budget as part of the Executive Office:

> to assist the President in the preparation of the budget and the formulation of the fiscal program of the government;
>
> to supervise and control the administration of the budget;
>
> to conduct research in the development of improved plans of administrative management, and to advise the executive departments and agencies of the government with respect to improved administrative organization and practice;
>
> to aid the President to bring about more efficient and economical conduct of the government service;
>
> to assist the President by clearing and coordinating departmental advice on proposed legislation and by making recommendations as

*The Reorganization Act of 1939 carried the terminal date of January 21, 1941; it was not extended. Presidential authority was next provided for by Title I of the First War Powers Act, 1941, which was quite similar to the Overman Act of 1918 and was limited to matters affecting World War II. The Reorganization Act of 1945, following the war, returned to the procedures of the Reorganization Act of 1939, with certain modifications. It was supplanted by the Reorganization Act of 1949, which provided for the disapproval of a reorganization plan by a majority of the authorized membership of one house of the Congress (in lieu of the former disapproval by concurrent resolution). Several subsequent extensions and amendments have been enacted.

to Presidential action on legislative enactments, in accordance with past practice;

to assist in the consideration and clearance and, where necessary, in the preparation of proposed executive orders and proclamations;

to plan and promote the improvement, development, and coordination of federal and other statistical services; and

to keep the President informed of the progress of activities by agencies of the government with respect to work proposed, work actually initiated, and work completed, together with the relative timing of work between the several agencies of the government, all to the end that the work programs of the several agencies of the executive branch of the government may be coordinated and that the monies appropriated by the Congress may be expended in the most economical manner possible with the least possible overlapping and duplication of effort.

The duties of four other divisions were also defined in Executive Order 8248: The White House Office, The National Resources Planning Board, The Liaison Office for Personnel Management, and the Office of Government Reports. (See Appendix C.) Section V of this order further defined the Budget responsibilities of the Bureau as follows:

The Director of the Bureau of the Budget shall prepare a consolidated budget for the Executive Office of the President for submission by the President to the Congress. Annually, pursuant to the regular request issued by the Bureau of the Budget, each division of the Executive Office of the President shall prepare and submit to the Bureau estimates of proposed appropriations for the succeeding fiscal year. The form of the estimates and the manner of their consideration for incorporation in the Budget shall be the same as prescribed for other Executive departments and agencies.

The Bureau of the Budget shall likewise perform with respect to the several divisions of the Executive Office of the President such functions and duties relating to supplemental estimates, apportionments, and budget administration as are exercised by it for other agencies of the Federal Government.

Daniel W. Bell went back to the Treasury as undersecretary on April 14, 1939, and Harold D. Smith, who was then director of the budget of the state of Michigan, was appointed Director of the Bureau of the Budget April 15, 1939. He served President Roosevelt during the difficult war period and later worked under President Harry S Truman until June 19, 1946. With the impact of war conditions, the Bureau staff was rapidly expanded to approximately 600—the highest level it has reached. Five divisions were formed: Estimates (budget preparation and apportionment); Administrative Management (organization and management studies); Fiscal (economic aspects and Budget Message); Legislative Reference (clearance of legislation); and Statistical Standards (coordination of statistical programs).

World War II brought a dramatic change in tempo to the Bureau. All policies were directed toward the one goal of winning the war. Taxes were raised as high as was thought could be practically done without diminishing the yield, and domestic expenditures were directed so far as possible toward attaining a military victory. With high income and excess profits taxes, government receipts of $21.4 billion in 1943 were more than three times the highest prewar figures of $6.6 billion in 1920 and $7 billion in 1941. During the next two years, receipts were six times the prewar figures—$43.5 billion in 1944 and $44 billion in 1945. Even so, there were successive budget deficits for these three years 1943-45 of over $50 billion each, greater than the total public debt at any time before 1941. There was another budget deficit of $20 billion in 1946, and the public debt reached a new high of $269.9 billion.

During the war period, the control over military expenditures was necessarily relaxed but the Bureau of the Budget took over additional duties. Executive Order 8512 of August 13, 1940, as amended March 3, 1942, assigned to the Bureau supervision of methods of financial reporting by government agencies. The Federal Reports Act of 1942 required the Director to coordinate federal reporting and statistical services to eliminate duplication, reduce the cost, and minimize the burden upon the public. Executive Order 9094 of March 10, 1942, charged the Bureau with coordination and planning federal mapping and chart-making activities. The Overtime Pay Act of 1942 started the Bureau establishing personnel ceilings as required by Congress. Executive Order 9384 of October 4, 1943, provided for Bureau review of federal public-works and improvement projects. The Government Corporations Control Act of 1945 extended the budgetary functions of the Bureau to wholly owned government corporations and provided for accounts to be maintained on a program basis.

This 1945 act was another turning point in governmental budgetary and accounting philosophy. It not only established the principle that corporate programs should be subject to regular budget review but also introduced the concept of business-type budgeting into the federal government. Corporate budgets were to be supported by accounts that provided full cost information, they were to be considered on a program basis, and the audits by the comptroller general were to be directed toward an appraisal of the corporation's performance rather than the mere legality and propriety of its expenditures, as had been traditional practice in the federal government.

During the entire period of the war, the United States was served by one of the ablest and most farsighted directors the Bureau has had. In 1945, during the last year of his office, Harold D. Smith wrote, in *The Management of Your Government* (cited earlier),

the fact that management in a democracy proceeds from the people does not in itself assure efficiency in carrying out governmental functions. Indeed, it has been said that inefficiency characterizes the government of a democracy and is the price paid for freedom, while in a dictatorship the people are compensated for the loss of their liberties by administrative effectiveness. The implication here is that, to gain efficiency in democratic government, management must obliterate individual liberties.

This implication is fallacious. . . . Under the democratic concept, the citizen is not only free, but he is encouraged to strive for personal advancement, to voice his thoughts, and to show his resourcefulness. Democracy draws its strength from the employment of the best talents and skills of free men and women.

Postwar Changes

Following the end of the war and the immediate postwar adjustments, fiscal 1947 and 1948 were years of surpluses with a sharp drop in expenditures and a reduction of the national debt to $252.4 billion by June 30, 1948. President Truman and his successor, Dwight D. Eisenhower, were both budget-minded men, and they maintained a tight rein on increases in established programs as well as on new programs, unless such programs met an urgent need or were required by the national economy.

One of the most important pieces of legislation enacted after the war was the Employment Act of 1946, which has had a significant effect on economic planning and budget policy. Section 2 stated:

It is the continuing policy and responsibility of the Federal Government to use all practicable means consistent with its needs and obligations and other essential considerations of national policy, with the assistance and cooperation of industry, agriculture, labor and state and local governments to coordinate and utilize all its plans, functions and resources for the purpose of creating and maintaining, in a manner calculated to foster and promote free competitive enterprise and the general welfare conditions under which there will be

afforded useful employment opportunities, including self-employ-
ment for those able, willing and seeking to work and to promote
maximum employment, production, and purchasing power.

The phraseology of this act, sometimes incorrectly referred
to as the "Full Employment" act, was carefully chosen. Congress recognized that full employment was unattainable because of the continual entry of young people into the labor
force, job transfers, shifts in population in some sections,
immobility of labor in other sections, and unemployables.
The Act stipulated that the federal government was to promote maximum purchasing power as well as maximum employment and production; clearly, control of inflation was
meant to receive equal attention.

James E. Webb was appointed Director of the Bureau of
the Budget on July 31, 1946, and served until January 27,
1949. After twenty years of legal and business experience, he
was first appointed as the executive assistant to the undersecretary of the Treasury, then Budget Director, and, in 1949,
Undersecretary of State. Frank Pace succeeded him as Director after ten years of legal experience and service for about a
year as assistant director of the Bureau of the Budget. Frederick J. Lawton, with many years of experience in the Budget
Bureau, was appointed Director on April 13, 1950, when
Frank Pace became Secretary of the Army.

In this period, new legislation gave the Bureau chiefs a
number of new duties. The Classification Act of 1949 required the Director to issue and administer regulations under
which agencies make systematic reviews of their operations
on a continuing basis. The Travel Expense Act of 1949 assigned to the Director regulatory functions with respect to
travel allowances. Executive Order 10033 of February 8,
1949, required the Director's approval for responses by federal agencies to statistical inquiries from intergovernmental
organizations.

After World War II, a number of significant steps toward the improvement of management and accounting control within the government were taken. In accordance with Public Law 162, approved July 7, 1947, the Commission on Organization of the Executive Branch was appointed by President Truman with Herbert Hoover as chairman. A number of different task forces were appointed, including one on fiscal, budgeting, and accounting activities, which submitted its report in January, 1949. A proposal of this task force, to return the budgeting organization to the Treasury under the direction of a new chief accounting officer, was not accepted by the Commission. However, the Commission did make significant recommendations for improvement in budgeting and in the appropriation structure, the principal ones, from a report dated February 15, 1949, being that: (1) a budget based upon functions, activities, and projects, designated a "performance budget," be adopted; (2) the appropriation structure be surveyed and improved; (3) budget estimates of all departments and agencies be separated between current operating expenditures and capital outlays; and (4) the President's authority to reduce expenditures under appropriations "if the purposes intended by the Congress are still carried out" be clearly established.

The recommendations of the first Hoover Commission resulted in legislation that greatly improved procedures. For example, the National Security Act of 1947 was amended in 1949 to provide for performance budgeting in the Department of Defense. Other 1949 amendments to the same Act authorized the establishment of comptroller positions in the Department of Defense and its component services and the establishment of working capital funds. The Budget and Accounting Procedures Act of 1950 recognized the need for accounting systems that would provide a reliable base for budgeting and management (see also Chapter V). By this Act, the President was given authority to prescribe the con-

tents and arrangements of the Budget, resulting in a simplification of presentation, the broadening of appropriations, and
progress in performance budgeting. Reorganization of the
Bureau of the Budget was effected in 1952 and resulted in
better coordination of the review function with its management, fiscal, and legislative responsibilities.

The Eisenhower Years

Joseph M. Dodge was serving as fiscal adviser to the undersecretary of the Army when General Eisenhower, after his
election as President in November, 1952, asked him to spend
the next two months reviewing the operations for fiscal 1953
and the proposed budget for fiscal 1954. He was appointed
Budget Director on January 22, 1953. An outstanding banker
and international expert on fiscal policy, he had been financial adviser to the U.S. Military Government in Berlin after
the war, had attended many ministerial meetings, and was
largely responsible for putting Japanese postwar finances on a
sound basis. During his tenure, the expenditures for fiscal
1953 of $74.1 billion were reduced to $67.5 billion in 1954
and $64.4 billion in 1955 with the end of the Korean War
and many improvements and economies.

Dodge had made the same promise that General Dawes,
the first Budget Director, had made—that is, that he would
take the job for a year but would be anxious then to return
to Detroit, Michigan, to his bank, from which he had been
away so much during the postwar years. Roland Hughes, his
deputy, succeeded him in April, 1954. Mr. Hughes was also
an experienced banker and budget officer and was for many
years controller of the National City Bank of New York. I
had known and worked with him on various committees of
the New York Chamber of Commerce, including the execu-

tive committee of which I was then chairman. Director Hughes asked me to come to Washington toward the end of April, 1954, to discuss some budget suggestions I had made, and, at that time, much to my surprise, the President asked me to become deputy director.

I had an exciting and grueling two years as deputy director, followed by two as Director. I was fortunate in having a strong and experienced staff: A. R. Jones, a certified public accountant from Kansas, was my deputy, and Percy Rappaport, also a C.P.A. but from New York, Ralph W. E. Reid, Robert E. Merriam, William F. McCandless, Roger W. Jones, William F. Finan, and Raymond T. Bowman were assistant directors. Among the many developments on which we worked were those growing out of the second Hoover Commission's report, entitled "Budget and Accounting," issued June 20, 1955, and based on the recommendations of a task force headed by J. Harold Steward, C.P.A., urging further strengthening of the Bureau of the Budget.

This report proposed:

> that the executive agencies report each year to the Bureau of the Budget and the President, on the conduct of their operations permitting comparison of the costs and efficiency of current operations with past performance, and should furnish suitable information relative to measures taken and planned to improve agency management.
>
> That after the Congress has granted an appropriation, allotments should be made supported by cost-based operating budgets furnished by the lower management levels, and followed by periodic reports to management, comparing budget projections with actual performance.
>
> That the executive budget continue to be based upon functions, activities, and projects adequately supported by information on program costs and accomplishment, and by a review of performance by organizational units where these do not coincide with performance budget classifications.

That the executive budget and congressional appropriations be in terms of estimated annual accrued expenditures, namely, charges for the cost of goods and services estimated to be received.

Additional recommendations included the establishment of the position of comptroller in all of the principal agencies and the suggestion that major subdivisions set up systems, recruit and train personnel, and prepare reports and budgets. All were strongly supported by the Bureau of the Budget, the General Accounting Office, and the Treasury Department.

The result was Public Law 863, approved on August 1, 1956, in the Eighty-fourth Congress, which provided that:

1. Agency accounts should be maintained on an accrual basis of accounting.*
2. Agencies should develop cost-based budgets in support of appropriation requests and for internal agency administration and operation purposes.
3. There should be, insofar as possible, consistency in the accounting and budgeting classifications of each agency and synchronization between su·h classifications and the agency's organizational structure, to the extent possible.
4. Supporting budget information on performance and program costs by organizational units should be provided when classifications do not coincide.
5. Each agency should work toward simplification of its administrative control of funds.

A related piece of legislation, Public Law 85-759—approved August 25, 1958, but which did not become law without a strenuous battle in Congress—enabled the Bureau to strengthen further its control over expenditures. It provided

---

*An accrual basis of accounting includes a service rendered or materials delivered at the date the liability of the government is determined rather than when the bills are received or the checks are issued. This is particularly important for work on long-term contracts under government specification.

for improved methods of stating budget estimates and for the inclusion of limitations on annual accrued expenditures, as follows:

> Whenever the President determines there has been established a satisfactory system of accrual accounting for an appropriation or fund account, each proposed appropriation thereafter transmitted to the Congress for such account pursuant to the provisions of this Act shall be accompanied by a proposed limitation on annual accrued expenditures. The President may include in the Budget, with any such proposed limitation on annual accrued expenditures, proposals for provisions authorizing the head of a department or establishment to make transfers within his department or establishment between such limitations on annual accrued expenditures; and such provisions may limit by amount or by per centum the size of any transfer so proposed.

Although it cannot be said that all the provisions of the laws just outlined have been put into effect, major steps have been taken in that direction, including accrual accounting. Most recently, the President's Committee on Budget Concepts has strongly urged the adoption of accrual accounting throughout the government and in the budget presentation. This should be possible within another year or two.

During 1957, A. R. Jones was appointed director of the Tennessee Valley Authority and Maurice H. Stans, then deputy postmaster-general, was appointed deputy director of the Budget. Stans also was a C.P.A. and a former president of the American Institute of Accountants. The following year, he succeeded me as Director.

In addition to the regular work, which is always exacting, two important projects were completed under Director Stans, a self-survey of the Bureau and a ten-year projection of federal expenditures. The self-survey was conducted by top Budget officials and made a number of suggestions for improved operations, most of which were put into effect. Although changes and improvements are continually being made, an exhaustive periodic review is useful. The ten-year projection was an important and interesting exercise and indicated the difficulty of long-range forecasts even with alternative range levels.

The 1960's

A special study of management improvement in the executive branch was also completed in the fall of 1960. For this report, a survey had been conducted in twenty-five departments and agencies through interviews with about nine hundred management officials by joint teams. Some eight hundred significant accomplishments in improved management were identified, "some of them constituting real breakthroughs involving meaningful savings in the cost of government."

With the change of Administration, President Kennedy appointed as Director David E. Bell, professor of economics at Harvard University and a former member of the staff of the Budget Bureau. He had also served as field director of the Agency for International Development in Pakistan. President Kennedy later felt that he needed Bell's experience in the foreign field and on December 20, 1962, appointed him Director of AID, where he made an exceptionally fine record. Kermit Gordon, a member of the Council of Economic Advisers, was appointed Budget Director. Gordon had also been a professor of economics, at Williams College, and had been a Rhodes scholar. He was succeeded in turn on June 1, 1965, by Charles L. Schultze, who had formerly been an assistant director of the Budget Bureau but more recently professor of economics at the University of Maryland. Schultze resigned in January, 1968, and was succeeded by Charles J. Zwick, an agricultural economist with a Ph.D. in economics who, after teaching at Harvard and with nine years of experience with RAND Corporation, had been assistant director of the Bureau of the Budget for the three years preceding his appointment as Director.

On January 21, 1969, Robert P. Mayo became Director of the Bureau of the Budget under President Richard M. Nixon. A graduate of the University of Washington, Mayo served as economist with the Department of the Treasury for more than twenty years, and he is thoroughly familiar with government finance. He has also had business and banking experience. Although the Bureau he heads was set up as an independent agency and the right arm of the President—responsible only to the President and located in his Executive Office—just thirty years ago, its duties and areas of operation have increased manyfold.

The present organization of the Bureau, now commonly called the BOB in Washington, is set forth in the next chapter. Subsequent chapters describe the Bureau's government-wide functions as it faces the problems of the 1970's.

III

The BOB Today:
Organization and Position

Since 1939, the Bureau of the Budget (BOB) has been a part of the Executive Office of the President. (See Chart 1.) The Director of the Bureau of the Budget is responsible to the President and to him alone. He is appointed by the President, and his appointment is neither submitted to nor confirmed by the Senate. He holds cabinet rank and is invited to attend Cabinet meetings, although not a member of the Cabinet. He is independent of all other agencies of the executive branch of the government and all other branches of the government.

The Director's position is much like that of the comptroller of a large corporation, although the latter is usually responsible to his board of directors rather than to his president. At the beginning of this century, in New England particularly, the treasurer of a company was often the chief executive officer, along with his financial and budget duties. In most businesses today, the treasurer is the custodian of the funds, depositing all receipts, making all payments on vouchers properly approved by the controller's office, and handling all securities and debt transactions. The comptroller is usually responsible for preparing the budgets, authorizing and ap-

Chart 1

EXECUTIVE BRANCH

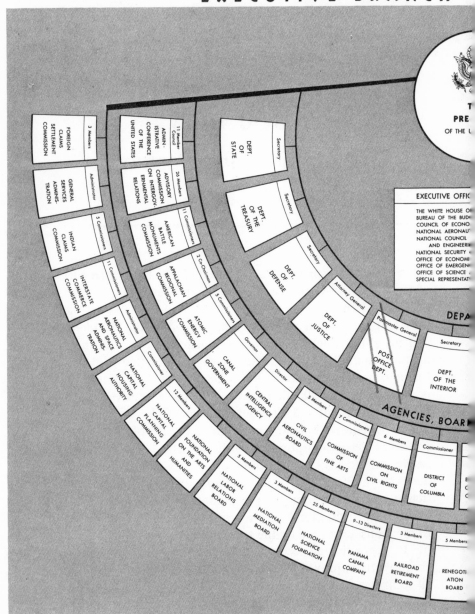

THE
PRE
OF THE U

EXECUTIVE OFFIC

THE WHITE HOUSE OF
BUREAU OF THE BUD
COUNCIL OF ECONO
NATIONAL AERONAUT
NATIONAL COUNCIL
AND ENGINEERI
NATIONAL SECURITY
OFFICE OF ECONOMI
OFFICE OF EMERGEN
OFFICE OF SCIENCE
SPECIAL REPRESENTAT

DEPA

AGENCIES, BOARD

FOREIGN CLAIMS SETTLEMENT COMMISSION

3 Members

GENERAL SERVICES ADMINS-TRATION

Administrator

ADMIN-ISTRATIVE CONFERENCE OF THE UNITED STATES

11 Members Council

DEPT. OF STATE

Secretary

INDIAN CLAIMS COMMISSION

5 Commissioners

ADVISORY COMMISSION ON INTERGOV-ERNMENTAL RELATIONS

26 Members

DEPT. OF THE TREASURY

Secretary

INTERSTATE COMMERCE COMMISSION

11 Commissioners

AMERICAN BATTLE MONUMENTS COMMISSION

11 Commissioners

DEPT. OF DEFENSE

Secretary

NATIONAL AERONAUTICS AND SPACE ADMINS-TRATION

Administrator

APPALACHIAN REGIONAL COMMISSION

2 Co-Chairmen

DEPT. OF JUSTICE

Attorney General

NATIONAL CAPITAL HOUSING AUTHORITY

Commissioner

ATOMIC ENERGY COMMISSION

5 Commissioners

POST OFFICE DEPT.

Postmaster General

NATIONAL CAPITAL PLANNING COMMISSION

12 Members

CANAL ZONE GOVERNMENT

Governor

DEPT. OF THE INTERIOR

Secretary

NATIONAL FOUNDATION ON THE ARTS AND HUMANITIES

CENTRAL INTELLIGENCE AGENCY

Director

NATIONAL LABOR RELATIONS BOARD

5 Members

CIVIL AERONAUTICS BOARD

5 Members

COMMISSION OF FINE ARTS

7 Commissioners

COMMISSION ON CIVIL RIGHTS

6 Members

DISTRICT OF COLUMBIA

Commissioner

NATIONAL MEDIATION BOARD

3 Members

NATIONAL SCIENCE FOUNDATION

25 Members

PANAMA CANAL COMPANY

9-13 Directors

RAILROAD RETIREMENT BOARD

3 Members

RENEGOTI ATION BOARD

5 Members

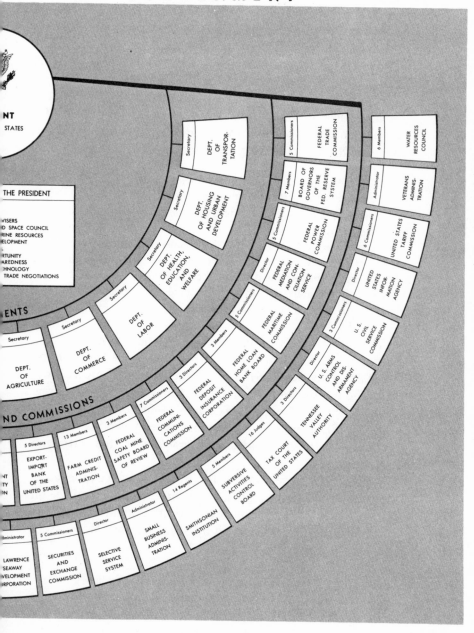

THE PRESIDENT

...VISERS
...ND SPACE COUNCIL
...RINE RESOURCES
...VELOPMENT
...
...RTUNITY
...AREDNESS
...HNOLOGY
...TRADE NEGOTIATIONS

NT
STATES

...ENTS

Secretary — DEPT. OF AGRICULTURE

Secretary — DEPT. OF COMMERCE

Secretary — DEPT. OF LABOR

Secretary — DEPT. OF HEALTH, EDUCATION, AND WELFARE

Secretary — DEPT. OF HOUSING AND URBAN DEVELOPMENT

Secretary — DEPT. OF TRANSPORTATION

...ND COMMISSIONS

5 Directors — EXPORT-IMPORT BANK OF THE UNITED STATES

13 Members — FARM CREDIT ADMINISTRATION

3 Members — FEDERAL COAL MINE SAFETY BOARD OF REVIEW

7 Commissioners — FEDERAL COMMUNICATIONS COMMISSION

3 Directors — FEDERAL DEPOSIT INSURANCE CORPORATION

3 Members — FEDERAL HOME LOAN BANK BOARD

5 Commissioners — FEDERAL MARITIME COMMISSION

Director — FEDERAL MEDIATION AND CONCILIATION SERVICE

5 Commissioners — FEDERAL POWER COMMISSION

7 Members — BOARD OF GOVERNORS OF THE FED. RESERVE SYSTEM

5 Commissioners — FEDERAL TRADE COMMISSION

...Iministrator — ...LAWRENCE SEAWAY ...VELOPMENT ...ORPORATION

5 Commissioners — SECURITIES AND EXCHANGE COMMISSION

Director — SELECTIVE SERVICE SYSTEM

Administrator — SMALL BUSINESS ADMINISTRATION

14 Regents — SMITHSONIAN INSTITUTION

5 Members — SUBVERSIVE ACTIVITIES CONTROL BOARD

16 Judges — TAX COURT OF THE UNITED STATES

3 Directors — TENNESSEE VALLEY AUTHORITY

Director — U. S. ARMS CONTROL AND DISARMAMENT AGENCY

3 Commissioners — U. S. CIVIL SERVICE COMMISSION

Director — UNITED STATES INFORMATION AGENCY

6 Commissioners — UNITED STATES TARIFF COMMISSION

Administrator — VETERANS ADMINISTRATION

6 Members — WATER RESOURCES COUNCIL

proving expenditures, and improving the management controls. Similarly, the Budget Director authorizes expenditures through the budget and the apportionment processes. The Treasury Department makes the disbursements, but the control and management power lie in the Budget Bureau.

Percy Rappaport, former assistant director of the Bureau, in an article in the *Journal of Accounting* (March, 1956), brought out the position of the Bureau as a sort of liaison between the agencies and the President—

> . . . a reviewing agency of things flowing up to the President from the individual departments whenever they do not fit into the assignments of the other parts of the Executive Office of the President. In performing this review function the Bureau attempts to judge whether the matter is ready for the President's attention, whether all angles of likely interest to the President are clearly identified, and whether in making his decision the President will have before him not only an indication of the expected results, but also possible alternatives he may want to consider.

The effectiveness of the Bureau depends upon the President and his confidence in the expertness of the Director and his staff. They act for the chief executive and protect him from the multiplicity of details that make up each small segment of the total budget. The line of authority runs down from the President—from the most experienced assistant director to the most recent college graduate on the staff—and back up to him.

The President's relation to the Bureau is well expressed in the following excerpt from a report by the Subcommittee on National Policy Machinery of the Senate Committee on Government Operations submitted by Senator Henry M. Jackson, October 16, 1961:

> The Budget Bureau will never win a bureaucratic popularity contest. The total program requests of the operating departments always far

exceed any budget a President can prudently approve. The Bureau must often be a no-sayer and help the Chief Executive trim agency programs to fit the Presidential cloth. Hence its reputation, even if undeserved, as the villain of the executive branch.

Each President must decide how he wants to use the Bureau.

A President can employ the Bureau mainly to keep a lid on expenditures. The Bureau, in such cases, is told to "hold the line"— but may be given little guidance concerning the Chief Executive's priorities and program goals.

A President, however, can employ the Bureau differently. He can use it as his "lengthened shadow" across the whole front of fiscal policy and program management. The Director of this kind of Budget Bureau sits in the innermost policy councils of the Presidency. Program planning and budgeting are seen as but different aspects of one process, which starts with the formulation of policy objectives and ends with costed and time-phased programs for action. The President regards the Bureau as his strong right arm in executive management.

A President will do well to use the Bureau of the Budget in this way.

Since the Budget Director is an assistant to the President, he must support the Administration's program. He participates actively in its development, of course, and has many opportunities to present his own point of view, but, if it becomes clear that he is not in agreement with the program of the President when it is developed, he should resign. The civil service staff will see that the work is carried out effectively.

Internal Organization

The Bureau of the Budget, one of whose major functions is to advise and assist the President on the organization and management of the entire executive branch, has had a difficult time deciding how to organize itself. The reason, of course, is that its role requires its staff, only a few hundred strong, to combine technical and professional competence in a variety of complex functional areas and an intimate knowledge of the whole range of federal agencies and programs. The problem has been to divide up the Bureau's staff and apportion its responsibilities so as to achieve the most effective blending of the functional and the agency, or program, bases of organization.

From 1939 to 1952, the Bureau's organization appeared to be based primarily on function. As previously noted, there were five divisions, each one charged with responsibility for one of the Bureau's main functions—budget preparation and review, fiscal, organization and management, legislative clearance, and coordination of statistical programs. However, the importance of agency and program specialization was recognized in the subdivision of the Estimates Division into a number of units, each of which had budget review responsibility for specified agencies and programs. These agency and program specialists, moreover, were extensively consulted by the other divisions in carrying out their functional responsibilities. In one instance, at least, involving the international area, budget and organization and management responsibilities were combined in one unit of the Estimates Division.

The current organization of the Bureau (see Chart 2) is a modified version of the scheme adopted in 1952. It gives more formal recognition than did the previous arrangement to agency and program specialization, although the functional basis of organization is still controlling. The Bureau staff is now divided about equally between six offices and six divisions. One office has general administration and related responsibilities. Each of the other five—Budget Review, Program Evaluation, Executive Management, Legislative Reference, and Statistical Policy—has general responsibility for one of the Bureau's major functions. Each of the six divi-

Chart 2

EXECUTIVE OFFICE OF THE PRESIDENT
BUREAU OF THE BUDGET

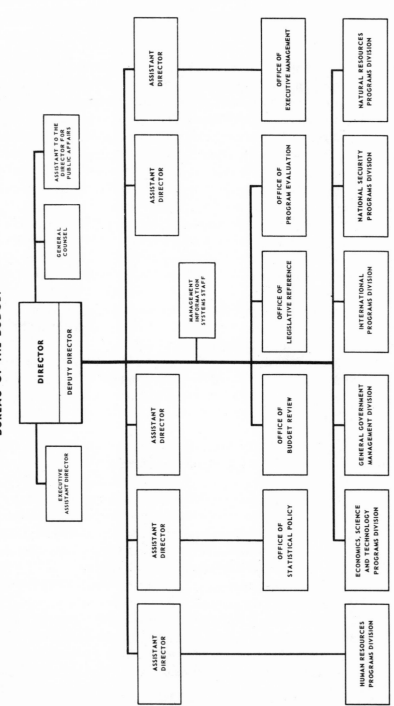

sions—National Security Programs, Natural Resources Programs, Human Resources Programs, Economics, Science, and Technology Programs, International Programs, and General Government Management Programs—is charged with carrying out the Bureau's functions in its program area.

Throughout the existence of the Budget Bureau, change has been one of its consistent and interesting characteristics. Organization, as well as leadership, has changed continually to meet new problems and developments in business and government. Thus, any detailed statement of its present organization is, of necessity, only illustrative. Further changes are always under consideration; some of them will probably become effective even before this book is published. For example, the whole system of accounting and accounting procedures will undoubtedly be adapted to electronic equipment before very long, possibly bringing about additional organizational adaptation.

What follows is a brief description of the structure of the Bureau as of July 1, 1969, with one new office in operation (and reflecting the increased importance of the planning-programing-budgeting system).

Office of the Director

The common management and service activities required for the effective operation of the Bureau of the Budget are centered in the Office of the Director. These activities consist of support operations for the Bureau's top management and the conduct of general administrative services.

The principal internal management functions of this office are personnel administration and position management, budget planning and control, personnel and documentary security, clearance of Bureau issuances, and analysis of particular operations in the Bureau to assure efficiency and economy in the performance of the Bureau's work. The general administrative services furnished centrally include the usual payroll and fiscal services; provision of office equipment and supplies and duplicating and graphics services; maintenance of messenger and mail services; distribution of reports and other materials needed by the offices and divisions; administration of records; and management of a specialized library for the professional staff.

A number of changes have been made in the Director's office over the past several years, and it will, doubtless, change again in response to the ever increasing pressure to make the Bureau fully responsive to the very big needs of a very big government. At present, the Director is assisted by a deputy director, five assistant directors (in addition to the assistant directors in charge of the separate offices listed below), an executive assistant director, a general counsel, an assistant to the Director for Public Affairs, a director of Administration, and a small working group called the Management Information Systems Staff.

Office of Budget Review

The Office of Budget Review is primarily responsible for the major task of the Bureau, the preparation of the federal budget itself. (See Chapter IV.) It has five staff directors in charge of five separate functions.

Budget Preparation. This section prepares the budget, supplemental estimates, and special compilations. The director (who is also an assistant director of the Bureau) and his deputy are responsible for the preparation of the material going into the budget, interim projection and analyses of expenditures, analyses of congressional action on budget proposals whether or not recommended by the Administration, and close liaison with the appropriations committees of the House and the Senate.

Planning and Analysis. The job of this section is to prepare or assign to divisions the preparation of projections and reviews, economic assumptions, and fiscal policy for budgetary use; to supervise the publication of the budget messages; to help prepare the bases for the estimates of tax and miscellaneous receipts; to prepare the data on federal receipts and expenditures for the national income accounts; and to provide analytical support for the Bureau in its relations with state and local governments and their fiscal problems. It also maintains liaison with the tax staffs of the Secretary of the Treasury and the staffs of the Council of Economic Advisers, the Federal Reserve Board, and other governmental and private agencies concerned primarily with fiscal and economic policy, and with congressional committees interested in these subjects.

Monetary and Credit Analysis. The duties of this group are to coordinate the federal credit policy involved in budgetary requests and legislative proposals, plans for sales of assets, and other substitution of private funds for federal credits; to review regulatory policy and assist in clearance of proposed legislation affecting private financial institutions; to analyze trends in general monetary policy and interest rates; to assist in the clearance of proposed legislation for government insurance programs (other than retirement and social insurance); and to analyze the effect of proposed government transactions abroad that relate to the balance of payments and to recommend actions to be taken. This staff maintains continuous liaison with the staffs of the Treasury Department, the Council of Economic Advisers, the Federal Reserve Board, and other government and private agencies concerned primarily with monetary and credit policy.

Resources Systems. Here the assignment is to direct efforts toward the improvement of the federal budget system for the governmentwide development of planning-programing-budgeting systems (PPB) and to see that they are used in the formulation of the annual budget. The group also provides assistance in legislative clearance, training programs, and consultation with representatives of federal agencies, state and local governments, foreign countries, and special interest groups.

Cost Analysis and Reduction. * This section develops techniques for analyzing resource requirements; promotes the use of cost analysis in the budget review process and throughout the executive branch; advises the Director on the progress made in the President's cost-reduction program; and provides a focal point for the development of user changes and the review of representation allowances, manpower use, restraints, and analyses on federal employment.

Office of Program Evaluation

Originally the Program Evaluation Staff of the Office of the Director was organized in the Budget Bureau in August, 1965, as part of the introduction of planning-programing-budgeting into the federal government. This office was upgraded to its present status in January, 1969. Its director is also identified as assistant director of the Bureau of the Budget for Program Evaluation. As such, he provides leadership for the development and implementation of the PPB system throughout the federal government. The Office of Program Evaluation participates in formulating and drafting the major program issues that must be analyzed during forthcoming and future budget cycles.

Offices of Executive Management, Legislative Reference, and Statistical Standards

The Office of Executive Management, the functions and organization of which are described more fully in Chapter V, is charged with the general responsibility for maintenance of

*This section has since been transferred to the Office of Executive Management.

and continuous improvements in federal management systems and proper interagency coordination. The Office of Legislative Reference analyzes all proposed legislation for clearance purposes. (See Chapter VI.) The Office of Statistical Policy is responsible for coordinating the wide-flung statistical services of the federal government. (See Chapter VII.)

The Divisions

Although the staffs of all six of the offices described above have continuous direct and indirect contacts with the different departments and agencies, much of the detailed day-to-day work with agency programs is done through the professional staff in the six divisions, to which approximately half of the total Budget Bureau staff is assigned. These extremely able civil servants are the support troops of the Bureau.

Each division deals with a broad segment of U.S. Government activities, bringing the Bureau's budgetary, fiscal, legislative, and management responsibilities to bear upon the programs that fall within that segment. The divisions review agency programs and budget requests, develop recommendations on the budget, and assist the Director in the control and review of the execution of the budget. They also analyze agency planning-programing-budgeting submissions and proposed legislation and executive orders, stimulate and assist the agencies in the improvement of management and organization, work on special projects involving long-range budgetary and organizational improvement, generally in cooperation with one of the offices, and propose improvements in the coordination of agency programs. The division organization as of July 1, 1969, was as follows.

National Security Programs. There are a division director, a deputy director, and assistant directors for Special Projects, the Army, the Navy, and the Air Force. This division covers the Department of Defense and a few related civilian functions. (See also Chapter VIII.)

Natural Resources Programs. The director of the division has under him an assistant to the director for PPB, an assistant director for special projects, and assistant directors for agriculture, interior, and water resources, which includes the Corps of Army Engineers' civilian functions. (See Chapter IX.)

Human Resources Programs. The division director supervises the work of a deputy director and special assistants for budget and special projects, an associate director for program coordination, and assistant directors for education, health, and medical programs as well as those of housing and urban development, income maintenance and veterans affairs, and labor and manpower. (This division and the following three divisions are covered more fully in Chapter X.)

Economics, Science, and Technology Programs. Assistant directors in this division are in charge of general management, economic development, transportation, space programs, general science, and atomic energy.

International Programs. The director of the division, and his deputy are in charge of the work of assistant directors for the Department of State and the U.S. Information Agency, economic assistance, military assistance, and intelligence.

General Government Management. This division has a director, a deputy director for programs, and a deputy director for management. There are assistant directors for Justice and the District of Columbia, postal property and fiscal, automatic data processing (ADP) management, property and supply management, and personnel management. The responsibilities in the areas of ADP, property and supply, and personnel were only recently transferred to this division from the old Office of Management and Organization. These duties are in the nature of management functions and are assigned to three separate branches of this division.

The ADP Management branch provides policies and standards used by federal agencies in the management and operation of their own data-processing activities, participates in Bureau reviews of these activities, and provides fiscal and policy control over the governmentwide programs of the General Services Administration with respect to the procurement, utilization, redistribution, and disposal of ADP equipment and of the National Bureau of Standards with respect to the development and recommendation of data-processing standards and the conduct of research in computer sciences and technology. It also maintains continuous liaison with the computer industry and professional and trade associations to assure that the latest trends and advances in computer technology are considered in the formulation of government policies and programs.

The Property and Supply Management branch conducts studies and develops recommendations in connection with management improvement, budget review, and legislative coordination on governmentwide problems relating to policies, regulations, procedures, and organization for federal real and personal property management, including purchasing and contracting; maintenance and repair; handling of surpluses; development of standards, specifications, and catalogues; motor-vehicle management; and public building programs. It also performs staff work on standardized government travel regulations and transportation of employees' household goods; working hours in metropolitan Washington, D.C.; federal employees' uniform-allowance regulations, and so on.

The Personnel Management branch conducts investigations and develops recommendations for more effective organization and systems—employment, pay, benefits, and status—relating to the management of federal government personnel and serves as a focal point of Bureau coordination with the Civil Service Commission.

The Bureau's Own Budget

The BOB budget for the three years covered in the 1969 budget message is set forth below in thousands of dollars:

Program by Activities	1967 Actual	1968 Actual	1969 Estimate
Office of Budget Review	$1,149	$1,163	$ 1,359
Office of Executive Management	926	929	1,263
Office of Legislative Reference	310	327	328
Office of Statistical Standards	649	597	693
Program Divisions			
Economics, Science, and Technology	490	541	583
General Government Management	697	724	844
Human Resources	909	978	1,049
International	584	644	643
National Security	757	757	813
Natural Resources	731	736	795
Executive Direction and Administration	1,610	1,846	1,940
Total program costs, funded	$8,813	$9,242	$10,310
Actual appropriation		$9,500	$10,000

The proposed increases were partly to provide for the adoption and utilization of a system of longer-range resources planning and the establishment of a management information system covering the status and progress of federal programs to complement and supplement the planning-programing-budget systems and aid in determining priority of projects and alternative courses of action. The severe budget cuts made this expansion impossible. However, allowances for the new Office of Program Evaluation out of funds listed under

"Executive Direction and Administration" above were expected to help in attainment of these goals.

Much greater increases were not proposed because of the serious budget stringency. It is unfortunate that the fiscal and management staff was reduced when the cause of the stringency is partly attributable to the lack of sufficient staff to foresee and prevent it. In my opinion, the Bureau at present is understaffed by at least 50 per cent. The proposed 1969 staff levels of the Bureau, which were greater than the current level, compared with those of the General Accounting Office (GAO) as follows:

	GAO	BOB
Management and top grades, GS-14 and up	572	229
GS-11-13, inclusive	1,725	115
Total numbers, all grades	4,499	546

This is not, of course, a criticism of the numbers of the General Accounting Office but of the inadequacy of the Bureau's small numbers. Without sufficient staff, the Bureau can neither fully meet its responsibilities nor seize its opportunities.

The BOB Staff

The staff of the Bureau must have administrative ability as well as technical skill in the areas that the divisions serve. Each member of a division staff is assigned to an individual agency and is expected to become familiar with all the operations of the agency or its sections or subagencies to which he has been assigned. He must become acquainted with the legislative background as well as the programs approved by Congress and the funds apportioned to each. At the time of budget preparation, he must spend his full time analyzing the needs for the future based on his review of the current programs and the developing needs of the agency that has become, in effect, his client. He is invited to be present at the agency presentation of its budget and also at the Budget Director's review and all conferences relating to his client's operations. He is consulted with respect to all legislation introduced or proposed that affects the agency's interests. He is expected to make suggestions with respect to improvements in management and organization to the Bureau's Office of Executive Management and is, of course, consulted about any plans for improvements that others have suggested.

In making staff assignments among the offices and the divisions, the Bureau leadership must remember that it is desirable to maintain continuity, if possible for several years in an assignment, but it is also useful to provide for rotation to bring in a fresh viewpoint and new ideas. It is particularly helpful in the division assignments if the staff assistant has had some previous experience or training in the area in which his client operates.

Security clearance is required for all staff members, and periodic reviews are made. Top-secret clearance is required for the Director and all of those connected with national security, atomic energy, and the intelligence community.

The background, education, and expertise of the Bureau staff are extremely varied. The staff includes scientists, educators, engineers, economists, certified public accountants, and lawyers. Practically all members of the technical staff hold at least one college degree and more than one-half have a master's degree or its equivalent. At present, there are twenty-nine who have doctorates, and there have been a number of Rhodes scholars. Many have been recipients of distinguished service awards.

In order to see how recent additions to the Bureau staff had specialized in college, a study was made during the first eight months of calendar year 1967, when 47 new professional staff members were added. Of these, 15 had specialized in economics, 12 having received graduate degrees; 10 had specialized in political science, with 3 having received graduate degrees; 6 had specialized in business administration, with 5 having received graduate degrees. The rest had specialized in engineering, science, or history. Of the total number, 6 had received law degrees, 4 graduate degrees in public administration, 2 in industrial relations, 1 in geology, 1 in education, and 1 in city planning.

Other recent studies have indicated that all members of the new staff have college degrees and well over one-half have at least one graduate degree. Courses in higher mathematics and accounting were usually included in either undergraduate or postgraduate work. An interesting sample case, one of the staff assistants in agriculture, had been a "dirt farmer" and for several years had made his living raising cattle. A highly trained mechanical engineer is presently in charge of budgeting for the naval forces, particularly their airlift and sealift capacities. A civil engineer on the staff is one of its greatest masters at drafting precise and clear organization orders. A West Point graduate is an expert in government organization, management, and personnel administration. Two psychologists are using their education and training in personnel work. A lawyer on the staff developed special capabilities in supply management and is now called upon if there are any questions in this field.

My own experience leads me to believe that there is no more capable staff than the Budget Bureau's to be found in either business or government. Interestingly, there are perhaps more people on the staff with general experience and qualifications than there are specialists. Other agency heads recognize the knowledge and expertise of the Bureau staff. I am sure that other Budget directors have found, as I did, that many new Presidential appointees in the executive branch call to ask for a rundown on the difficult problems with which their departments are confronted.

Although the operations have changed substantially since my time as Director, the unchanging mission of the Bureau is today what was authorized in Executive Order 8248 issued September 8, 1939. A recent promotion booklet of the Bureau describes that mission as being to provide direct staff assistance to the President of the United States in five major areas of responsibility:

Formulation, presentation, and execution of the President's annual budget;

Improvement of Federal management and organization including financial management systems, inter-agency coordination of operations and development, and maintenance of general management systems;

Analysis of proposed legislation and Executive orders and review of legislation enacted by the Congress before Presidential action to approve or disapprove it;

Coordination and improvement of Federal statistical programs;

Planning and evaluation of Federal substantive programs.

This, it concludes, is an unusually demanding assignment "encompassing the entire range of federal activity. Solution of issues requires many different skills. The objective of the Bureau's staff work is analysis and recommendation, aiming for synthesis, not just compromise, among the various alternatives."

IV

Budget Preparation
and Presentation

The fundamental decisions on every new budget relate to the programs to be carried out to meet the national needs—the choice of objectives, the determination of the level, and the estimated receipts available to carry them out. The budget, including the legislative program, reflects the President's proposals with regard to all the programs of the government for each succeeding year—and his taxation policy as well.

No other government in the world has a similar budget system. During my period of service as Director, delegates from many other countries called to find out how the Bureau operated. It was difficult for them to understand its functions and operations. The whole U.S. system of budget preparation and submission, in which they seemed to be particularly interested, is so different from that of a parliamentary government, in which there is no separation of powers. A parliamentary government's budget is presented by a prime minister or fiscal officer and is either accepted or rejected in total. Rejection indicates a lack of confidence in the government, and resignations are expected, or new elections must be held. In the U.S. system, the Bureau of the Budget prepares the budget for the President to submit to Congress, where it is thoroughly reviewed. Substantive additions and deductions are made, both to present and proposed programs, and new programs may be added, necessitating constant revisions in the Budget as originally proposed. Such changes are unheard of abroad.

The government's programs must be considered within the framework of economic and fiscal policy as well as national needs, with attention to the impact of federal activities and taxation upon the nation as a whole and upon differing regions and industrial groups. Although the budget is basically a set of well-balanced proposals, not merely a collection of forecasts, its development in the over-all economic setting requires the use of the best available techniques of forecasting and projection. With the increase in federal lending and loan guarantee activities, as well as in the light of international monetary developments, the relation of government programs to monetary and credit policy has become a matter of great importance.

Budget preparation also requires the evaluation of the "input"—the application of resources—available to achieve the desired program output. This requirement means that there must be a thorough examination of budgetary requirements for personnel, space, travel, matériel, contractual services, and the other pertinent elements, just as surveillance of budget execution must be maintained in order to see that money, men, and materials are not wasted and that their utilization produces planned results. For this important process, the Bureau has come to lean heavily on the planning-programing-budgeting system, first broadly utilized in the Department of Defense under Secretary Robert S. McNamara.

The object of PPB is simply to apply accounting and economic analyses to help arrive at the best decisions in the allocation of available resources. Actually an extension of what used to be called cost analysis and cost-effectiveness studies, it is geared to over-all programs that cross over and, in many cases, disregard agency or service lines. It is now being adopted throughout the government under the direction of the Bureau and with the encouragement of the General Accounting Office, in the hope that, as President Johnson told members of the Cabinet and heads of agencies on August 25, 1965, once in operation it will enable us to:

1. identify our national goals with precision and on a continuing basis;
2. choose among those goals the ones that are most urgent;
3. search for alternative means of reaching those goals most effectively at the least cost;
4. inform ourselves not merely on next year's costs—but on the second, and third, and subsequent year's costs—of our programs;
5. measure the performance of our programs to ensure a dollar's worth of service for each dollar spent.

The Budget Bureau is not a policy-maker, but it can serve as a stimulus to desirable new programs and act as a check on undue enthusiasm for expansion of established programs and new ventures in times of budget stringency. Although all programs are subject to the decision and direction of the President, the Bureau is expected to exert a positive influence, not to act as an echo. This spirit is reflected in Director Robert Mayo's testimony before the Joint Economic Committee on June 12, 1969:

Allocating limited resources among alternative uses is the very essence of budgeting. In federal budgeting there are two levels of resource allocation and priority determination: first, between the private and the public sectors; and, second, within the public sector.

A detailed evaluation of programs guides us in the recommendations that the executive branch makes to the Congress for the federal sector. The final allocations are, of course, the responsibility of the executive branch and the Congress acting in concert. These allocations within the federal sector reflect political, economic, and social decisions, and, therefore, measure our national priorities.

Obligational Authority and Expenditures

The first step in the inauguration of a new program by Congress is an "authorization." This is the enactment of substantive legislation providing the legal basis for a specified program. It usually starts with the introduction in the House or the Senate of a bill that is then referred to a committee. If this bill is enacted, the next step will be the request for an appropriation; this is called "obligational authority" and is an authorization to incur obligations and to make payments out of the U.S. Treasury. It is usually for the current year only but can be made a "no year" appropriation, which enables it to be carried forward. New obligational authority, or NOA, becomes newly available each year.

In the early days of the Budget Bureau, the greater part of the expenditures was for services rendered in the same year for which the authority was granted. Today, a substantial part of federal expenditures is for construction, complex equipment, research and development, loans, purchase of commodities, strategic materials, and other programs that may extend over several years. This change, together with the increased importance of U.S. participation in international activities, the worldwide character of U.S. defense efforts, and the rapid technological advances on planes, missiles, and all types of transportation and delivery of weapons, has increased the need for large advance authorizations and resulted in considerable time lag between new obligational authority and expenditures.

Each new Congress is faced with the fact that its predecessors have committed it to expenditures that it cannot control. This has actually rendered the preparation of the budget for a single year at a time obsolete. Today, advance planning for at least five years is necessary.

The Budget Bureau is always working on three different budgets. The President is required to submit his annual Budget Message to Congress for the fiscal year that will begin the following July 1 within fifteen days of the convening of Congress in January. This time lapse is to give both the Senate and the House of Representatives at least five months for consideration and enactment of the necessary authorizations before the next fiscal year begins, although recently they have often overrun the beginning of the new fiscal year by several months. In this Budget Message, the President also submits revised estimates for the then current fiscal year based on legislation enacted by the previous session of Congress and on revisions required by new developments throughout the world. In addition, the actual figures for the fiscal year ending the previous June 30, which by now have been determined, are also included.

Just as soon as the Message has been presented to Congress, and while representatives of the agencies are appearing before the committees of Congress to explain the detailed requests for the fiscal year beginning July 1 next, the Bureau continues to develop the outline of guidelines for the following fiscal year beginning seventeen months later.

Budget Guidelines

"Guidelines" as used by the Bureau of the Budget means suggestions for the preparation of new budget requests. These guidelines point out programs that need particular attention for either new or increased efforts to meet developing problems, improvements in direction or efficiency, and the increases or decreases considered desirable in appropriations or expenditures, or even the entire elimination of programs because they are no longer required or must be dropped because of budget stringency. Additional programs are always under consideration—either those previously under discussion and postponed or new ones to meet new needs that have developed. As an example, the subjects recommended in April, 1969, by the Budget Director to the Department of Health, Education, and Welfare (HEW) for close analysis were as follows:

Health
   Hunger and Malnutrition
   Increasing the Production of Physicians
   Health Services Research and Development
   Community Mental Health Services
   Health Insurance

Education
   Experimental Education Programs
   Student Aid
   Program Evaluation Plan
   Institutional Costs and Financial Status
   Analysis and Data System for Elementary and Secondary Education

Welfare
   Relationship of the Social Security Benefit System to Current Prices and Earnings
   Effectiveness of the Social Services Provided to Public Assistance Receipts
   Utilization of the Minimum Benefit Under Social Security to Support the Income of Needy Beneficiaries
   Short-term Assessment and Long-term Evaluation Plan for the Work Incentive (WIN) Program

In addition to study reports on each subject, HEW was asked to prepare an over-all program memorandum for each of the three major study areas. These documents were to be submitted with the budget request material and were to summarize the results of the individual studies and discuss other issues requiring a decision in the current budget cycle. For each study subject, additional detailed suggestions were provided. (See also Chapter X.)

The guidelines often include a suggested range of expenditures and areas in which some special consideration seems to be needed. The formulation of these guidelines is of considerable importance. They are based in part on the results and estimates of the three fiscal years covered in the President's previous message. But they are also based on the Administration's long-range policies and programs, on forecasts of future conditions throughout the world, on estimates of what the gross national product (GNP) will be, on the prospects for high-level employment, on the anticipated income under present laws on various assumptions, and on possible increases or decreases in taxation.

The forecasts are prepared by the planning staff of the Budget Bureau, the Council of Economic Advisers, the Treasury Department, the State Department, and the Defense Department primarily, but they are discussed with all the other departments and with congressional leaders. Under President Eisenhower, budget proposals were aired at several Cabinet meetings before they were formalized. He was very anxious to get the full support of his Cabinet and principal advisers; although differences in view were fully expressed, he made it very clear that once a decision was reached he expected complete loyalty and whole-hearted support. Under Presidents John F. Kennedy and Lyndon B. Johnson, the budget programs and figures were broken up and discussed in smaller meetings of the persons directly affected. The foreign programs were taken up particularly with the departments of State, Treasury, and Defense. Domestic programs were taken up with the departments and congressional representatives concerned, but few general presentations were made.

Agency Requests

After the general guidelines have been established, it becomes the responsibility of the executive agencies to put together their preliminary budget estimates for the budget year that will not commence for another twelve to fourteen months.

Each agency must consider the following questions:

1. What is the necessary level of current programs that must be continued in the next budget year? What would be the effects of possible cuts? What increases are desirable and how necessary are they? What new programs should be considered? How important are they? Do they meet the developing needs of the country? Are they the proper function of the federal government, because the citizens themselves cannot do them at all or as well as the federal government? Are the states and municipalities not able or willing to undertake them?

2. What resources are now available in the form of unused obligational authority, expected receipts from user charges,* or reimbursements from other agencies, and the use of stores and supplies on hand? What commitments have been entered into for which obligational authority has not yet been provided?

One of the weaknesses of governmental accounting in the past has been that expenditures have been recorded only on a

---

*A user charge is exactly what the term implies. For example, the National Parks Service collects user charges from campers. The federal gasoline tax and aviation fuel tax are user charges, restricted to the support of federal highway programs and airport development, respectively.

checks-issued basis (indeed, at one time, on a checks-cleared basis). Accrual accounting, however, has been approved by Congress and is gradually being put into effect, with complete adoption scheduled for fiscal 1972.

The departments and agencies used to submit by June or early July, preliminary estimates of what their recommendations would be for the following fiscal year (commencing twelve months later). Between 1961 and 1965, planning figures were prepared in the Bureau after informal discussion with the agencies but without any formal submissions by them. Under the present planning-programing-budgeting system, the major agencies submit an updated program and financial plan (PFP) between February 15 and July 15.* The PFP, a comprehensive summary of agency programs in terms of their outputs, costs, and financing needs over a planning period covering the budget year and at least four future years, has become the basic planning document of the agency PPB system. The figures it shows are assembled by the Budget Bureau and discussed with the President, who may also discuss the totals with individual department heads and budget officers. Changes may be made in the guidelines, and then the preparation of the detailed budget requests is resumed.

After discussions with the Bureau staff, the agency head decides upon his program recommendations and submits his budget requests with a revised PFP to the Bureau on or before September 30, together with supporting program memoranda and special analytic studies. The agency requests are then thoroughly analyzed by the Office of Budget Review and the division staffs, which have been following current agency programs very closely. Hearings are held. Summaries are prepared for the President, and he is kept advised of all important differences between the agencies and the Bureau and the possible consequences of alternatives. The totals of

*Here briefly summarized, the preparation and submission of annual budget estimates is explained in full in BOB Circular A-11, excerpted in Appendix C.

the proposed expenditures are again compared with the expected receipts and the programs are reviewed in relation to a new forecast of the economic and international outlook. The Council of Economic Advisers is kept advised with respect to all programs having a significant effect on the economic outlook, especially those that should be considered alongside the possible effects of any international incident, extended strikes, or unusual domestic developments.

In the hearings conducted by the Bureau of the Budget for each department or agency after the receipt of their estimates and the preliminary review by the Bureau staff, the Director or deputy director is on hand when the presentation is made by the agency head, who explains the policy questions of the greatest importance and brings out the salient points in which their departments are most interested. The heads of the subsidiary operating divisions or offices then describe their needs as foreseen. The budget officer of the agency indicates how these policies and needs can best be met by the budget figures presented.

After the agency presentations, the Bureau staff again reviews the requests in depth. The next stage is what is called the "Director's review." The Director and his deputy or some of his assistants hear the Bureau staff present their appraisal of each agency's needs and their reasons for questioning the amounts proposed. These reviews and the agency presentation take up most of the Director's time during October and November. After he has given careful consideration to the differences and has determined his recommendations, he advises the President and the effect of the alternatives is again discussed. The President has been kept advised of the principal points of difference as the hearings with the different agencies have progressed. The Director is, of course, guided by the President's views in the positions taken, but, after the agency has been advised of the Bureau's decision, there is no appeal except to the President.

After agreement is reached with each department and agency, the budget figures are set up in type. Proofs are prepared and cleared as soon as possible, partly to spread the volume of work in the Bureau and in the Government Printing Office and partly to speed the decision-making process. Last-minute changes can be made up to the end of December, but it becomes increasingly difficult after the first of that month.

Many of the budgetary decisions are not easy, and there is not as much latitude as might appear from the magnitude of the figures. There are certain necessities, such as interest payments and the daily conduct of the federal government. There are certain priorities in defense, veterans, and health programs. Many farm programs have been determined a year in advance, when support prices were announced before new plantings were made. Many contracts for future delivery and long-term construction programs requiring periodic payments have been placed. By deducting the amounts for such programs as these, the range of flexibility is determined. The Bureau's staff addresses itself primarily to reaching a fair balance among programs of the different agencies in similar and in widely different fields both at home and abroad.

The Budget Message and Congressional Reaction

While the departmental and agency hearings are being held, the Budget Message itself is in course of preparation to summarize and emphasize the most important developments. Before the message is completed, there is another over-all look at the total figures. Will the total expenditures that seem reasonable and necessary after months of analysis and study come within the expected receipts? Will new taxes be necessary and, if so, what recommendations will be made to Congress? Will another deficit be acceptable or even tolerated, and by how much will Congress probably cut or expand the Administration's requests?

The Budget Message itself is usually drafted by the Director and his assistants and is reviewed by the White House staff. It receives a lot of Presidential attention to be sure that it adequately sets forth the President's policies and dovetails with but does not duplicate what is included in the State of the Union Message (which usually precedes it) or the Economic Report (which follows it).

The annual-budget document contains the estimates of the President as to anticipated receipts under present legislation and his proposals to Congress for changes in taxes, postal rates, and other user charges. It likewise contains his estimates of the expenditures under present legislation and obligational authority already granted, together with his requests for new obligational authority, and his estimates of expenditures to be made therefrom during the next budget year.

During the months following the delivery of the Budget Message in January, all the requests are thoroughly examined by Congress. The Director usually appears before the House Appropriations Committee as a whole, accompanied by such of his staff as he thinks may be required to make the initial presentation and answer questions. He also appears before the subcommittee that deals with the expenditure requests for the Budget Bureau itself. The Director and his staff are always available for questions by individual congressmen and senators. Each department head, together with his staff, also appears to testify and justify all his proposals before the appropriation committees of both the House and the Senate.

Authorizations must be requested from the substantive committees, meeting as a whole, and appropriations from the appropriation subcommittees assigned to the particular agency—all of which means the repeated appearance of the department and agency heads and time spent in preparing as well as testifying. This is necessary under present congressional procedure to acquaint the committee members with the programs and the reasons for the requests that have been submitted. Joint hearings by the several committees concerned have often been suggested, but these are rarely held because they interfere with congressional prerogative.

The members of Congress naturally are anxious to find out the real views of the agency heads about their programs and whether their initial requests submitted to the Budget Bureau have been accepted or reduced. The President is equally anxious not to have any serious differences of opinion disclosed, since he has the responsibility for submitting the over-all budget figures that he considers desirable and necessary to carry on his programs.

This difference of viewpoint between Congress and the executive has been troublesome from the beginning. In *The National Budget System* cited earlier, W. F. Willoughby stated that administrative officials appearing before the committees on appropriations of Congress, "have difficulty in refraining from urging larger appropriations for their services than those carried in the budget." He noted that President Warren G. Harding found it necessary to admonish officials on this point in the following language:

I have noticed from the hearings before the Appropriation Committees of Congress that some of the officials of the Government have not yet realized that under the Budget and Accounting Act the estimates which are before Congress are those submitted by the Chief Executive. The officials to whom I refer were apparently of the impression that the estimates which their respective departments or establishments submitted to the Bureau of the Budget were the official estimates which they were authorized to advocate before the congressional committees. I trust this erroneous impression will not prevail hereafter. If Congress desires estimates other than those submitted by the Chief Executive, it has reserved unto itself in the Budget and Accounting Act the authority to request such estimates and defined the method of obtaining them. But the administrative officials, who are operating under the Executive, are expected to subscribe cordially and loyally to the budget estimates, and I do not hesitate to say that the repetition of an advocacy of an estimate before the Congressional Committees in excess of the executive recommendation, will be looked upon as sufficient reason to give consideration towards severance of employment with the Government.

Today, the head of an agency, asked the direct question by a member of the House or Senate, "Are you satisfied with the amount of the request for your agency in this year's budget figure?" would obviously be lying if he said "Yes" when he felt the amount was inadequate. Under established rules, however, if he says "No," he is required to indicate why and can then close with the statement that he has accepted the amount of the request in view of the many other demands upon available funds and because he supports the program of the President. If he chooses any other course he will eventually end up with trouble for his agency and for the Bureau of the Budget.

The entire appropriation process is fraught with difficulties for all concerned. After the appropriation subcommittees of the House and the Committee as a whole have considered and approved each appropriation bill—of which there are now fourteen—these are discussed on the floor. Amendments are offered and sometimes adopted, necessarily without the thorough study and review that has been given to the preparation of the budget or the committee reviews. This whole procedure is repeated in the Senate and, after passage, the appropriation bills go to conference to iron out differences, if possible, in order to reach a compromise version to send to the President for signature.

In Congress, Its Contemporary Role (New York: New York University Press, 1967), Ernest S. Griffith describes the appropriating process as one in which "legislative intent can be enhanced and promoted" or, conversely, "hampered or strangled altogether." He writes that

if appropriations are to be considered in detail, there are not days, weeks, and months enough to cover the ground. If it is in lump sums, who is to judge whether the amount is too much or too little to attain the end? Whole sections of expenditure, especially in the military, are shrouded in secrecy and must be accepted largely on faith. Occasionally, functions declining in their magnitude or largely obsolete are retained year after year at their old figure, principally for want of a substantive analysis of the work itself. Then, too, the approach employed by the executive retains the fiction of the equal importance of all items in the estimates, and what would be enormously valuable assistance from the Bureau of the Budget or the agency itself, in assessing priorities, is not forthcoming. Duplications, especially in research and intelligence, are covered up through emphasis on minor differences. Their detection is the more difficult because they usually fall within the province of different subcommittees, and it is in the subcommittees that the detailed examination of estimates takes place. Pressures from the interests involved and from their congressional spokesmen are overtly and subtly exerted. At any time a Spartan decision in the direction of economy on the part of the committee may be overthrown in a quick vote on the floor or by the committee of the other house, which may hold a different view.

Money to Spend

The relation of appropriations or authorization to spend to actual outlays is shown in Chart 3. After the appropriation bills become law, the Bureau of the Budget again enters the picture and apportions the funds by calendar quarters so as to prevent, as far as possible, the necessity for deficiency appropriations. Seasonal variations occur in many programs, notably agriculture, and must be taken into account when the quarterly apportionments are made. The Bureau has the right to establish reserves, and, as a matter of caution, frequently uses this right. Or, if the Director considers that a program is not advanced far enough to require the expenditure of the seasonally allocated portion of the annual appropriation in the first quarter of the fiscal year, he can apportion less than that amount. The agency head has the right of appeal to the President but is not likely to use it unless he feels that it would seriously imperil the success of the program. In the case of an anticipated over-all budget deficit, the withheld reserves may not be apportioned at all. The executive branch is not obliged to use all the money appropriated if the head of the agency concerned considers it unnecessary.

Chart 3

1969 Budget – Relation of Authorizations to Outlays

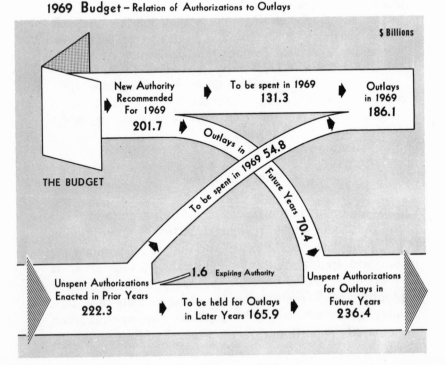

There have sometimes been complaints from congressmen that too much control is exercised by the Budget Bureau, particularly in its occasional apportionment of less than the whole amount of appropriated funds, which may be due to reasonable caution or to the President's unwillingness to accept an increased appropriation or added-on obligational authority greater than he requested. In such cases, the Budget Director has sometimes been condemned by members of Congress, but, when supported by the President, he has been able to sustain his position. Although the executive branch cannot make expenditures without an appropriation by Congress, it is not obligated to spend all money appropriated if the President considers such expenditure unwise or unnecessary. However, the Bureau of the Budget must give consideration to the objectives of an authorized program in some other way when money is withheld.

Supplemental and Deficiency Appropriations

The question of supplemental budget requests and deficiency appropriations submitted after the President's Budget Message has plagued Congress for a century. It is obvious that the budget estimates presented to Congress six months before the beginning of a fiscal year and eighteen months before the end cannot be exact estimates of what will be required to carry out the programs planned. Some supplemental budget requests are always necessary, but Congress has looked suspiciously at "supplementals" that indicated carelessness in preparation of the original request or deliberate understatement, and it has regarded deficiency appropriations with extreme disfavor. A supplemental is a request, made after the budget has been submitted, for an additional appropriation deemed necessary in order to carry out a program already authorized but for which the funds appropriated are inadequate. A deficiency appropriation is a request for an appropriation to make up an overexpenditure of amounts previously appropriated. In an attempt to curb the deficiency outlet, Congress passed the so-called Anti-Deficiency Act, in force since February 27, 1906, which states in part:

> No executive Department or other Government establishment of the United States shall expend in any one fiscal year, any sum in excess of appropriations made by Congress for that fiscal year, or involve the Government in any contract or other obligation for the future payment of money in excess of such appropriations unless such contract or obligation is authorized by law. . . . Any person violating any provision of this section shall be summarily removed from office and may also be punished by a fine of not less than one hundred dollars or by imprisonment for not less than one month.*

This proved to be useful in preventing gross abuses, although its penal provisions have not been invoked.

A deficiency appropriation is very embarrassing to the Administration, which has to request Congress to approve the overexpenditure. As the fiscal year progresses, each department watches its current commitments against its apportionments so as to be able to take steps to reduce them for the next quarter if it is unwilling to request a supplemental appropriation or fails to get its approval from the Budget Bureau or Congress.

Commission on Concepts

The President's Commission on Budget Concepts was appointed on March 17, 1967, to make a thorough and objective review of the federal budget and to make recommendations on budget concepts and presentation. David M. Kennedy

*See Appendix B for other parts of this Act.

was chairman and Robert P. Mayo was staff director when the Commission was appointed. The Commission reported on October 10, 1967, and many of its recommendations were adopted in the 1969 budget. The most important was for a unified summary budget statement "to replace the present three or more competing concepts" that had been in use up to that time.

The 1967 budget had presented primarily the administrative budget, which included all receipts and expenditures relating to the government operations exclusive of trust funds. This was reconciled with the consolidated cash statement by including all federal trust funds and by changing from a checks-issued to a checks-paid basis. This combined total was in turn reconciled with the national income accounts by eliminating loans made and repayments of loans and by adjustments to an accrual basis wherever the figures were available; it is the one now used in arriving at the federal sector included in the gross national product and in determining the national income.

The 1968 budget attempted to simplify the presentation by stressing the national income accounts as better reflecting "the impact of the Federal Budget on the flow of income and production in the economy."

The 1969 budget discarded the form of both the 1967 and the 1968 presentations to show everything in the form recommended by the Commission—that is,

1. Budget appropriations
   a. Proposals for action by Congress—what has heretofore been called new obligational authority (NOA).
   b. Proposals not requiring action by Congress—including both obligational authority enacted in prior years carried forward and certain expenditures, such as interest on the public debt, that are automatically approved when the debt limit is fixed by Congress.

2. Budget receipts, expenditures, and lending
   a. Receipts less expenditures, excluding lending
   b. Loan disbursements less repayments
3. Means of financing
   a. Borrowing from the public (including sale of partici-
      pation certificates)
   b. Reduction of cash balances, etc.
4. Outstanding federal securities and loans
   a. Federal securities, gross and held by public
   b. Federal credit programs
      (1) Direct loans
      (2) Guaranteed and insured loans

Changes other than in the form of presentation recommended by the Commission, effect to which was also given in
the 1969 budget, were: (1) inclusion of federal trust fund
transactions; (2) exclusion of government-sponsored activities
that are now completely privately owned, such as the federal
land banks; (3) exclusion of receipts and expenditures of the
local District of Columbia government; (4) exclusion of notes
issued to international lending organizations in lieu of cash;
(5) exclusion of subscriptions, drawings, and other net
changes in the U.S. position with the International Monetary
Fund, which is treated as a depository, and (6) sale of participation certificates no longer to be treated as an offset to
expenditures but as a means of financing.

The inclusion of the trust funds with the receipts and
expenditures of the administrative budget in accordance with
the recommendations of the President's Commission on Budget Concepts is clearly an improvement in the over-all reporting by the federal government. However, it is important not
to forget the differences among (1) trust fund receipts where
the government acts as a fiduciary in disbursing earmarked
taxes, (2) customs and excise taxes that are available for any
purpose but in their enactment had definite policy aspects

related to trade or consumption, and (3) income taxes designed to allocate the remaining costs of government where the burden will be the lightest. For example, the consolidated expenditures of the federal government for the six most recent fiscal years, 1965-70, show that the expenditures for health and welfare have doubled ($27.2 billion to $55.0 billion), largely out of trust funds. Defense expenditures have increased more in amount but just under 65 per cent ($49.6 billion to $81.5 billion). To deduce therefrom that Congress and the Administration intentionally reduced the proportion of total government expenditures devoted to defense would be wide of the mark.

The important recommendation that all the accounts now on a checks-issued basis should be put on an accrual basis has been accepted and will be reflected as soon as possible, although the Department of Defense and some other departments have not as yet put their accounts on that basis. This change is in accordance with a law enacted in 1956.

Carl W. Tiller, a special adviser on budgetary development in the Bureau charged particularly with the implementation of the recommendations of the President's Committee on Budget Concepts, outlined progress to May 15, 1968, before a meeting of the American Society of Military Comptrollers on that date. He explained that the installation of an accrual basis of accounting throughout the government meant recording materials received or services rendered when they became the liability of the government, whether or not a check had actually been issued. The Treasury and Defense are working together on a trial basis to iron out the bugs that may develop. It was hoped, he said, to make the transfer effective for all government activities for fiscal 1970.*

Action has so far been deferred on Commission recom-

*This did not prove possible, but, when the transfer becomes effective, it will prevent the previous practice of accelerating or slowing down payments by check just before the end of the fiscal period.

mendations that (1) the interest subsidy on loans at rates less than the Treasury borrowing costs be specifically disclosed as an expenditure in the budget and measured on a capitalized basis at the time of the loan and (2) further subsidy, because of the risk element, be recognized by a provision for losses charged off as new loans are extended.

Both of these recommendations are sound. The disclosure of the computation in itself might have some effect on congressional action. The recording of such computations, however, involves additional work. Perhaps the approximate effect might be disclosed in the Budget Message without passing it through the accounts.

V

The Management Function

The possibility of assigning to an agency within the government the responsibility of improving the operations and management of the executive branch was brought out for the first time during the Administration of President Taft, but it did not gain much ground for some time.

The Bureau of Efficiency, established in 1916, has been referred to in Chapter I. Its purpose was to investigate the duplication of statistical and other work in order to improve efficiency in the operations of the government, but it did not prove to be very effective as a separate organization and was abolished in 1933, its records being transferred to the Bureau of the Budget. Meanwhile, the Budget and Accounting Act of 1921 had given the Bureau of the Budget certain management responsibilities, which were not exerted for a number of years. Then the Brownlow Committee (described in Chapter II) began its study of efficiency in government. Its report on January 8, 1937, included recommendations for the expansion of the White House staff and the development of the managerial agencies of the government, particularly those dealing with the budget and efficiency research. Finally, under the Reorganization Act of 1939, by Executive Order 8248 of September 8, 1939, the President placed upon his newly established Executive Office certain management responsibilities and delegated them to the Bureau of the Budget, which was directed

> To conduct research in the development of improved plans of administrative management, and to advise the executive departments and agencies of the Government with respect to improved administrative organization and practice.
>
> To aid the President to bring about more efficient and economical conduct of Government service.

Under this directive, Director Harold D. Smith set up the Division of Administrative Management, with Donald C. Stone, now dean of the Graduate School of Public and International Affairs of the University of Pittsburgh, in charge.

Director Smith pointed out in 1945 that this division was charged particularly with making studies of the organization, activities, and methods of business of the departments and establishments "with a view to securing greater economy and efficiency in the conduct of the public service." He said that

> It would be physically impossible for the Bureau to help the various agencies of our government solve all their organizational and management problems, and it would be unwise to attempt to do so. Therefore, the Bureau encourages the departments to give more continuous attention to the internal improvement of their own administrative practices. This requires the development of improved business methods and procedures; it requires that instruction be given the agencies in the use of these improved devices of management.

Organizational Changes, 1948-67

In 1948, the Director of the Bureau of the Budget, the Secretary of the Treasury, and the comptroller-general agreed to undertake a joint program to improve systems of accounting and financial management throughout the government. The Bureau of the Budget established an accounting group in the Division of Administrative Management to give full time to this program. In 1956, this accounting group was transferred to the newly established Office of Accounting and the staff was expanded; in 1959, its name was changed to the Office of Financial Management in recognition of its broader function and the need for the development of financial systems to integrate programing with budgeting, accounting, and financial reporting. This office also developed internal audit facilities in the agencies.

At the same time, the whole Division of Administrative Management established by Director Smith was superseded by the Office of Management and Organization. Its duties were enlarged to deal with a wide range of management problems, including organizational studies, the development of reorganization plans, studies of methods and procedures, manpower utilization surveys, and the development and dissemination of guidance material in the management field. It provided forums for the discussion of management problems and provided consultation and advice to the agencies. It also fostered the development of management and organization staffs within the major federal agencies.

Another internal reorganization of the Bureau in 1967 brought about major changes with regard to the management function. Several of the activities of the Office of Management and Organization were transferred to other parts of the Bureau and the office was abolished. Responsibility for dealing with governmentwide problems in personnel, procurement, and automatic data processing were transferred to the newly established General Government Management Division. The cost-reduction function was transferred to the Office of Budget Review. The government organization function was transferred to the newly established Office of Executive Management. The Office of Financial Management was also abolished; its functions were to be absorbed by the Office of Executive Management, but, as events proved, there was not sufficient staff to carry them out.

This 1967 reorganization of the management functions of the Bureau of the Budget resulted in a major reorientation of some of the functions as they had previously been carried on. One of its major effects was to give more emphasis to the coordination of intergovernmental problems, particularly those dealing with the Johnson Administration's Great Society programs involving the coordination of federal activities at the state and local government levels. However, the means for bringing about operational coordination of federal programs at the state and local levels has not as yet been fully developed.

Present Difficulties

In its present stage of development, under the concepts of the 1967 reorganization, it can only be concluded that the Bureau, as the management arm of the President, has not been performing a service commensurate with the management responsibilities set forth in the Budget and Accounting Act of 1921 and the Budget and Accounting Procedures Act of 1950. This leads to the question as to whether the management function now vested in the Bureau could be performed more effectively in a separate office in the Executive Office of the President. It is a question about which differences of opinion exist. It is undoubtedly true that the many demands upon a Director of the Bureau of the Budget concerning the day-to-day budget problems detract from his ability to give adequate time and attention to management. Furthermore, under the 1967 reorganization, the management functions have been dispersed to various organizational units of the Bureau, adding coordination problems within the Bureau.

The importance of management certainly requires the full-time direction and leadership of an experienced, competent individual not burdened with other responsibilities. Some of the functions now vested in the General Government Management Division relating to governmentwide policy matters on automatic data processing, procurement and supply, and personnel should, in my opinion, be entrusted to such a person, along with the functions relating to cost reduction now vested in the Office of Budget Review.* His staff should be charged with identifying the management and organization problems within and between federal agencies. Delay of a year in finding a man to head up this important division has had a serious effect on its operations.

My own suggestion has been to establish eventually a statutory second deputy director within the Bureau of the Budget, to be appointed by the President and to give his whole time to management and organization. Establishment of a new position within the Executive Office, outside the Bureau and responsible only to the President, would undoubtedly add needed prestige to the management role. However, it would also mean the establishment of some duplicate facilities, since the new office would not have available to it the staffs in the divisions familiar with the personnel and operations of the different agencies. Furthermore, it would burden the President with one more organizational unit whose head would be asking for his time and support.

Certainly, there is much to be done. Over the past few years, Presidents have proposed and Congress has enacted a whole range of major new programs dealing with education, health, poverty, manpower-training, urban development, and pollution control. The interagency and intergovernmental nature of these programs has brought with it special problems

*See footnote on page 51.

in the organization and management of the executive branch. The problems are nationwide but the means best suited to solve them vary in the different cities and neighborhoods throughout the United States. Studies are required to determine the mixture of education, housing, skills improvement, and social services needed in each locality. These federal programs must be coordinated at the local level to assure an integrated response to the specific needs of each locality.

The management problem is to coordinate not only the programs of several separate federal agencies but also those of the states, cities, counties, other local jurisdictions, and many private organizations. Coordination and cooperation must be vertical, among many levels of government, as well as horizontal, among the many agencies of each level of government. The primary reason for the establishment of the Office of Executive Management was to equip the Bureau to work on solutions to this important problem of public administration today.

New Emphasis on the Office of Executive Management

President Nixon has appointed Dwight A. Ink as full-time head of the Office of Executive Management and assistant director of the Bureau. Ink has had wide experience in management, and he is making plans to expand the work as fast as the staff is made available to him. The organizational set-up will undoubtedly be modified later, but present responsibilities in his office are divided among Ink himself and two assistant directors—one for legislation, reorganization plans, and executive orders, the other for program and administration. There are three separate staffs for organization, financial management, and operational coordination and management.

Budget Director Mayo began to emphasize the importance

of improvements in executive-branch organization early in his tenure. One particularly significant effort in improving executive-branch field structure and operations should be mentioned. This is the standardization of regional boundaries and regional office locations for the five agencies—the departments of Health, Education, and Welfare (HEW), Housing and Urban Development (HUD), and Labor, the Office of Economic Opportunity (OEO), and the Small Business Administration (SBA)—that are most directly involved in programs to solve our urban problems. Regional councils composed of the regional directors of these five agencies have been established to better coordinate federal response at the regional level to state and local needs. In addition, the President has directed the Bureau of the Budget, in cooperation with other federal agencies, to study the total field structure of the agencies involved in cooperative federal-state-local programs with a view to improving all interagency and intergovernmental cooperation.

Although numerous steps have been taken or initiated within the Budget Bureau to strengthen the capabilities of state and local chief executives to coordinate federally assisted programs through improved data, advance consultation on regulations, support of central overhead costs, the development of planning machinery, and speedier delivery of funds and action on applications, and although other actions await White House or congressional decisions, much remains to be done to improve government coordination and management. Little has been done to establish a consistent pattern of delegations to the field to facilitate coordination at that level. Little progress has been made on the fundamental problem of consolidating related categorical-grant programs into broader, more flexible programs, although the Bureau staff has it very much in mind. For example, Bureau staff members are participating in a planning coordinating committee established by HUD and representing the several federal agencies that have grant programs aiding or requiring development planning.

On April 19, 1969, the Office of Executive Management reported that a number of important budget and interagency programs designed to improve the delivery of federally assisted services under Presidential directives were actively under way. In addition to those already mentioned, these activities included the streamlining of federal-aid processes and decentralization of decision-making authority, simplification of grant administration and technical requirements, and implementation of the Intergovermental Cooperation Act of 1968.

This legislation, enacted in the last session of Congress, called for providing information on federal grants-in-aid to governors and state legislatures, waiver of single-state agency requirements, federal provision of information and technical services to states and localities on a reimbursable basis, simplification of financial requirements placed on states, and advance consultation with state and local government on federal and federally assisted projects. At the time of writing, drafts of Budget Bureau circulars implementing this Act were out for comments by federal agencies and state and local government representatives. Issuance of circulars was anticipated within thirty days.

Legislation, Reorganization Plans, and Executive Orders

The assistant director for legislation, reorganization plans, and executive orders in the Office of Executive Management (a position occupied for many years now by Fred Levi) serves as the BOB's expert on reorganization of federal agencies, regrouping or shifting of functions assigned to agencies, the presentation of plans or proposals resulting from major management studies or surveys, the development of major legislation and executive orders involved in federal reorganization, and the establishment of new federal agencies by action of the President and Congress.

One of the important powers of the executive branch that was established by the Reorganization Act of 1939 was the ability to prepare and submit to Congress reorganization plans that would become effective unless disapproved by a majority of both houses of Congress. If the committee to which it was referred had not rejected it within ten days, any member could move to discharge the committee from further consideration. This was later amended so that the plan would fail if disapproved by a majority of the full membership of either house and later, by another amendment, if disapproved by a majority of either house. The authority to establish new departments by Reorganization Plan was cancelled and the President's whole authority to submit reorganization plans expired December 31, 1968. However, it was later renewed and extended until April 1, 1971.

An interesting example of how the preparation of reorganization plans works is provided by the history of Reorganization Plan 3 of 1967 "to provide a better government for the citizens of the Nation's Capital." For many years, there had been a steadily increasing demand for "home rule" by residents of the District of Columbia. Before 1967, the District was governed by three commissioners who were appointed by the President but came under the direct supervision of the committees of Congress. Many proposals for improvements, including some measure of self-government, had been advanced from time to time, and a number of bills had been introduced but not enacted into law.

Late in 1966, representatives of the District, the White House Office, and the Bureau of the Budget held a number of meetings to thrash out the problems involved and to determine a course of action to be recommended to the President. The objective at that time was to find a way of improving the

District government, short of Home Rule. It was concluded that the most practicable procedure would be to handle it through a reorganization plan.

With the help of an analysis of all statutory functions of the Board of Commissioners of the District of Columbia prepared by Irving Bryan, formerly of the District Corporation Counsel's Office, Bureau of the Budget staff members next prepared a draft reorganization plan of some sixty pages. Its distribution at this stage was severely limited, but extensive consultations about the basic features of the reorganization plan took place, particularly with congressional committee chairmen, committee members, and committee staff members. Various corrections and modifications flowing from this procedure were incorporated into the final reorganization plan.

The President sent this plan to Congress on June 1, 1967, and it was referred to the committees on government operations of the two houses. Since no action was taken to disapprove the plan, as proposed, within sixty days of continuous session of Congress following presentation of the plan, it automatically became effective under Chapter 9 of Table 5 of the U.S. Code but, under a provision contained in the plan itself, its main provisions did not become operative until the Commissioner of the District of Columbia and six members of the District of Columbia Council had entered office under the plan. The District is today governed under that plan, although efforts to move to home rule have found increasing support.

Other Work of the Management Office

Studies and the development of recommendations for the solution of federal and intergovernmental organization and central coordination problems are conducted by the govern-

Outside . . .

The Executive Office Building, at Pennsylvania Avenue and 17th Street, N.W., Washington, D. C. Once the State, War, and Navy Building, it now houses part of the Bureau of the Budget and other sections of the executive office of the President.

Inside . . .

The present Director of the Bureau of the Budget, Robert P. Mayo (right, facing camera), and Special Assistant to the Director Roger Jones (to Mayo's right) at work in the Director's office.

Some

former

Budget

directors . . .

The author, with President Dwight D. Eisenhower at Gettysburg, Pennsylvania, December, 1957, putting the finishing touches on the 1959 budget.

David E. Belle (right) with Secretary of the Treasury C. Douglas Dillon.

The New York Times

Kermit Gordon, Director of the Bureau of the Budget, 1962–65, and now President of the Brookings Institution.

Director Maurice Stans (right) watches as George Viault, Administrative Officer, swears in Elmer Staats (now Comptroller-General of the United States) as Deputy Director of the Bureau of the Budget.

Charles Schultze   explaining some points to
President Lyndon B. Johnson

and testifying before a Senate committee.

ment organization staff. Its functions include the organization of new or extensively revised federal programs, the creation of new departments and agencies, and the reorganization, consolidation, and improved formal coordination of existing agencies and programs at headquarters and field levels.

The operational coordination staff and the management systems staff were combined into a single unit effective November 7, 1968, and designated as the operational coordination and management systems staff. This combined staff assumed all the functions previously performed by the two staffs. It makes field evaluations of the responsiveness of federal programs to varying state and local needs and of the efficiency and effectiveness of federal programs that are cooperatively administered and financed, and it establishes and maintains communication with state and local officials, federal field-office staffs, and private institutions and individuals. It also is responsible for developing and improving the management systems needed to administer large multi-agency federal programs when these programs are designed to be carried out in partnership with state and local governments. The staff has begun to work with the principal agencies involved in the management of urban community and social development programs to find new techniques of voluntary cooperation and workable methods for the application of management systems.

The financial management staff is charged with promoting the development and use of effective financial management systems throughout the government and developing financial policies for uniform application on interagency, intergovernmental, and industry problems in various areas. The development of cost principles for grants and contracts with educational institutions and state and local governments has been assigned to this staff, as has the development of policies and guidelines for the purpose of determining whether commercial or industrial products and services for government use should be carried out by independent contractors or by government personnel. A further responsibility is to review the General Accounting Office audit reports on executive-branch operations and to coordinate efforts to ensure appropriate executive-branch action on audit findings. This staff also reviews and approves agency regulations for administrative control of funds and for recovery of erroneous payments, and it participates in the Joint Financial Management Improvement Program, which is conducted by the Bureau of the Budget, the General Accounting Office, and the Treasury Department in cooperation with the executive agencies.

Joint Financial Management

Part II of the Budget Accounting and Procedures Act of 1950, referred to briefly in Chapter II, is known as the Accounting and Auditing Act of 1950. Section 111 states that it is the policy of Congress that

a. The accounting of the Government provide full disclosure of the results of financial operations, adequate financial information needed in the management of operations and the formulation and execution of the Budget, and effective control over income, expenditures, funds, property, and other assets.

b. Full consideration be given to the needs and responsibilities of both the legislative and executive branches in the establishment of accounting and reporting systems and requirements.

c. The maintenance of accounting systems and the producing of financial reports with respect to the operations of executive agencies, including central facilities for bringing together and disclosing information on the results of the financial operations of the Government as a whole, be the responsibility of the executive branch.

d. The auditing for the Government, conducted by the Comptroller General of the United States as an agent of the Congress be directed at determining the extent to which accounting and related

financial reporting fulfills the purposes specified, financial transactions have been consummated in accordance with laws, regulations, or other legal requirements, and adequate internal financial
control over operations is exercised, and afford an effective basis for
the settlement of accounts of accountable officers.

e. Emphasis be placed on effecting orderly improvements resulting in simplified and more effective accounting, financial reporting,
budgeting, and auditing requirements and procedures and on the
elimination of those which involve duplication or which do not serve
a purpose commensurate with the costs involved.

Most significantly, Section 111(f) assigns a "continuous program for the improvement of accounting and financial reporting in the Government" to the comptroller-general of the
United States, the Secretary of the Treasury, and the Director of the Bureau of the Budget.

Elmer B. Staats, comptroller-general of the United States
and formerly deputy director of the Budget, in testimony at
a hearing before a special studies subcommittee of the Committee on Government Operations of the House on July 17,
1967, recalled how this group, which became known as the
Joint Financial Management Improvement Program, was
formed:

When Mr. Webb became Director of the Budget, he was very much
interested in this matter, and I think it is of some significance that
he and Lindsay Warren* were good friends, and Mr. Webb also knew
the Secretary of the Treasury very well because he had worked in
the Treasury Department. All three agencies were operating under
somewhat different ground rules in this area.

An informal arrangement was established in about 1948 or 1949,
and Congress then recognized the need in 1950 and provided in the
1950 legislation that the Comptroller General of the United States,
the Secretary of the Treasury, and the Director of the Bureau of the

*Lindsay Warren was comptroller-general from 1940 to 1954.

Budget conduct a continuous program for the improvement of accounting and financial reporting in the Government.

The reason I mention this earlier history is that the Congress really enacted into statute an arrangement that had been pretty well worked out informally by the heads of the three principal agencies prior to that time.

Mr. Hardy: This statutory language did not exactly give legitimacy to the committee that had already been established, but it did call on the three agencies to run these programs, is that right?

Mr. Staats: That is right.

Section 112 of the 1950 Act goes into further detail giving the authority to the comptroller-general, after consultation with the Secretary of the Treasury and the Director of the Budget "concerning their accounting, financial reporting, and budgetary needs, and considering the needs of the other executive agencies," to prescribe "the principles, standards, and related requirements for accounting to be observed by each executive agency."

Although the 1950 Act indicates clearly that the comptroller-general must consult with the Secretary of the Treasury and the Director of the Budget concerning their accounting, financial, and budgetary needs before prescribing principles and standards, Section 113 provides that the head of each executive agency shall establish and maintain systems of accounting and internal control in conformity with the principles, standards, and related requirements prescribed by the comptroller-general. The theory underlying these provisions is contrary to generally accepted management organization today. In my opinion, the executive branch should be required to establish the principles and accounting records of the agencies subject to meeting the information requirements of the General Accounting Office and the Congress of the United States. The legislative branch, represented by the GAO, should not be directly responsible for prescribing the system. However, it is good organization and sound management to have the auditing done by the comptroller-general outside the executive branch, since this system gives Congress adequate control over both the reporting and the auditing.

The present procedure has not yet caused any major difficulty—mainly because of the close and friendly relations between the members of the group and the inadequate staff of the Bureau to pursue this work in relation to its other responsibilities.

Accounting Systems

On March 17, 1965, Congressman William L. Dawson submitted a report entitled "Submissions of Agency Accounting Systems for GAO Approval," which dealt with the responsibility of the General Accounting Office under the 1950 Act to approve the system of central accounting and reporting required by Section 114 of the Act. He stated that, fourteen years after the statute had been enacted by Congress, 128 organizations within the civil departments and agencies had accounting systems subject to approval by the comptroller-general. Only forty-one of those systems had been approved; parts of systems in fifteen other civil-agency organizations had been approved. In the Department of Defense, only the accounting system covering the civil functions of the Army Corps of Engineers had been approved in full. I think that, if the Bureau of the Budget had been empowered to prescribe and oversee the installation of the accounting systems, much more rapid progress would have been made.

The following year, on September 19, 1966, hearings were held before a subcommittee of the Committee on Government Operations of the House at which Comptroller-General Staats was present and made a more complete report of the program and the reasons for the delay. Staats referred frequently to the work of the Bureau of the Budget. On July

17, 1967, another hearing was held before the Subcommittee on Government Operations of the House at which, in addition to statements and testimony by the Comptroller-General and others, Phillip S. Hughes, deputy director of the Budget, made the following statements with respect to the development of better accounting systems and getting them approved by the Comptroller-General:

> As you know, this work is carried out in large part through the joint financial management improvement program, a cooperative effort conducted under the combined leadership of the Bureau of the Budget, the General Accounting Office, and the Treasury Department, working in cooperation with the Civil Service Commission and the operating agencies. The primary points of responsibility and the detailed work involved in accounting systems improvement inevitably rest on the operating agencies—which are responsible for development and maintenance of such systems; and on the GAO for its cooperative work and approval responsibilities. The Bureau of the Budget's limited size and diverse responsibilities require that our role be primarily one of leadership, stimulation, and periodic review of status. The major credit for progress made should go to the staff of the GAO and of the operating agencies directly involved.

Hughes also went on to explain how the Bureau staff worked with the operating agencies:

> The lead role in our accounting systems improvement activities is carried by our staff Office of Financial Management. Mr. Armstrong, who is with me here, is the Chief of that Office and, as Mr. Staats indicated, has been chairman of the steering group for the joint financial management improvement program. The Office of Financial Management provides guidance and assistance on financial systems problems to budget examiners in our line divisions and, through them, to individual agencies. As a generalization, we endeavor to work with the agencies to stimulate improvement actions. Under these arrangements, the amount and nature of participation by the different staff vary according to the nature of the problem.

The Bureau of the Budget is not staffed—nor do we believe it should be—in a manner that would permit it to actually develop an accounting system for an agency. Nor are we equipped to review the detailed accounting systems submitted by operating agencies to the Comptroller General for approval.

Although Hughes's statement supports the present situation, in my opinion the Bureau should be staffed, authorized, and expected to help develop and set up an accounting system within each of the agencies to meet its own needs.

On May 24, 1966, President Johnson issued a memorandum to the heads of executive agencies, in which he stated:

I have a strong and continuing interest in the development of businesslike financial systems throughout the Federal Government. Such systems are essential to assist in carrying out a basic pledge of this administration—to get a dollar's value for a dollar spent.

The Budget Director will issue more detailed instructions with respect to this program. Your full support is needed. I want every manager—the general manager and the financial manager alike—to feel and respond to your personal demands for the use of highest quality, business-type financial information systems.

With increased assistance by the central agencies and a positive action program on your part, we can readily achieve what is contemplated in the Budget and Accounting Procedures Act—the utilization of the best business practices in the day-to-day management of our Government.

Simultaneous with the release of the President's memorandum, the Bureau issued Bulletin 66-6, requiring each agency to take prompt and vigorous action toward modernizing its financial management system. Each agency was requested to

reexamine the adequacy of its accounting systems against current published requirements, review the status of developmental work, and take action to speed up needed improvements. These efforts should be organized in firm projects for completion of necessary developmental work within specified time periods, and coordinated with plans for submission of accounting systems to the Comptroller General for approval as soon as practicable.

Another bulletin, 66-8, was released in June, 1966, requesting agency reports on accomplishments and the status of their financial management improvement programs. More recently, the Bureau of the Budget, in Bulletin 67-11, called for reports on the status of financial management systems and improvements completed in fiscal year 1967. The difficulty with this procedure is that the Bureau does not have any staff to check the agency reports or to assist the agencies in the actual installation of the accounting improvements in the financial management program. The particular emphasis on planning-programing-budgeting in the agencies resulted in the setting up of a special task force within the Office of Budget Review in the Bureau to see that progress was made in this area.

The Twentieth Annual Report of the Joint Financial Management Improvement Program, dated December 20, 1968, highlighted a number of developments that its members (including, by invitation, the chairman of the Civil Service Commission) believed had helped to improve the budget process and control over expenditures:

A great deal of work has been done on developing the planning-programming-budgeting programs. Near the beginning of fiscal year 1968, the Bureau of the Budget began formal work looking toward the establishment of a management information system for the Bureau and the Executive Office of the President. Study by an internal task force was followed by creation of a Management Information Staff in the Bureau of the Budget. It is expected that a contract for consulting services in establishing such a system will be entered into during fiscal year 1969. Such an information system is likely to include both program data and financial data and become a part of the systems of both budget formulation and budget execution.

Meanwhile, steps have been taken to develop a more comprehensive computer system in the Bureau for use in processing agency submissions of data for the 1970 budget. This represents an extension of the automation of the budget compilation processes that was initiated several years ago.

Management Functions in the Director's Office

Several new projects located in the Office of the Director are directly concerned with the management function. Some of these involve the Management Information Systems Staff, described briefly in Chapter III. Examples of the activities of this staff initiated in the summer and early fall of 1968 included study for the design of an information system to support and help integrate the newer PPB processes with the more traditional appropriations-budgeting processes. A contract was signed with McKinsey and Company in September, 1968, to assist the Bureau in identifying additional ways to improve the manner in which information is collected and processed to support the decision-making needs of federal-program officials in planning, operating, and evaluating federal programs. The contract, for $400,000, was for the first two phases of a four-phase effort. The principal products were to be a preliminary design concept for an integrated budget-PPB management-information system, a preliminary governmentwide classification structure, and an identification of additional steps that the Bureau might take to enlarge and extend the PPB concept on a governmentwide basis. A voluminous report on the first two phases was received on June 30, 1969, and is now under thorough study.

Another project of the Management Information Systems Staff is to attempt to develop a program progress-reporting system for approved federal programs. Over the years, a number of *ad hoc* attempts have been made to systematize the program evaluation process by using a formalized and regularized progress-reporting system that would relate program performance and results to input resources and costs. However, no operating and comprehensive system yet exists.

The development of an advanced information retrieval and computational system for the Council of Economic Advisers (CEA) is yet another effort. By virtue of its strategic role and mission as the President's key economic-advisory group, the CEA must retrieve and assess a wide variety of basic socioeconomic, financial, statistical, program, and other information from numerous federal information systems and data series, as well as the systems and series of private-sector groups. As a first step in assisting the CEA to better organize its information systems, the Bureau undertook to inventory the information needs of the Council for decision-making, computational, and analytical requirements. This system would be designed on a modular basis, providing first for a modest capability that later could be expanded into a more sophisticated capability, possibly with remote inquiry facilities.

Relationship of the Office of Program Evaluation to the Management Function

In January, 1969, the Program Evaluation Staff of the Office of the Director was elevated into a separate Office of Program Evaluation, headed by an assistant director responsible for a wide range of activities related to the manner in which the different parts of the federal government develop and utilize program budgeting. Specifically, the Office of Program Evaluation promotes and coordinates the identification and analysis of policy and program issues, both within the Bureau and jointly with the agencies. It provides leadership for improving program evaluation systems and related public information, consulting, and educational services. It also helps to develop a comprehensive and compatible governmentwide program structure, in part through overviews showing the likely impact of various programs on the economy and national goals.

Another of its major tasks is to assist the BOB divisions in their definitions of policy and program issues, preparation of program overviews, and evaluation of agency program memoranda, special analytic studies, and financial plans. Staff members assigned to this office maintain liaison with the agencies with respect to all these matters, as well as to education, training, and career-development programs for agency analytic personnel.

Thus, while the Office of Program Evaluation does not have specific responsibility for the structure and management of federal agencies, it does have responsibility for helping to ensure that the agencies are adequately organized and equipped to engage in program budgeting and systematic analysis. To the extent that the planning-programing-budgeting system represents a way of approaching decisions, and to the extent that its implementation requires adequate staff resources, this office is deeply involved in the continuing effort to improve federal management.

VI

Legislative Reference

Every year, a multitude of bills are introduced to Congress by representatives and senators on their own behalf or on behalf of their constituents. These bills have to be reviewed and referred to all the agencies affected in order to obtain their views. The President, in regular and special messages during the year, makes a series of recommendations for legislation to carry out his program. These proposals must be checked in advance with the agencies affected, so as not to run contrary to agency objectives and programs. Many other bills are introduced, at the request of the various departments and agencies, to suggest ways to carry out their budget programs, and these also have to be coordinated and referred to the agencies that might be affected, in order to obtain their approval. The small staff of the BOB's Office of Legislative Reference is responsible for all these chores of review and reference. Its job, ascertaining and coordinating the views of the executive agencies with respect to legislation introduced or to be introduced, is known as clearance.

The clearance function of the Bureau dates back to the Budget and Accounting Act of 1921. Richard E. Neustadt has pointed out that when President Harding approved the Budget and Accounting Act on June 10, 1921, the Federal agencies lost their historic freedom to decide for themselves what appropriations they should ask of Congress; now the President alone was to decide with a new staff agency, the Budget Bureau, to help him to do it. . . . It is significant of this community of interest (i.e. with the Congressional Committees on Appropriations) that the required proposal for some form of central clearance came not from the new Budget Bureau, but from the House Appropriations Committee.*

Budget Circular 49, issued by Budget Director Dawes on December 19, 1921, outlined the procedure to be followed. The pertinent paragraphs are:

a. Before any request or recommendation of this character, originating in or sponsored by any executive department or independent establishment of the Government, is sent to either House of Congress, or to any committee thereof, it shall first be submitted to the Director of the Budget, who shall make recommendations with respect thereto, to the President. And no such request shall be submitted to either House of Congress, or to any committee thereof, without having first been approved by the President. When so approved, the request or recommendation to either House of Congress, or to any committee thereof, shall recite the fact that such approval has been obtained.

b. Whenever any request or measure proposing legislation, with the purpose or effect set forth above, shall be referred to any executive department or independent establishment for advice or expression of opinion thereon, the head of the executive department or independent establishment concerned shall ascertain, through the Director of the Budget, whether or not such recommendation, request or measure is in accord with the financial program of the President. And such advice or expression of opinion when transmitted shall include a statement whether the proposed legislation is or is not in such accord.

*Richard E. Neustadt, "Presidency and Legislation: Planning the President's Program," *The American Political Science Review* 49, 4 (December, 1955).

c. That copies of such requests, recommendations, or proposed measures referred for advice as in subparagraph (b) shall be promptly furnished to the Director of the Budget for the information of the President.

This circular had been cleared by the House Appropriations Committee. However, it was not enforced until President Coolidge appointed General Lord as Budget Director in 1924. Lord was able to secure nearly full compliance, which continued through President Hoover's term, in spite of the oncoming Depression.

With President Roosevelt's clean sweep of Administrative positions and the inauguration of many new programs, the full clearance process was not enforced; only the clearing of proposals for appropriations and all bills carrying authorizations for appropriation with the President through the Bureau of the Budget was required.

After the Brownlow Committee's report of January, 1937, and during the service of Daniel W. Bell as Budget Director, Budget Circular 336 was issued in December, 1937. Its pertinent part reads:

There shall be sent to the Bureau of the Budget, for consideration of the President before submission to the Congress, or any committee or member thereof, the original and two copies of each recommendation or report, concerning proposed or pending legislation (other than private relief legislation), requested from or advanced by any executive department, independent establishment, or other Government agency (including the municipal government of the District of Columbia and Government-owned or Government-controlled corporations), or any officer thereof. When such recommendation or report thereafter is submitted to the Congress, or to a committee or member thereof, it shall include a statement as to whether the proposed legislation is or is not in accord with the program of the President.

Before any person in his official capacity as officer or employee of any executive department, independent establishment, or other

Government agency (including the municipal government of the District of Columbia and Government-owned or Government-controlled corporations) shall advocate or oppose legislation (other than private relief legislation) before any committee of the Congress, he shall ascertain from the Bureau of the Budget through the Budget officer of his organization whether such legislation is or is not in accord with the program of the President, and he shall so inform the committee.

The new rules were enforced by an increased staff organized in the Division of Coordination, which, after the Reorganization Act of 1939, became the Division of Legislative Reference. During 1939, in the first session of the Seventysixth Congress, the Bureau of the Budget processed 2,448 agency reports setting forth agency views on pending bills. The most recent figure, for the First Session of the Ninetieth Congress, is 5,858.

During World War II, some of the clearance function was performed by and through the Office of War Mobilization, a process that lasted into the postwar period until the appointment of James E. Webb as Director. Working closely with the White House staff, the legislative clearance system, through the Budget Bureau, again became effective and included positive drafting as well as negative clearance of Administration proposals. Direct questions from Congress, so-called direct referrals, became frequent in the Eightieth Congress.

The Division of Legislative Reference had its name changed to Office of Legislative Reference in 1952; remaining in charge was Roger Jones, who had an intimate knowledge of the legislative procedure and close contacts with the Hill as well as with the agency staffs. The transition from President Truman to President Eisenhower was a smooth one notable for the full cooperation of the two Presidents and that of the two directors, Frederick J. Lawton and Joseph M. Dodge. Roger Jones continued as Chief of Legislative Reference, and his office became a key influence in translating

Presidential policy into legislative enactment, especially in housing and social security.

To be or not to be "in accordance with the program of the President" is a traditional phrase dating back at least to President Franklin D. Roosevelt. It undoubtedly has been used to encourage or shut off legislation desired or opposed by the White House without relating to any particular authorized goals. Each President, however, has announced his general objectives in his election campaigns and has set them forth in some detail, as well as in general terms in his State of the Union and Budget messages and economic reports. Each President's announced goals have become his program.

Ernest S. Griffith, Director of the Legislative Reference Service of the Library of Congress from 1940 to 1958, made some pertinent comments on the subject of the President's program in his book *Congress: Its Contemporary Role.* He notes that an interesting byproduct of Presidential programs has been the leverage these procedures give a President over his departments and agencies. And why, he asks, has Congress not only not resented these programs but increasingly welcomed them? He answers:

> Several factors are operative at this point. In the first place, the great majority of items had been before Congress for a number of years. Presidential endorsement became a matter to some extent of timing, the identification of the right moment for throwing his weight back of a proposal. In the second place, Congress with its increasingly developed and available expertise has felt much more secure in dealing with such recommendations. It is able to screen, amend, reject, substitute, or accept, after full hearings and exhaustive analysis. Under these circumstances, especially as there is nothing to prevent Congress adding items, if it wishes, the "President's program" nonetheless plays a most convenient role in furnishing an outline agenda for the session. Back of the messages may well lie very considerable informal consultations with key congressmen, a give and take which furnishes the initial step in consensus building.

The importance of a legislative plan or program has been emphasized also by Richard E. Neustadt. He points out the great difficulties in all transitions between Presidents. President Eisenhower, for instance, did not present to Congress any legislative program at all in the spring of 1953. While the President and many members of his staff, including Joseph Dodge (soon to become the Director of the Budget), had been invited by President Truman to work closely with his staff between election and inauguration, they felt that it would be unwise to propose any complete program so soon after taking over the Administration. In his article in the *American Political Science Review,* cited earlier, Neustadt does say, however, that

early in 1954, President Dwight D. Eisenhower presented to the Congress—and the country and his party—some 65 proposals for new legislation, over and above appropriations. This presentation was a massive affair. First came six weeks of well-publicized preliminaries: cabinet deliberations, congressional briefings, press conferences, and a fireside chat. Then, in three annual messages to Congress—a State of the Union Address, a Budget Message, and an Economic Report—the President set forth his bundle of proposals, elaborating certain aspects, outlining the rest. Along with these came seven supplementing special messages, each filling in details on some particular: Taft-Hartley, farm price supports, social security, health, housing, atomic energy, foreign aid, and trade. And following the messages Administration-approved bills, conveyors of the ultimate details, were introduced in Congress.

Throughout, one theme was emphasized: here was a comprehensive and coordinated inventory of the nation's current legislative needs, reflecting the President's own judgments, choices, and priorities in every major area of Federal action; in short, his "legislative program," an entity distinctive and defined, its coverage and its omissions, both, delimiting his stand across the board. And—quite explicitly—this stand was being taken, this program volunteered, in order to give Congress an agenda, Republicans a platform, and voters a yardstick for 1954.

Frequently, legislation is introduced or contemplated that is not directly related to any policies previously announced. It then becomes necessary to formulate a policy acceptable to the President that can be applied to such cases. Clearance with the different agencies helps both to formulate the policy and to obtain a consensus on what will further or hinder its success. The White House staff is constantly in touch with the legislative leaders throughout the session and they in turn participate through weekly meetings attended by the Director or other representatives of the Budget Bureau in the formulation of policy and specific legislation to be pressed or opposed.

The Office of Legislative Reference today acts as the clearing agency for legislation to be drafted and submitted, for analyses of bills that have already been introduced in Congress, for obtaining departmental views on these bills, for determining the relationship of legislation to the program of the President; and for coordinating the departmental viewpoints to be expressed in testimony. All this requires wide use of the division staffs in the Bureau who are familiar with the programs of the different agencies to which they have been assigned. It also requires the full cooperation of the staffs of the various departments and agencies and close working arrangements with them.

One of the important needs for the services of this Office arises when one agency wishes to have a bill introduced or to testify before Congress in favor of a bill that might conflict with the views and programs of another agency. Not only are the agency comments analyzed, but, in addition, an independent review is made by the Bureau staff to determine whether the proposed bill conforms with the rest of the program of the President. That is, it is looked at to determine whether it advances the objectives of the Administration as a whole rather than only those of one agency whose objectives might conflict with programs proposed or under consideration by other agencies. It is also necessary for this Office to consider the administrative implications of proposed bills and their broader import. Long experience enables Bureau staff members to detect organizational defects in bills as well as conflicts with existing programs, overlapping programs, or unworkable proposals. For example, the Bureau is always on the alert for legislative provisions that would complicate departmental administration by vesting authority in subordinate officers rather than an agency head.

During the preparation of the various Presidential messages, the Office of Legislative Reference is consulted and is in a position to advise and assist in readying the necessary legislation to carry out the program when it becomes necessary. This means, in effect, that the Bureau participates in every aspect of development of the Presidential legislative program.

Congressional committees and federal agencies not immediately concerned are more and more consulting the Office of Legislative Reference about the relationship of proposed or pending legislation to the program of the President. A very close liaison with congressional committees and the individual members of Congress is necessary; this primarily covers the substantive committees but also applies to the appropriation committees. One of the most difficult problems is to coordinate the testimony of the heads of departments and agencies when they are asked to appear before the committees. In such cases, close coordination is necessary with the other offices and divisions of the Bureau and with the White House staff, since members of Congress are anxious to obtain independent views of witnesses regardless of their impact on the program of the President.

Another function of this Office is to keep track of legislation pending before the substantive committees of Congress and arrange for testimony, if needed, to further the progress of bills supported by the Administration. The staff of the office does not submit testimony directly unless asked to do so by the Committee, but it prepares the way for the appearance of the Director or other officers of the Bureau to supplement the appearance of the agency heads or other experts.

Differences of opinion between the staff of the Bureau and of the agencies are usually resolved without the need of consultation between the Office of the Director and the agency boss. On occasion, however, the President is advised, and he may participate in any policy decisions that are required.

As an illustration of how clearance works, let us take the frequent case of an agency wishing to sponsor a bill in Congress. If the subject is important, the agency may seek Presidential endorsement by having the President mention it in one of his regular messages or in a special communication. The draft bill is sent to the Bureau in accordance with well-established procedures. There it is reviewed and a determination is made on what additional data and information is needed and, in particular, what other agencies have substantial interests and should be asked to comment. Meanwhile, Bureau and other executive-office staff analyze the bill and identify the issues.

All the agencies whose views are asked may favor it or at least may have no objection. What is more likely, however, is that one or more will propose substantive or technical amendments or perhaps a complete substitute. Divergent views may be reconciled by telephone or by letter, or, if it is appropriate, a meeting of the interested agencies may be arranged by the Bureau staff. If the bill is important and differences are substantial and cannot be worked out, key members of the White House staff, even the President himself, may be brought into the discussion.

After review and analysis, including analysis of the views

of other agencies and White House and other executive-office staff, the Bureau may advise the reporting agency that (1) there is no objection to the pending legislation or its views of it, (2) the pending bill is consistent with Administration objectives or in accord with the President's program, or (3) the bill conflicts with an important Administration objective or is not in accord with the President's program.

One interesting recent example is the procedure that led to the establishment of Redwood National Park in California, proposed for many years by various conservation groups and for which various bills had been introduced from time to time. The present Act originated in H.R. 13011 introduced in the Eighty-ninth Congress on February 23, 1966. It had been drafted at the suggestion of the Department of the Interior and had been cleared by the Bureau. Other bills were introduced in the same Congress as S.2962, H.R.13009 and H.R.13929. Hearings were held on S.2962 by the Senate Committee on Interior and Insular Affairs, but no further action was taken on the bill. After a few minor changes, the President resubmitted another bill, which became S.2515, and hearings were held by the Committee on Interior and Insular Affairs. The Secretary of the Interior on March 11, 1967, submitted a report to Speaker of the House John W. McCormack, in which he explained the proposals at some length and ended with the submission of a man-years and cost-data statement and the paragraph "The Bureau of the Budget has advised that the presentation of this proposed legislation would be in accord with the program of the President." Other bills were introduced during the spring of 1967, and the Secretary of the Interior, asked for his views, gave them to the Chairman of the Committee on Interior and Insular Affairs on June 26, 1967, calling for some modification in the original proposal and ending with the following paragraph: "The Bureau of the Budget has advised that there would be no objection to the presentation of this report and that enactment of H.R. 10951 would be in accord with the program of the President."

The views of the Secretary of Agriculture were also requested. As an illustration of the type of agency report cleared by the Office of Legislative Reference, it is reproduced below, slightly shortened.

Department of Agriculture
Washington, D.C.

June 27, 1967

Hon. Wayne N. Aspinall
Chairman, Committee on Interior and Insular Affairs
House of Representatives

Dear Mr. Chairman:

As requested in your letter of May 9, 1967, here is our report on H.R. 7742, H.R. 8383, and H.R. 8776, identical bills to authorize the establishment of the Redwood National Park and Seashore and the King Range National Conservation Area in the State of California, to provide for the acquisition of Point Reyes National Seashore, and to provide economic assistance to local governmental bodies affected thereby.

These bills have three major objectives. First, they would establish a Redwood National Park and Seashore in Del Norte and Humboldt Counties, California. . . .

The second major objective would be the establishment of the King Range National Conservation Area. . . .

Finally, these bills would increase to $44,500,000 the authorization for the acquisition of lands and interests in lands for the Point Reyes National Seashore.

On February 23, 1966, the President proposed to the Congress the creation of a Redwood National Park in northern California. Legislation to establish the park was submitted to the 89th Congress by the Department of the Interior on that day. It was introduced as H.R. 13042. No action was taken by the committee on H.R. 13042.

In his message of January 30, 1967, on protecting our national heritage, the President again recommended the establishment of a Redwood National Park. On March 11, 1967, the Secretary of the Interior submitted legislation to establish such a park. That proposal has been introduced as H.R. 10951.

H.R. 10951 would provide for establishing a Redwood National Park of not more than 45,200 acres as depicted on the drawing numbered NP-RED-7102A, dated February 1967, which would be on file and available for public inspection in the office of the National Park Service. It would also provide for the transfer of not more than 31,000 acres in the King Range area to the State of California. It does not seek to treat the financing of acquisition for Point Reyes National Seashore.

This Department recommends the enactment of H.R. 10951 rather than the other bills mentioned above.

The Bureau of the Budget advises that the enactment of H.R. 10951 would be in accord with the President's program.

Sincerely yours,

ORVILLE L. FREEMAN

In the meantime, the views of the Bureau of the Budget had been requested again, and the following letter was submitted:

Executive Office of the President
Bureau of the Budget
Washington, D.C.

May 17, 1968

Hon. Wayne N. Aspinall
Chairman, Committee on Interior and Insular Affairs
House of Representatives, Longworth Building
Washington, D.C.

Dear Mr. Chairman:

Your letter of November 27, 1967, requested a report from the

Bureau of the Budget on H.R. 13508, a bill "to authorize the establishment of the Redwood National Park in the State of California, and for other purposes," and S. 2515, which is the same except that it does not contain the detailed restrictions on the land exchange authorities in section 3(b) of the Senate bill.

The Bureau of the Budget concurs with the report which the Department of the Interior is submitting to your committee on these bills.

Establishment of a Redwood National Park, along the lines discussed in the Interior report, would be in accord with the program of the President.

Sincerely,

PHILLIP S. HUGHES
Deputy Director

The Committee on Interior and Insular Affairs recommended the enactment of S. 2515 as amended. It was subsequently passed and became Public Law 90-545, which was approved on October 2, 1968.

Case studies of important legislation are very interesting, but they extend over many months or years and cannot be given full justice here. Two case studies relating to an FBI retirement bill and the Foreign Service Act of 1946 are set forth in great detail in a book entitled *Public Administration and Policy Development,* edited by Harold Stein (New York: Harcourt, Brace & World, 1952). Other interesting studies have been published in the Inter-University Case Program (New York: Bobbs, Merrill) and still others are readily available in *Congressional Quarterly.*

The following summary of requests, reports, and bills gives an idea of the workload created by the Bureau's legislative clearance function.

	88th Congress	89th Congress	90th Congress 1st Session
Congressional requests for Bureau views	2,358	2,853	1,856
Agency reports for clearance	8,124	9,294	5,858
Agency draft bills	1,042	1,072	752
Private bills	886	1,006	572
Total	12,410	14,225	9,038

This does not include some legislative coordination and clearance functions of the Bureau, such as responding to requests for information, coordinating agency testimony, and handling enrolled bills.

The Office of Legislative Reference has one further function, that of relating agency views on enrolled bills. After Congress has completed its work on a bill, the bill is enrolled and sent to the President for his approval. The Constitution provides that the President shall take action within ten days after receipt of the bill (not including Sundays). The interested agencies have only this short period in which to prepare written analyses and recommendations, including the preparation of a signing statement or the draft of a veto message in case either is recommended. The Bureau then prepares a memorandum to the President on the enrolled bill, summarizing the issues and the various views and recommendations.

As can be readily imagined, in connection with their work in the legislative area, Bureau officials and staff members spend a substantial amount of time in testifying before congressional committees, attending committee hearings, and working informally with committee staff on pending legislation.

VII

Statistical Policy

In earlier years, the nation's principal federal statistics were derived from the decennial census of population, initiated in 1790. Beginning in 1810, the census included questions on manufacturing activity, and, by the end of the nineteenth century, it carried inquiries on agriculture, minerals, and state and local government operations. During World War I, Allyn A. Young, then president of the American Statistical Association, the leading professional statistical organization, stated:

> Our national participation in the war has brought with it an enormous demand for prompt and exact statistical information. . . . The statistical activities of the Federal Government in times of peace cover in the main only those phases of national life which are deemed to be of public and especially of political moment. Thus the Federal Government, in its statistical work, has touched the current of our national life at only a relatively few points and at some of these only intermittently.

More progress was made in the private than in the public sector, until a committee on government statistics and information services, known as COGSIS, was formed jointly in

119

June, 1933. by the secretaries of several federal departments, the American Statistical Association, and the Social Science Research Council. At the suggestion of COGSIS, the President, on July 27, 1933, created by executive order the Central Statistical Board to formulate standards for and effect coordination of the statistical services of the federal government incident to the purposes of the National Industrial Recovery Act. Stuart Rice was appointed its chairman, Morris Copeland its executive secretary—both of them great names in this field.

The Bureau of the Budget was first charged with responsibility for statistical services in Reorganization Plan One, which took effect on July 1, 1939, and shifted the Central Statistical Board to the Bureau. Executive Order 8248, signed by the President on September 8, 1939, directed the Bureau "to plan and promote the improvement, development and coordination of Federal and other statistical services." Rice was placed in charge of this work, as head of the organization that became the Office of Statistical Standards—now called the Office of Statistical Policy. Later developments that enlarged the Bureau's responsibility in this area and strengthened its power were: (1) the Federal Reports Act of 1942, to eliminate duplication of data requests and introduce standard reporting concepts; (2) Executive Order 10033, to coordinate inquiries from international organizations; and (3) the Budget and Accounting Procedures Act of 1950, followed by Executive Order 10253, for the improved gathering, compiling, analyzing, publishing, and disseminating of statistical information by federal agencies.

In 1942, a business advisory council was established in response to the Bureau's request to leading business organizations to provide a means for developing closer relations with business groups furnishing and using economic statistics. This group is now known as the Advisory Council on Federal Reports. In 1945, a labor advisory council was appointed, and still later the Bureau participated in the establishment of the Federal Statistics Users' Conference to present the views of business, labor, agricultural, and professional groups on the federal statistical system.

At the request of the Hoover Commission, the National Bureau of Economic Research made a study and report in 1948 on the statistical services of the federal government, and the American Statistical Association subsequently appointed an advisory committee to the Bureau to provide a continuous review of major statistical issues. Rice was succeeded as assistant director of the Bureau in charge of the Office of Statistical Standards in 1955 by Raymond T. Bowman; both are past presidents of the American Statistical Association.

The Employment Act of 1946 established the Council of Economic Advisers, which, with the Joint Economic Committee of Congress, did much to emphasize the need for more and better integrated statistics upon which to base policy decisions.

One of the basic features of the Bureau's long-run program for the improvement of economic statistics has been its periodic provision for the critical examination of major statistical series by special review committees. These included two committees—appointed by the National Bureau of Economic Research at the request of the Office of Statistical Standards —dealing with statistics underlying the national economic accounts in 1957 and price statistics in 1960. The President's Committee to Appraise Employment and Unemployment Statistics made its report in 1962, and the Review Committee for Balance of Payment Statistics completed its review and reported in 1965. Each of these basic appraisals of an important segment of national statistics was the subject of hearings before the Subcommittee on Economic Statistics of the Joint Economic Committee. The testimony of expert witnesses who had been invited to comment on the problems that were involved added significantly to the value of the appraisals made by the distinguished review committees.

In explaining the reasons for requesting the National Bureau of Economic Research to undertake a critical appraisal of national economic accounts, Dr. Bowman stated:

> The various national accounting systems not only serve special purposes in themselves, but in addition, provide a consistent frame of reference for seeing that necessary associated data match appropriately. They also reveal what data are lacking and what data are inadequate, inaccurate, or not prompt enough.
>
> It was with these objectives in mind that the Bureau of the Budget requested the National Bureau of Economic Research to undertake a review and appraisal of our national economic accounts. As the agency responsible for coordination and improvement of Federal statistical programs, we sought expert guidance for a better-integrated program to meet the needs of basic economic analysis.
>
> In our opinion the report does provide an excellent source of guidance and should aid materially in developing a truly useful and valid Federal statistical program.

In turning to the National Bureau of Economic Research to obtain a critical appraisal of price statistics, the Budget Bureau indicated the direction that Dr. Bowman wanted the review to take by specifying that it should

> take into account not only the needs of the Government but also those of the general public, including business, agriculture, labor, and private research organizations. Attention should be given to the need for data reflecting current economic conditions and also to the need for basic information required for meaningful historical analyses and studies of price and cost relationships. Some attention should be given to the special problems which arise as a result of the use of the indexes for wage adjustments and price supports.

The report of the Price Statistics Review Committee contained recommendations dealing with general problems related to the construction of all indexes and special problems related to the consumer price index, the wholesale price index, and the indexes of prices received and paid by farmers. The importance of these indexes and the problems associated with their use were underlined in the following statement from the report:

> The CPI (Consumer Price Index) is becoming an integral part of the area of collective bargaining, through its extensive use of wage escalation. The WPI (Wholesale Price Index) is receiving an increasing role in business contracts covering even fairly short periods of time. The Indexes of Prices Paid and Received by Farmers are at the foundation of agricultural price-support policies of the Federal Government. . . . The important legal commitments which rest on the indexes normally lead the parties to press for strict comparability in the concepts and procedures employed in compiling the index. . . . Strict comparability in the items priced and the weights assigned to commodities can be achieved only at the cost of making an index number increasingly obsolete. It would be possible to make up a consumer price index, for example, that priced only goods that were very similar in 1930 and 1960, but it would have to disregard the majority of the goods consumed in either year, and its course over time would be a mere caricature of the movements of a good consumer price index. The periodic revision of price indexes, and the almost continuous alterations in details of their calculation, are essential if the indexes are to serve their primary function of measuring the average movements of prices.

Extensive hearings on the price statistics report were held by the Joint Economic Committee. Senator John Sparkman, who opened them, said: "Price changes have an important bearing on many public and private economic policies, and have been a matter of continued interest to the Joint Economic Committee."

Statistics dealing with employment and unemployment, so important in judging the heart of the economy, were initially prepared separately from different sources by both the Department of Commerce and the Bureau of Labor Statistics. Commerce obtained data from a monthly household survey while Labor collected monthly data from employers and utilized information available from the administration of the unemployment-compensation systems. The monthly results sometimes did not agree. One day, while I was in the Bureau, President Eisenhower called me into his office to point out two different figures that had just been issued for unemployment. He asked the Bureau to look into the difference, tell him what the matter was, and see that it was corrected. The Office of Statistical Standards took the lead in attacking this problem and after some months of negotiation worked out a solution, which was approved by the President. The nature of the new arrangement was summarized by the Bureau in the June, 1959, issue (No. 258) of its monthly publication, *The Statistical Reporter,* as follows:

> On July 1, 1959, responsibility for the publication and analysis of labor force statistics based on sample surveys of the population will be transferred, with the approval of the Congress, from the U.S. Department of Commerce to the U.S. Department of Labor. The Bureau of the Census will continue to collect and tabulate the data as an agent of the Bureau of Labor Statistics.

In testifying before the Subcommittee on Economic Statistics of the Joint Economic Committee on June 7, 1967, Dr. Bowman referred to this centralization of responsibility for employment and unemployment statistics as a source of improvement in the data but noted continued public questioning of the series:

> In the summer of 1959 a major realignment of function occurred. Responsibility for planning, analysis and publication of the employment and unemployment statistics obtained from the household survey was transferred to the BLS while the Census Bureau continued

to collect the data as agent. In effect, BLS became more completely the responsible agency for employment and unemployment statistics. Meanwhile, the wealth of detail expanded, and seasonal adjustment of the series was introduced to enhance its use as an economic indicator. Nevertheless, the continued high level of unemployment fostered continued doubt over the reliability and adequacy of the unemployment series.

In the fall of 1961, the President, at the recommendation of the Bureau of the Budget and the Department of Labor, appointed a committee of distinguished nongovernment economists and statisticians to appraise employment and unemployment statistics. The report of this committee, made in September, 1962, led to important improvements in the sample of the monthly series and in needed analytical and experimental work. Effective implementation of the committee's recommendations was expedited by the public discussions and testimony resulting from hearings on the subject held by the Joint Economic Committee.

Another illustration of the use of a committee of outside experts to evaluate an important area of government statistics is the Review Committee for Balance of Payments Statistics, appointed by the Director of the Bureau of the Budget in April, 1963. This committee was asked to consider "basic conceptual problems, problems of presentation and analysis, and technical statistical problems of data collection, estimation and related matters." Its recommendations, amplified by the comments of other experts testifying on the report at hearings held by the Joint Economic Committee, provide important guidelines for the continued improvement of statistics having to do with balance of payments.

In addition to having expert committees review and appraise statistical measures of significant economic activity, the Bureau initiates changes in statistical organization and responsibility that are designed to achieve progressive improvement and better coordination of government statistical programs. The shift of responsibility for employment and unemployment statistics to the Department of Labor has already been noted. Other significant changes include: (1) the centralization of responsibility for construction statistics in the Bureau of the Census (a project under study when I was in the Bureau); (2) the shift, to the Census Bureau, of responsibility for department-store statistics (from the board of governors of the Federal Reserve System) and for the conduct of the monthly series on manufacturers' shipments, inventories, and orders (from the Office of Business Economics in the Department of Commerce); (3) the focus of responsibility for planning and coordinating input-output statistics on the Office of Business Economics, for scientific manpower statistics on the National Science Foundation, and for carrying out recommendations of an interagency study group on petroleum statistics on the Department of the Interior. New organizational units have been established with responsibility in specified areas: the National Center for Health Statistics, concerned with illness, injuries, and impairments, health examinations and health records, as well as vital events; and the Center for Educational Statistics, which plans, among other activities, to develop "an educational model to indicate capabilities and inconsistencies in educational statistics."

The Bureau's efforts to improve selected areas of statistics information have not always been successful. For example, statistics on crime and delinquency have never been perfected. Dr. Bowman has testified that the Office of Statistical Standards worked "closely with the National Crime Commission, particularly its Task Force on Crime Assessment, on developing better statistics and establishing a national crime statistics center." The lack of satisfactory progress in this area reflects, in part, the fact that, except for violations of federal law, crime prevention, detection, and punishment are matters of state and local responsibility. As Dr. Bowman noted, the "principal function that the Federal Government can serve is to collect data on as nearly a uniform basis as possible so that a state or locality can compare its record with others and with national averages."

Improvement and coordination of statistics in a decentralized statistical system such as that of the United States requires the use of standard classifications, procedures, and definitions if it is to increase the comparability of data from different agencies. Today, the Office of Statistical Policy leads the development of uniform statistical standards for use by all agencies. Among the more important standards are the standard industrial classification of establishments by activity, covering the entire economic field; the standard metropolitan statistical areas, definitions of some 230 metropolitan areas; the standard enterprise classification of enterprises by activity; the standard commodity classification for transportation statistics; and the statistical classifications of commodities imported into and exported from the United States. Work is also under way through an interagency group sponsored by the Office of Statistical Policy to develop a standard occupational classification.

Since 1955, a consolidated statement of the budgets for major statistical programs of the federal government has been included as one of the special analyses associated with the annual budget document. The preparation of the annual budget provides an opportunity to review the principal statistical programs of the federal agencies by broad subject fields as well as on agency lines. The review provides a means of evaluating the usefulness of statistics in given areas and points the way to a balanced and effective statistical program for the government as a whole. Funds for the principal statistical programs in fiscal 1969 amounted to a total of $158.4 million.

Achieving the objectives of the Federal Reports Act of 1942 constitutes another principal function of the Office of Statistical Policy. Under this Act, the Bureau is charged with the responsibility of coordinating federal reporting services and eliminating duplication and reducing the cost of such services to the government and nongovernment respondents by minimizing the burden of furnishing data to federal agencies. The Act provides that every agency of the federal government (except a few specified exemptions) must obtain approval of the Bureau of the Budget for any data request to be sent to ten or more respondents. This review of data requests has eliminated hundreds of requests and lessened the burdens on business—which are heavy enough as it is. An outstanding example of savings resulting from this review and coordination is the greater use of administrative records, including tax returns, which has eliminated the need for the Census Bureau to obtain data in the economic censuses from some 2 million small firms with few employees.

In carrying out its review responsibility, the Bureau has the benefit of advice on industry-reporting practices and on the probable cost to industry respondents incurred in preparing replies through its Advisory Council on Federal Reports, which takes an active interest in this part of the Bureau's work.

The Office of Statistical Policy serves as a center for coordination of statistical matters between U.S. Government agencies and international organizations and for ensuring that requests from certain international organizations for statistical data are consistently handled and that comparable data are supplied by the various agencies. It cooperates with the State Department in drafting and clearing, among interested government agencies, U.S. position papers and instructions to U.S. delegations concerning international statistical matters and in formulating recommendations on the nature and extent of U.S. participation at various international statistical conferences. The Office of Statistical Policy also publishes a monthly bulletin called *Statistical Reporter*, which deals primarily with current developments in federal statistics in all the departments of the executive branch and includes reference to publications by the U.N. statistical office and other statistical agencies.

In spite of heroic efforts on the part of the Bureau to improve and coordinate the economic statistics for the federal government, all admit that the present system is far from satisfactory. The Subcommittee on Economic Statistics of the Joint Economic Committee, in its report of August 7, 1967, stated that

> on the basis of testimony, the subcommittee concludes that the present methods of operating our statistical programs have become obsolete in the sense that the need for integration and data availability have outstripped progress. At the present time, statistical programs require radical improvement to take advantage of modern technology and to meet the new and rapidly expanding needs of policy and analysis.

One far-reaching suggestion has been made by Dr. Bowman and others, calling for the establishment of a national statistics data center. Such a scheme has been brought within the range of practicability by the new generation of computers, but many questions must be settled before it is implemented. Transfer of data to such a center and retrieval from it must, obviously, safeguard information concerning individual persons and businesses. Clearly, also, what quantitative information can usefully be stored must be determined.

VIII

The Budget Bureau
and the
Department of Defense

For each of the last three years (1967-69), the military expenditures, including trust funds, of the Department of Defense have amounted to over 40 per cent of the total U.S. budget outlays. The percentage for fiscal 1970 will be about the same. (See Chart 4.) About two-thirds of the proposed expenditures will be made from new obligational authority requested in the budget, the balance from obligational authority carried over from earlier years. (See Table 1.)

It is impossible to discuss U.S. defense programs without pausing to stress the great contribution of the nation's allies in manpower, equipment, and bases to the common defense effort. It is my belief that our mutual assistance programs have probably been the cheapest expenditures we have made in terms of protection obtained, except for Southeast Asia. The U.S. expenditures there are now included in the total military budget under the heading "Special Vietnam," as Table 1 indicates.

Because of its size and paramount importance to the safety of the country, the Defense budget gets more top-level study, review, and discussion than any five other departmental bud-

TABLE 1. DEPARTMENT OF DEFENSE MILITARY EXPENDITURES[a]

	1967 Budget Message	1967 Actual	1968 Actual	1969 Estimate
Personnel	$18,150	$19,787	$21,954	$23,665
Operation and maintenance	14,980	19,000	20,578	22,106
Total operations	$33,130	$38,787	$42,532	$45,771
Procurement	15,970	19,012	23,283	24,337
Research, development, and test and evaluation	6,400	7,160	7,747	7,545
Military construction	1,120	1,536	1,281	1,508
Family housing	545	482	495	630
Civil defense	100	100	108	82
Revolving and management funds and other	-115	512	2,091	-1,945[b]
Deductions for offsetting receipts			-164	-140
Trust funds		20		2
Total	$57,150	$67,466	$77,373	$77,790
Total excluding Special Vietnam	($46,965)	($47,333)	($50,826)	($48,978)

[a]The 1968 and 1969 figures are from the 1970 Budget Message. All figures are in millions of dollars.

[b]In the original Budget Message for fiscal 1968, presented to Congress by President Johnson on January 24, 1967, "Revolving and management funds and other" was estimated to require net payments to the public of $346 million. The actual figures reported two years later, after it became certain that there would be a record-breaking deficit for fiscal 1968 in any case, were increased to $2,091 million with an almost off-setting credit to fiscal 1969, in which year it was desired to show a surplus.

gets together. Under President Eisenhower, the Security Council gave consideration to the budgets of the different armed services and the recommendations of the Joint Chiefs of Staff. During the Kennedy and Johnson administrations, these were taken up directly by the President.

Every President devotes a tremendous amount of time to the nation's defense posture and the plans and expected de-

Chart 4

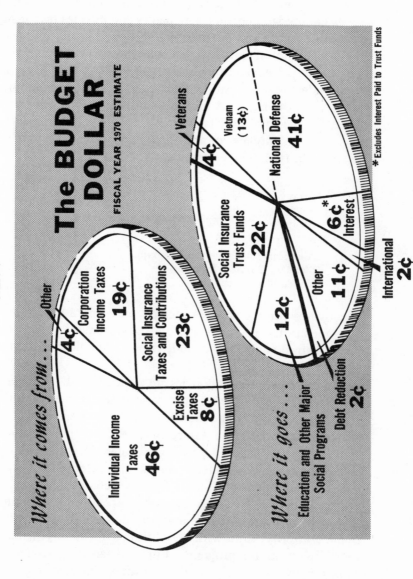

The BUDGET DOLLAR

FISCAL YEAR 1970 ESTIMATE

Where it comes from....

Individual Income Taxes **46¢**

Excise Taxes **8¢**

Social Insurance Taxes and Contributions **23¢**

Corporation Income Taxes **19¢**

Other **4¢**

Where it goes....

Education and Other Major Social Programs **12¢**

Debt Reduction **2¢**

Other **11¢**

Interest **6¢***

International **2¢**

National Defense **41¢**

Vietnam (13¢)

Social Insurance Trust Funds **22¢**

Veterans **4¢**

* Excludes Interest Paid to Trust Funds

velopments. Programs must be long-range. It takes five years from the approval of the construction of a big aircraft carrier to its commissioning, and new planes and missiles take many years to develop and put into production. The magnitude of the dollar amounts involved can be better realized by separating the actual expenditures by the armed services from the total budget and comparing them with the gross expenditures of some of the largest American industrial companies. In fiscal 1967, the total purchases, wages, and operating expenses, in millions of dollars, of the three services and of four selected industrial giants were:

Army	$18,906
Navy	16,679
Air Force	19,227
General Motors	$17,092
American Telephone and Telegraph	7,816
Standard Oil, New Jersey	6,930
United States Steel	3,989

The figures for the services include only military personnel and operations, maintenance, and procurement. Those for the industrial companies include research and depreciation as well.

The nation's military policies are decided by the President, the Secretary of Defense, the service secretaries, and the Joint Chiefs of Staff and modified by the congressional committees, particularly the Armed Services and Appropriations committees of the House and Senate. The total dollar amounts of the U.S. defense budget are determined by the policies these men set. Budget Bureau recommendations are primarily related to comparisons of expenditure programs: first with programs already authorized, second with obligational authority, third with expenditures of earlier years, and fourth with future programs. But they are also related to consideration of maintaining a proper balance between worldwide policy objectives and domestic programs. The views of the Bureau staff are expressed only to the President or his advisers or through the budget process.

The total obligational authority in billions of dollars that had been requested for the past three years for major mission-oriented defense programs (including military assistance to the nation's allies) is as follows:

	1967 Actual	1968 Actual	1969 Estimate
Strategic forces	$ 6.9	$ 7.6	$ 9.1
General purpose forces	32.7	32.4	33.2
Intelligence and communications	5.3	5.7	6.0
Airlift and sealift	1.9	1.9	1.6
Guard and reserve forces	2.7	3.2	2.7
Research and development	4.8	4.4	4.7
Central supply and maintenance	7.1	8.2	8.8
Training, medical, and other general personnel activities	8.5	10.0	10.3
Administration and associated activities	1.5	1.3	1.5
Military assistance funded by Department of Defense	1.6	1.8	2.7
Adjustment for retired pay accrual	-.4	-.3	-.1
Total	$72.5	$76.2	$80.6

The size of the programs and the importance of the time element in the assembly and review of the figures have made it essential to work out a technique for the Budget Bureau's procedures for the Defense Department that differs from that for the civilian agencies. The members of the trained technical staff of the Bureau's National Security Programs Division, almost all of whom have themselves had military service, spend the whole year on the analysis and review of current and future operating programs and plans.

Procedures Under President Eisenhower

The procedures worked out for the review of military proposals by the Budget Bureau under President Eisenhower were as follows: The general guidelines laid down in the spring of the year were considered by the headquarters staff of each of the services and by the Defense Department staff in Washington. These agencies, together with the Joint Chiefs of Staff, the Department of State, the Budget Bureau, and the Council of Economic Advisers, participated in the final formulation in the National Security Council of these guidelines, which were then distributed, together with individual requests for suggestions, throughout the worldwide operating military units. When suggestions were received, they were compiled and reviewed thoroughly in the appropriate service comptroller's office, and preliminary estimates were then prepared for discussion with the Budget Bureau, the Secretary of Defense, and the Joint Chiefs in June or July. When the suggestions from all services had been discussed, general goals were set and approved by the President. After that, the detailed requests were prepared and again reviewed by the comptroller's office and the staff of the Secretary of Defense. The totals usually substantially exceeded the amounts that could be approved without affecting the programs of the other departments and requiring additional revenues, so the service secretaries and their staffs usually made substantial cuts before October, when revised presentations were made to the staffs of both the Budget Bureau and the Comptroller of the Department of Defense over a period of several days. The presentations included technical discussion of all the promising new weapons, slides and movies of their design and performance, comments on their effectiveness by officers who had used them, and consideration of the purpose for which they were needed. Representatives of the Joint Chiefs also participated and copious notes were made. Much of the material was classified, and only persons directly concerned with the operations or Budget needs took part. Late in November, the Director of the Budget and the Secretary of Defense discussed again all the important issues with their deputies and representatives of the National Security Council and the office of Science and Technology.

Present-Day Procedures

The joint review procedure today is much the same as it was under Eisenhower, with two important exceptions: (1) the review of the budget in the fall takes off from a previously approved long-range program that has been developed and modified as necessary throughout the year and (2) the Secretary of Defense, who has been concentrating on the major issues under consideration throughout the spring and summer, prepares or approves a series of major-decision documents known as draft Presidential memorandums.

Very early in his tenure, Defense Secretary Robert S. McNamara and his first comptroller, Charles Hitch, made a special effort to redefine the Department of Defense programs in mission-oriented or "output" terms rather than the traditional budget categories defined on a functional basis. As a result, Defense budget totals today are broken down into ten major programs conforming to major force structure and support missions. These major programs are aggregated on a "building-block" basis, which starts from program elements such as B-52 squadrons, armored divisions, or antisubmarine aircraft-carriers. These aggregations are reviewed in the services and in the Office of the Secretary of Defense, and future requirements are compiled to form the Five Year Defense Program. When the Secretary of Defense gives his stamp of approval, this represents the approved program of the Department of Defense from which the services and the operating commands are not allowed to deviate. The programing procedure also includes specific instructions for requesting changes in the program, which must be approved by the Secretary of Defense or his deputy.

The joint review process in the autumn is supposed to concentrate on problems of pricing, production feasibility, and development status of weapons systems. It has been very difficult to complete the programing and major decision process on schedule, so many of the major decisions of the Secretary and the President still have not been reached by November and December. As a result, late in the 1960's, Assistant Secretary and Comptroller of the Department of Defense Robert Anthony spearheaded financial management improvements, particularly in the operations area, called Project PRIME (Priority Management Effort). These improvements are designed to make the budget process in operations conform more closely to the programing process by providing management personnel in the services themselves, the major commands, and down to the installation level with review tools expressed in program terms and including military personnel as an integrated element of cost. Under the new system, implemented in fiscal year 1969, operating budgets will be requested, reviewed, and released in program terms at all echelons.

The cycle of decision-making for the financing of future military requirements is now a continuous process. The Secretary of Defense stated that preparations for the budget for the fiscal year 1972, which starts July 1, 1971, would begin in October, 1969. Based on their evaluation of the worldwide situation and supported by a special analysis by the intelligence community, the Joint Chiefs of Staff will prepare a Joint Strategic Objectives Plan (JSOP) recommending a five-year strategy. After consideration by the President, the National Security Council, the Bureau of the Budget, the Council of Economic Advisers, and his other advisers, a Strategic Guidance Memorandum will be drafted by the Secretary of Defense. This will be studied by the military services and the staff of the Secretary, with further conferences, so that a revised decision paper can be prepared by mid-January, 1970, on the strategic concept that will guide the preparation of the budget for fiscal 1972. The Joint Chiefs of Staff will then prepare and release a revised JSOP, which is costed in rough terms. During the spring, also, a series of requirements studies are conducted by the services, the Joint Chiefs, and the Office of the Secretary of Defense. These requirements studies address major force-structure and weapons-systems questions. The assistant secretary of defense in charge of systems analysis is very heavily involved in these studies, and his staff prepares a series of issue papers, or draft Presidential memorandums, on segments of the Defense program for his review, so scheduled that he may make the major program decisions before the budget figures come in from the services in October for final review. Director Mayo, in a statement before the Joint Economic Committee, recently explained the huge amount of work involved in this process, which, he said:

> will culminate within the Department of Defense with a series of 400 to 500 program-budget decision documents. Each document addresses a separate budget issue and consists of a concise description of the issue, a statement of the internal Department of Defense cost estimate, and a discussion of possible alternatives, as well as a brief description of the rationale for each alternative offered.

The Defense Department today is accomplishing a great deal in coordinating the services and requiring as much common procurement and uniform specifications as is practical. This coordination, an objective of the Bureau for many years, is difficult to accomplish, because each service is constantly making improvements to meet its own specialized requirements. Where it can be effected, however, it provides a valuable check on the relative importance of proposals by the services and perhaps makes for more effective operation than if the services were integrated and combined into one operating organization. It encourages initiative and creative rivalry at the same time that it moderates the sometimes excessive demands by individual units.

Problems of Rivalry and Duplication

Some competition between the separate services is good, and it is natural that each feels its preeminent importance and makes claims for new opportunities that open up, such as those in outer space. The enormous size of U.S. defense operations throughout the world and the wide distribution of forces and equipment means that any individual's intimate knowledge is limited to a narrow fraction of the total operations of a single service in any one area. This fact makes it particularly difficult to measure the relative value of a unit or to eliminate operations no longer required. It is especially true in eliminating installations within the United States. As soon as word gets out that any abandonment is even under consideration, there is a deluge of protests from local interests—the mayor of the nearest town, its Chamber of Commerce, members of Congress.

For example, a few years ago agreement was reached between the Bureau and the Defense Department on closing two large military hospitals, one in Arkansas and the other in Massachusetts, that were no longer needed. New adjacent facilities were quite adequate. However, the interests affected were successful in blocking this economy move by getting a directive written into an appropriations bill covering many billions of dollars, stating that none of these funds could be used if either of the two hospitals were closed down. I could give a number of similar examples.

Secretary McNamara made an effective drive to eliminate facilities no longer in use and to reduce and eliminate the procurement of items no longer necessary. Although his efforts to reduce such waste were more effective than any previous attempts, the results were still far from what he wished to accomplish, and the war in Vietnam has prevented further progress, at least for the time being.

The United States spends a tremendous amount of money on military research and development—over $7 billion a year. Here, too, is a lot of waste. New ideas have to be developed up to a point often representing a heavy investment before any conclusion can be reached as to their effectiveness. Great vigilance is required to prevent unnecessary spending when future progress looks doubtful. Hundreds of new ideas are produced each year, not only by the research and development programs, but also in the field. They include new inventions and improvements in current hardware, both offensive and defensive, as new enemy weapons are encountered or as intelligence indicates that they are under production. One of the Bureau's many useful functions is to question the relative importance of different items that are under development and reaching procurement stage but seem to be designed for similar objectives and, hence, to represent possibly unnecessary duplication in costs.

There is always opposition from some quarter to technological changes that will mean reduction in the numerical strength of forces, even though fire-power strength may be greatly enhanced thereby. Other important obstacles to budget savings are that the alumni of the different services are naturally loyal to them and anxious to see their own branches of the service grow in stature and importance, that many of the contractors become strong advocates not only of the products they have developed but of the branch of the services they are supplying, that many members of Congress have served in one of the services and have not only predilections toward it but also channels of information to and from it. Even newspaper-writers and columnists have their service favorites. All this tends to bring pressure on the budget officers and the operating chiefs. Their painstaking efforts to balance conflicting claims and arrive at sound decisions are not always adequately appreciated by Congress or the country.

An especially complicated set of conflicting forces exists for a proposed program to build a fleet of fast deployment logistics (FDL) ships, large floating warehouses to be loaded with the heavy equipment of Army units and stationed near potential trouble spots, so that, if the Army units are deployed, their equipment will be available much more quickly than if it had to be shipped on conventional freighters from the United States. The FDL ships are advocated principally by the Army, but, since they are ships, they appear in the Navy's budget. The Navy, however, is only lukewarm about the FDL program, preferring to have its funds invested in combatant Navy ships. Merchant Marine interests oppose the program because of its potentially adverse effect on the need for conventional freighters. The Air Force, although not directly involved, favors the FDL ships because, without them, the case is weakened for the C-5A transport planes designed to fly the men whose equipment is on the ships. Congressmen line up on one side or the other, depending on their service affiliations, the presence of shipyards in their states or districts, and their views on the underlying question of whether American military forces should be prepared to move quickly into a troubled area. The program was deleted from the 1968 fiscal year budget; it was up for consideration again in 1969.

Similar conflicting pressures exist with respect to aerial support to infantry units. The choice is between helicopters and fixed-wing aircraft. Although this choice theoretically should be made on the basis of such considerations as maneuverability, vulnerability to enemy action, accuracy of fire, and speed of response to infantry requests for assistance, as a practical matter the debate has been heavily influenced by the fact that helicopters belong to the Army and fixed-wing aircraft belong to the Air Force. The Advanced Aerial Fire Support System (a fancy term for helicopters) item in the Army budget represents a victory for the Army point of view.

Similar conflicts arise *within* a service. For example, with the increased range of modern aircraft, a good case can be made for retiring the small aircraft-carriers, whose role in combat would be to detect and sink enemy submarines and to rely instead on shore-based aircraft to do the job. The cost of shore-based aircraft is much less than the cost of an equivalent number of carrier-based aircraft. Within the Navy, the issue is not debated entirely on its merits; the emotions of the "black-shoe" or ship-oriented officers and the "brown-shoe" or aircraft-oriented officers are also a factor. Indeed, some propose the easy solution of providing *both* carrier-based and shore-based aircraft. This solution would ease the Navy's emotional problem—but at a high cost to the taxpayer.

Carriers figured in an interesting review in which I participated when the Bureau took a hard look at the Navy's fiscal 1956 request for two of these vessels of the *Forrestal* class (cost about $200 million each, fifteen then in operation) and twelve more *Polaris* submarines (cost about $40 million each, sixteen then in operation or under construction). It seemed to the Bureau staff that the purpose of these very different types of ships for carrying out strategic missions was similar, that experience should have indicated by then which was superior, and that it would be wiser to concentrate on one type. After several conferences and discussions with Navy officers and staff, the Bureau personnel came to believe that its inquiry was not only justified but, in fact, confirmed by the opinions expressed. Since a great deal of money was involved, it was suggested that the Navy review its needs and that the Director would be glad to approve additional construction of either one vessel or the other, but not both. The Secretary of the Navy and the Secretary of Defense appealed to the President, and the whole situation was reviewed with him again. At the conclusion, the President said that he thought both types of ships were useful; his opinion was that carriers would be more effective deterrents than submarines in preventing the spread of brush-fire conflicts that might break out around the world and that carriers, protected by sufficient submarines, would also be valuable in any retaliatory action that might become necessary. He did not think that experience to that date could be used to justify the Navy concentrating on only one of the types for all future procurement, and he therefore suggested that the Bureau approve the authorization of one additional carrier and six more Polaris submarines. His decision, of course, settled the question, but it also served to direct more careful attention to the relative merits of each type of equipment for presentation of additional information the next year. It also reduced the total dollars involved to substantially what the Budget Bureau had suggested.

Testimony by former Budget Director Schultze and Director Mayo in June, 1969, before the Joint Economic Committee of Congress on the military budget and national economic priorities indicated that for several years the Bureau had not been questioning military priorities to the same extent that it had those of the civilian programs. Although the staff members of the Bureau who were continuously assigned to Defense programs throughout the year made the same independent review of proposals for procurement and missions as in the past and their joint review of service requests with the staff of the comptroller of the Department of Defense, and although the recommendations of the Bureau staffs and the priorities involved were also discussed at the Director's review, McNamara as Secretary of Defense took over responsibility for direct presentation of his own recommendations to the President.

The Secretary kept a very tight grip also on all the operations of the services, but, until 1966, the Bureau's viewpoint was not at odds with his proposals. With the escalation of the war in Vietnam, the proposals from the armed services' operations control began to have more weight with the President and the priorities seemed to have been determined without much regard to the views of the Secretary or the Director. This, according to Director Mayo, has now been changed. Mayo said that the Defense budget, like all others, will go to the Budget Bureau, which will have final say (subject to appeal to the President by the department head, as previously). A recent example was the acceptance by the Defense Department of the Bureau's recommendation that the $3-billion Manned Orbiting Laboratory be canceled.

The Military-Industrial Complex

In order to have a reliable supply of presently required matériel and an on-going research program to develop new types of equipment and facilities, it is necessary for the armed services to work very closely with American industry. The staffs of the Secretary of Defense and the Bureau of the Budget watch this work equally closely, in an effort to be sure that competitive bids are being properly sought by the services for procurement and that cost overruns are kept down as much as possible. The problem of undue influence has always been very much in the minds of the President, the Secretary of Defense, and Bureau officials, and in 1969 it became an issue in Congress as well and in the press. More and more, the public has been questioning defense expenditures and expressing opposition to the enormous military budget.

President Eisenhower was one of the first to recognize the dangers inherent in the vast size and wealth of the defense industry. In his farewell address on January 17, 1961, he sounded a warning that I believe summed up the situation better than anything we have heard since. It has been referred to often by writers but seldom quoted at length. Because of its significance, in both a contemporary and a historic sense, pertinent passages are reproduced below:

> A vital element in keeping the peace is our military establishment. Our arms must be mighty, ready for instant action, so that no potential aggressor may be tempted to risk his own destruction.
>
> Our military organization today bears little relation to that known by any of my predecessors in peacetime, or indeed by the fighting men of World War II or Korea.
>
> Until the latest of our world conflicts, the United States had no armaments industry. American makers of plowshares could, with time and as required, make swords as well. But now we can no longer risk emergency improvisation of national defense; we have been compelled to create a permanent armaments industry of vast proportions. Added to this, three and a half million men and women are directly engaged in the defense establishment. We annually spend on military security more than the net income of all United States corporations.
>
> This conjunction of an immense military establishment and a large arms industry is new in the American experience. The total influence—economic, political, even spiritual—is felt in every city, every State house, every office of the Federal government. We recognize the imperative need for this development. Yet we must not fail to comprehend its grave implications. Our toil, resources and livelihood are all involved; so is the very structure of our society.
>
> In the councils of government, we must guard against the acquisition of unwarranted influence, whether sought or unsought, by the military-industrial complex. The potential for the disastrous rise of misplaced power exists and will persist.

We must never let the weight of this combination endanger our liberties or democratic processes. We should take nothing for granted. Only an alert and knowledgeable citizenry can compel the proper meshing of the huge industrial and military machinery of defense with our peaceful methods and goals, so that security and liberty may prosper together.

IX

Natural Resources Programs

Programs to develop and maintain the great American heritage in natural resources have always had the sympathetic interest and encouragement of the Budget Bureau, although it has sometimes been accused of being short-sighted and stingy in this regard. The special budgetary problems involved, however, are often difficult, and, for this reason, as well as because of the importance of these resources to all citizens, are here given a separate chapter.

The Natural Resources Programs Division of the Bureau covers the agencies developing, operating, and otherwise concerned with natural resources. These include the Department of Agriculture, the Department of the Interior, and their many direct and related bureaus, commissions, and authorities, plus the Civilian Branch of the Corps of Army Engineers and the Tennessee Valley Authority.

In budget terms, the most important characteristic of these agencies has been the keen interest and effective control that Congress has exercised over them, in contrast to which the influence of the Budget Bureau has been relatively small. The congressmen and senators from the West, particularly, have been actively concerned with all the farm, reclamation, and development programs and have had great influence in Congress for many years; the restraints that the Bureau has tried to impose have been largely disregarded, and programs and budget requests submitted by the President in the area of natural resources on behalf of the executive agencies have been upgraded or disregarded when they did not coincide with the wishes of pressure groups. (This is one of the reasons for the frequent shifts in plans and in programs and their multiplicity.) Only recently has the urban dweller had the attention he deserves.

The requested authority and estimated expenditures (in millions of dollars) for the natural resources category in the Budget Message for fiscal years 1967-69 are shown in Table 2.

TABLE 2. NATURAL RESOURCES EXPENDITURES
AND NET LENDING

Program or Agency	Expenditures and Net Lending			Recommended NOA and LA for 1969[a]
	1967 Actual	1968 Estimate	1969 Estimate	
Expenditures				
Land and water resources				
Corps of Engineers[b]	$1,301	$1,341	$1,313	$1,283
Department of the Interior				
Bureau of Reclamation[b]	300	291	299	288
Power marketing agencies[b]	133	147	153	151
Federal Water Pollution Control Administration	130	190	248	326
Office of Saline Water[b]	17	31	41	30
Office of Water Resources Research	6	9	11	13
Bureau of Indian Affairs	106	113	112	113

TABLE 2 *(cont.)*

Program or Agency	Expenditures and Net Lending			Recommended NOA and LA for 1969a
	1967 Actual	1968 Estimate	1969 Estimate	
Bureau of Land Management[b]	87	83	76	76
Tennessee Valley Authority	102	109	150	50
Soil Conservation Service, watershed projects	108	106	93	61
International Boundary and Water Commission	27	22	15	9
Federal Power Commission and other[b]	17	22	25	24
Subtotal land and water resources	$2,335	$2,465	$2,536	$2,424
Forest resources				
Forest Service[b]	461	495	470	486
Bureau of Land Management	21	22	22	22
Recreational resources				
Bureau of Outdoor Recreation[b]	68	105	160	134
National Park Service and other[b]	126	140	148	110
Fish and wildlife resources[b]	136	153	158	158
Mineral resources				
Bureau of Land Management	48	50	50	50
Bureau of Mines and other[b]	73	83	80	76
General resource surveys and administration[b]	275	250	239	191
Interfund and intragovernmental transactions	−22	c	−1	−1

TABLE 2 *(cont.)*

Program or Agency	Expenditures and Net Lending			Recommended NOA and LA for 1969a
	1967 Actual	1968 Estimate	1969 Estimate	
Applicable receipts from the public	-1,410	-1,348	-1,381	-1,381
Subtotal expenditures	$2,113	$2,416	$2,483	$2,271
Net lending				
Land and water resources	18	15	6	4
Other	1	1	1	
Total	$2,132	$2,432	$2,490	$2,275

[a] Compares with new obligational authority (NOA) and lending authority (LA) for 1967 and 1968, as follows—NOA: 1967, $3,262 million; 1968, $2,488 million. LA: 1967, $17 million; 1968, $14 million.

[b] Includes both federal funds and trust funds.

[c] Less than $500,000.

Source: 1969 Budget Message.

The Agriculture Budget

The Department of Agriculture dates back to 1862—the year when it became the eighth executive department. In reviewing the Agriculture Department's programs, the Bureau staff must consider certain factors not encountered in other agencies. The prices of farm products fluctuate with the quantities of the crops produced in this country and abroad, unless support is given. The total volume depends on the acreage planted, which is decided at the beginning of the season or even earlier, in the light of prices for the crops carried over and subsidies proposed; thereafter, it is affected by the amount of fertilizer used, pest control, fluctuations in rainfall and temperature, shortages of labor at harvest time, spoilage of produce, and transportation and marketing difficulties. After the harvest, prices are affected by the volume of production not only in the immediate area but also in other parts of the country and around the world. Grains, the nation's biggest agricultural volume, are easily transported or can be stored at will up to warehouse capacity. Over the years, Congress has tried to stabilize production and prices by every conceivable form of subsidy, price support, bonus for increased yields, and bonus for destruction of produce and withdrawal of land from cultivation. In spite of this situation, the rapid mechanization of the farms, the increased use of fertilizers and improved seeds, the widespread use of irrigation, and improved sprays for pest control have all helped to increase agricultural production. It is even greater than the increase in the national population.

Three fundamentally different approaches have been considered by the Bureau in dealing with the agricultural budget: (1) all government controls and subsidies could be withdrawn and the law of supply and demand left to regulate the quantities produced and the price; (2) the prices of farm products could be kept high or raised further if necessary to keep production at a level sufficient to meet the requirements of the population; and (3) all controls could be removed from production, acreage, and prices, and the farmer would be directly subsidized to make up his losses and help him pay for the increasing cost of mechanization and everything he has to buy. All three policies have been tried in whole or in part and in various combinations.

Farm production was greatly stimulated during World War II, and since then the United States has had a technological revolution on the farms like the Industrial Revolution two generations ago. During the first ten postwar years, tremendous surpluses of many products (particularly the grains) were accumulated, leading to restrictive policies. With the backing of the Budget Bureau, Secretary of Agriculture Ezra Taft Benson, in the middle 1950's, fought valiantly for the lowering of price supports, which seemed to benefit the large operators rather than the marginal farmer for whom they were primarily intended. However, the substitution of flexible price levels for subsidies paid to the marginal farm operators was at that time opposed by congressional representatives from the farm states.

Since 1960, the huge stocks of surplus grains have disappeared, largely because of foreign assistance shipments and so-called supply adjustment programs. Grain shipments to India, for example, under Public Law 480, have averaged over a million bushels a day; the accumulated rupee equivalent of $800 million received as part consideration for these shipments, to be spent by the United States in India, is still largely unused.

The changes in American farm population since World War II have been staggering. According to the U.S. census of population classified as urban, rural-farm, and nonfarm, the farm population between 1950 and 1960 dropped from 23 million to 13.5 million, or from 23.7 per cent to 10.7 per cent of the total U.S. population. According to the most recent current population surveys of the Bureau of the Census, rural-farm families amount to 3 million, or only 6.9 per cent of the total, as compared to 4.7 million in 1960.

Of the 4.7 million farm families in 1960, 2 million, or less than half, produced 90 per cent of the products marketed, while the other 2.7 million families marketed only 10 per cent of the total produced. This pointed up the benefits of the Department of Agriculture's "rural development program," encouraged by the Budget Bureau in increasing the "off-the-farm income" of these 2.7 million families, which already received half their annual income from sources other than farming, such as part-time employment in the hundreds of commercial and manufacturing enterprises springing up in rural communities, from tourist accommodations, campers, and fishing privileges, and from handicrafts and so on. Decentralization of industry for reasons of labor availability, transportation difficulties, and accessibility to markets could eventually solve or mitigate the marginal farm problem without taking the farmers off the soil.

The 1969 Budget document states that the "Federal agriculture programs are designed to support and enlarge the contribution of our farm and rural economy to the nation's over-all economic prosperity." The new obligational and lending authority (in millions of dollars) requested for fiscal 1969 and the expenditures for the three years 1967-69 are shown in Table 3.

TABLE 3. AGRICULTURE AND AGRICULTURAL RESOURCES EXPENDITURES AND NET LENDING

Program or Agency	Expenditures and Net Lending			Recommended NOA and LA for 1969[a]
	1967 Actual	1968 Estimate	1969 Estimate	
Expenditures				
Farm income stabilization				
Price support and related programs	$1,652	$2,703	$2,775	$3,275
Conservation reserve, cropland conversion, and cropland adjustment programs	196	211	200	195
Removal of surplus agricultural commodities	145	175	178	407
National Wool Act	35	64	63	64
Sugar Act	82	86	87	82
Other[b]	157	190	156	156
Subtotal farm income stabilization	$2,267	$3,428	$3,459	$4,178

TABLE 3 *(cont.)*

Program or Agency	Expenditures and Net Lending			Recommended NOA and LA for 1969[a]
	1967 Actual	1968 Estimate	1969 Estimate	
Financing rural electrification and rural telephones	12	13	13	13
Agricultural land and water resources				
Soil Conservation Service, operations[b]	111	115	117	117
Agricultural conservation program payments (including CCC loans)	216	217	203	100
Other	26	30	30	25
Financing farming and rural housing				
Farm Credit Administration[b]	−21	−48	−64	
Farmers Home Administration and other[b]	11	74	96	92
Research and other agricultural services				
Present programs[b]	570	623	675	661
Proposed legislation for inspection fees			−13	−13
Interfund and intragovernmental transactions	−5	−5	−6	−6
Applicable receipts from the public	−32	−34	−36	−36
Subtotal expenditures	$3,156	$4,412	$4,474	$5,131
Net lending				
Farm income stabilization	262	−29	24	24

TABLE 3 (cont.)

Program or Agency	Expenditures and Net Lending			Recommended NOA and LA for 1969[a]
	1967 Actual	1968 Estimate	1969 Estimate	
Financing rural electrification and rural telephones[c]	232	279	360	234
Financing farming and rural housing				
Farm Credit Administration trust funds	671	749	771	541
Farmers Home Administration and other[b]	56	−100	−20	426
Subtotal net lending	$1,221	$ 899	$1,135	$1,225
Total	$4,377	$5,311	$5,609	$6,356

[a]Compares with new obligational authority (NOA) and lending authority (LA) for 1967 and 1968, as follows—NOA: 1967, $4,318 million; 1968, $4,383 million. LA: 1967, $1,405 million; 1968, $1,450 million.

[b]Includes both federal funds and trust funds.

[c]Figures for 1968 and 1969 reflect legislative proposals to establish a cooperative telephone bank and revolving funds for the electric and telephone programs of REA.

Source: The 1969 Budget Message.

Commodity Credit Corporation

Within the Department of Agriculture, there is one large agency engaged in making loans, purchasing commodities, and granting subsidies, which takes the full time of several members of the Budget Bureau staff. This is the Commodity Credit Corporation (CCC), authorized in 1933 and strengthened by the Agricultural Act of 1949. It has a capital stock of $100 million, owned by the U.S. Government, and has authority to borrow at any time up to $14.5 billion.

The position of the Bureau in relation to the Corporation is difficult for a number of reasons. The 1949 Act makes price support mandatory for the basic commodities—corn, cotton, wheat, rice, peanuts, and tobacco—plus many non-basic commodities, including tung nuts, honey, milk, butterfat, the products of milk and butterfat, and barley, oats, rye, and grain sorghums. The National Wool Act of 1954, as amended, also requires definite price support for wool and mohair and price support for other basic commodities—discretionary but with important catches. For example, whenever the price of either cottonseed or soybeans is supported, the support price of the other must be set at such level as the Secretary determines will cause them to compete with each other on equal terms on the market. From a budget point of view, this requirement removes any authority of the Bureau over this part of the agriculture Budget except to see that the congressional mandate is not exceeded. It places a very important limit on the power of the Bureau and the President, and their power is restricted even further by the timing of the actions required in the commodity programs.

The actual transactions by the Commodity Credit Corporation have averaged over $6 billion for each of the last three years. The losses incurred since the Corporation was formed have been colossal. Through June 30, 1967, they were, in billions of dollars:

Net realized losses	$34.0
P.L. 480 foreign-aid grants in commodities	17.5
International Wheat Agreement	1.5
All other (wool, special milk, barter, animal disease)	2.5
Total	$55.5

What is bad from a budget point of view is that these losses are not all written off when realized. Of the realized losses to June 30, 1967, almost 20 per cent had not yet been written off or absorbed.

The principal methods of providing price support are loans to and purchases from producers. With limited exceptions, price-support loans are nonrecourse. The commodities serve as collateral for the loan and, upon its maturity, the producer may deliver such collateral to satisfy his obligation without further payment, unless there is a deficiency in quantity or quality or unless he is guilty of fraudulent representation.

Since the Department of Agriculture has the exclusive right to set the support price for wheat and other crops, both Congress and the President lose control over an indeterminate amount of produce and money. In one sense, even Congress has lost control over this part of the budget. A dollar commitment for the subsidy would be safer for all concerned.*

It is true that the situation has improved in recent years. The present-day farm programs leave considerable discretion to the executive branch (much more than in the 1950's) in establishing price-support levels and acreage allotments, which provides a better opportunity for the Bureau of the Budget to review the impact on the budget of departmental proposals and to make alternative recommendations to the President. It also gives the Bureau an opportunity to solicit the views of the other federal agencies such as the Council of Economic Advisers. But, with prices fixed by the Department of Agriculture a year ahead, it is very difficult to effect even desirable economies.

The wheat-marketing year runs from July 1 to June 30. The decision on the commodity support program for wheat for the next year is made late in May or early in June—before the crop for the current year has been harvested.

The Department of Agriculture initiates the process by estimating the current year's production, the carry-over, and

*The United States is not alone in this predicament. Subsidies to French farmers in the Common Market have been the greatest source of difficulty in working out a common policy for the six member countries. The result all over the world of commodity price support has been to accelerate the concentration of production into larger and larger units, not to reduce the cost to the urban consumer.

the utilization (domestic and foreign) during the next marketing year to determine how much new production might be desirable. A number of alternative programs (each with different allotment levels, support rates, and diversion features) are considered, and the Secretary selects one, which he then proposes to the President. These are merely reviewed by the Bureau, the Council of Economic Advisers, and, at times, by other interested agencies. After the President makes his decision, the Secretary announces the program, and the price is fixed without any further possible action by the Bureau or the President. The budget estimates are based on crop estimates in the November crop report and the latest marketing and stock reports. Outlay estimates are somewhat tentative because the actual expenditures depend on how many farmers participate in the program and on the size of the crop. Price support and diversion payments are influenced by the number of participants. The sign-up takes place in March, so the budget figure is only a rough estimate. Outlays for loans and other price-support operations are influenced by the size of the crop and the market price. The winter wheat crop is planted at the time the budget is prepared, but no production estimates on it are available. The spring wheat crop has not been planted. The estimates used at the time the original program decision was made are used to estimate the budget outlays, unless there has been a significant unanticipated development. The decision on the program determines the outlays and is made outside the regular budget process six months before the budget is printed and from eleven to fifteen months before the expenditures actually are made.

The cotton-marketing year runs from August 1 to July 31. The decision on the cotton crop is made in November or December, along lines quite similar to the procedure employed in the wheat program. The department initiates a proposal, the Bureau and other interested agencies review the alternatives and comment, the President decides, and the Secretary announces the program. The budget outlay estimates are based on conditions existing at the time the decision is made, and, as in the case with the wheat program, the actual outlays are determined by the participation, the size of the crop, and the market price. The cotton program decision is made about the same time as other budget decisions are being made but outside the regular budget process. The outlays occur in the next fiscal year, some nine to thirteen months after the decision is made.

Under the supply-adjustment-price-support programs now in effect for the major commodities (wheat, feed grains, and cotton), the support price is set at about the world market price; domestic market prices generally stabilize at about this level, unless shortages occur. The farmer is directly subsidized by payments (price support and acreage diversion) to plant within given acreage limitations.

These direct payments now represent the major portion of the price-support budget and are largely predictable. It is still difficult to predict production and consumption for the price-supported commodities, but, with the lower support prices, the impact on the budget of missing the estimate is not as great as it used to be.

The direct-payment route has one important budget advantage over the other methods used to support income: It clearly reveals the amount of the subsidy and who is getting it, thereby focusing public attention on the real issue—who is being subsidized and why. But the burden on the taxpayer and the multiplicity of programs are still of concern to the Bureau.

Other Significant Agriculture Programs

The other programs of the Department of Agriculture are not as comprehensive or costly as those of the Commodity Credit Corporation. With none of them, however, are the effects of the Bureau's efforts to economize noteworthy. There are so many programs developed over the years and so many new ones proposed that they overlap to some extent or are geared to the same objectives. Programs costing more than $50 million each, over which little budget control is possible, with the amounts proposed in the fiscal 1969 budget, are as follows:

Agricultural Research Service	
Research and demonstration	$136,273,100
Plant and animal disease and pest control	88,647,500
Cooperative State Research Service, research, investigation, and experiment	62,179,000
Extension Service, employment of state and county workers	77,082,500
Soil Conservation Service	116,313,000
Consumer and Marketing Service, protection and distribution	119,846,000
Special Milk Program	104,000,000
School Lunch Program	184,443,000
Food Stamp Program	225,000,000
Agricultural Stabilization and Conservation Service	143,933,700
Sugar Act Program (financed by consumers)	82,300,000
Agricultural Conservation Program	195,500,000
Cropland Adjustment Program	85,700,000
Conservation Reserve Program	109,500,000

One appropriation that the Bureau thoroughly approves is the $12 million for administrative and operating expenses of the Federal Crop Insurance Corporation. This is a good program for insurance protection against losses from insect and wildlife damage, plant diseases, fire, drought, flood, wind, and other weather conditions. Premiums paid by the producers have substantially covered the indemnities for losses but not the overhead expenses. The program for fiscal 1969 will provide crop insurance approximating $854 million on many commodities in thirty-nine states. Premium income has exceeded indemnity costs in eleven out of nineteen years of operation, although at the time of writing losses were expected to exceed premium income for the 1967 crop year.

An important Department of Agriculture program, which has extended electricity until 99 per cent of all farms in the United States now have electric service available, is that of the Rural Electrification Administration. Although it has been very valuable, it is now operating with an indirect subsidy to which the Bureau of the Budget objects. The REA in 1968 received authority to borrow from the Secretary of the Treasury up to $304 million for its rural electrification program and $120 million for its rural telephone program. These loans are made at 2 per cent interest, although the Treasury is paying more than two and a half times that figure, and operating expenses have been absorbed by the government as well, to the extent of between $12 million and $13 million for each of the last three fiscal years. Part of the new capital advances benefit local industries, which are extending into the farm areas for construction of generating facilities, and to "heavy up the lines." These activities may be desirable from an economic point of view, both for the industry and for the labor supply, but the Bureau has questioned whether the benefit justifies the interest subsidy, or the capital loans during a period of serious national budget deficit. In any case, the President's Commission on Budget Concepts has recommended that the interest subsidy be shown and provided for.

The Forest Service of the Department of Agriculture has an important responsibility for administering the national forests and fighting fire and insects. Its programs have been approved by the Bureau for many years, and the incremental value of increases has been carefully measured.

The programs of the Farm Home Administration are principally direct loans on farms and operating loans for equipment, fertilizer, and seed. Some of these, the Bureau believes, could be converted into insured or guaranteed loans. Recently, rural-water and waste-disposal grants were authorized, to supplement the larger programs of the Federal Water Pollution Control Administration of the Interior Department.

The Bureau is endeavoring to centralize control over the many cross-agency programs that have been started in recent years. Very similar programs have been initiated within and across agency lines for the purpose of meeting developing needs more rapidly than by attempting to enlarge previous programs. The staff of the Bureau is trying to appraise the relative value of similar plans and also to minimize the number of competing programs. The Department of Agriculture has many activities that are firmly established and have been investigated and approved by Bureau staff expert in the areas. County agents are one example; throughout the states they furnish useful advice to farmers. However, there is an urgent need for a thoroughgoing study of all Department of Agriculture programs with a view to consolidation and closer congressional appraisal of the variety and value of the widespread federal activities in view of changing national needs. So far, no one Presidential Administration has had the support necessary in Congress to overhaul the structure and reconsider all agricultural policy objectives.

Water Resources

The federal government had long been interested in the development of water resources for navigation, irrigation, flood control, power, and other uses when President Franklin D. Roosevelt issued Executive Order 9384 on October 4, 1943, to systematize plans and reports in this area. This basic document (included in Appendix C) superseded Executive Order 8455 of June 26, 1940.

At that time, the Bureau of the Budget, finding that there were serious inadequacies in federal policies and standards for natural resources, outlined the scope of a study.

However, not until after the establishment in 1950 of the Water Resources Policy Commission as an *ad hoc* group to develop natural resources policy was a detailed report submitted. The President referred the three-volume report to the Bureau of the Budget for study and an interagency Water Review Committee was then established under the chairmanship of Edward Ackerman of the Bureau. Deep-seated differences in agency viewpoints were found to exist, and agreement could not be reached on an Administration bill to carry out any recommended procedures.

On December 31, 1952, the Bureau of the Budget issued Budget Circular A-47, outlining certain guides and standards for federal projects "for the conservation, development, and use of water and related land resources," and, in 1954, the Presidential Advisory Committee on Water Resources Policy was set up.

More recently, on July 22, 1965, under the Water Resources Planning Act, the Water Resources Council was established. It is composed of representatives of the departments of the Interior, Agriculture, Army, and Health, Education, and Welfare, along with the chairman of the Federal Power Commission, and it is charged with conducting a continuing study and bi-annual assessment of the nation's water supplies and requirements.

The Director represents the Bureau of the Budget at meetings of the Water Resources Council, and Bureau personnel work closely with the Council staff and its several committees and task forces in the coordination and resolution of complex problems in water resources. The Council has responsibility for comprehensive river-basin planning, improvement of project formulation and evaluation, and assessment of the national water requirements and supply that might be made available. Examples of work initiated by the Bureau and being undertaken by the Council are cost-sharing on flood protection projects, the development of criteria to determine when flow augmentation for water quality is desirable, improvement in the method of estimating water-quality benefits, and cost-sharing for improved water quality.

Budget outlays (in millions of dollars) for water resources and related developments for the last three years by agencies are shown in Table 4. The Administration and Congress are committed to spending over $11 billion on these projects in future years after fiscal 1969. However, the 1969 budget documents state that provision is to be made for continuing construction of ongoing water-resource projects at minimum rates. While no ongoing projects will be stopped in 1968 or 1969, actions taken in the current fiscal year and the stringent budget recommendations for 1969 will, in many cases, delay completion schedules.

TABLE 4. WATER RESOURCES AND RELATED
DEVELOPMENTS EXPENDITURES

Type and Agency	1967 Actual	1968 Estimate	1969 Estimate
Flood control works			
Corps of Engineers, Civil	$ 332.2	$ 398.4	$ 332.5
Grants	12.1	25.7	69.1
Bureau of Reclamation	10.0	13.6	5.4
Soil Conservation Service (mostly grants)	66.8	70.1	60.6
International Boundary and Water Commission	1.3	1.9	2.8
Tennessee Valley Authority	4.8	10.7	11.7
Subtotal flood control works	$ 427.2	$ 520.4	$ 482.1
Beach erosion control, Corps of Engineers, Civil	1.3	3.2	1.1
Irrigation and water conservation works			
Bureau of Reclamation	$ 155.5	$ 118.6	$ 109.3
Loan and grant program	16.8	14.2	7.5
Soil Conservation Service (mostly grants)	14.7	12.0	9.8
Bureau of Indian Affairs	11.5	8.5	4.5
Subtotal irrigation works	$ 198.5	$ 153.3	$ 131.1

TABLE 4 *(cont.)*

Type and Agency	1967 Actual	1968 Estimate	1969 Estimate
Navigation facilities			
Corps of Engineers, Civil	$ 272.3	$ 261.2	$ 216.1
Saint Lawrence Seaway Development Corporation	a*	3.2	8.5
Tennessee Valley Authority	0.7	0.1	
Subtotal navigation facilities	$ 273.0	$ 264.5	$ 224.6
Multiple-purpose dams and reservoirs, hydroelectric			
Corps of Engineers, Civil	$ 338.3	$ 334.1	$ 320.6
Bureau of Reclamation	25.3	38.5	50.2
International Boundary and Water Commission	8.1	8.8	7.9
Tennessee Valley Authority	31.6	25.5	9.7
Subtotal multiple-purpose facilities	$ 403.3	$ 406.9	$ 388.4
Thermal-electric powerplants, Tennessee Valley Authority	$ 65.0	$ 126.4	$ 170.8
Power transmission facilities			
Tennessee Valley Authority	$ 63.0	$ 65.8	$ 60.9
Bureau of Reclamation	31.5	35.7	35.2
Bonneville Power Administration	105.8	114.6	116.2
Southwestern Power Administration	3.4	4.2	5.2
Subtotal power transmission facilities	$ 203.7	$ 220.3	$ 217.5
Water-supply and waste-disposal facilities			
International Boundary and Water Commission	$ 0.1	$ 0.1	$ 0.9
Federal Water Pollution Control Administration (grants)	84.7	111.8	154.2
Farmers Home Administration (grants)	11.1	27.0	33.8
Bureau of Reclamation	8.4	4.1	14.5
Department of Housing and Urban Development			
Grants	6.0	90.0	130.0
Net lending	24.0	16.0	19.0

TABLE 4 *(cont.)*

Type and Agency	1967 Actual	1968 Estimate	1969 Estimate
Subtotal water supply and waste disposal	$ 134.3	$ 249.0	$ 352.4
Total	$1,706.3	$1,944.0	$1,968.0

[a]Less than $50,000.
Source: The 1969 Budget Message.

The Corps of Engineers and the Bureau of Reclamation

The Corps of Engineers, which is part of the Department of the Army, is the largest water-resources agency, and five staff members are assigned by the Bureau to study Corps proposals and review their justifications. The Corps has very important responsibilities for civil works related to construction, development, and control of water resources. It also conducts studies of navigation, flood control, and beach erosion before any projects are undertaken. Currently, the Corps of Engineers is making surveys for 99 navigation, 160 flood-control, and 10 beach-erosion projects and planning to initiate 7 navigation, 25 flood-control, and 2 new beach-erosion surveys. Research studies are undertaken jointly with Atomic Energy Commission on the use of nuclear explosives in public-works projects. It is engaged in hundreds of reservoir, flood-control, and multiple-purpose projects, although none as big, singly, as those of the Bureau of Reclamation, the next largest water resources agency.

This Bureau, a part of the Department of the Interior, constructs and operates facilities to irrigate lands, furnish municipal and industrial water and power, and assist in flood control in the seventeen western states and Hawaii. Its planning and operations are quite similar to the Corps of Engineers, although in more restricted areas. Four BOB staff members are assigned to this work; they also cover the federal power administrations. The estimated total costs of the largest projects now under construction by the Bureau of Reclamation, which will take many years to complete, are:

Central Valley Project, California	$1,973.4 million
Columbia Basin, Washington	1,399.5 million
Missouri River Basin	1,298.9 million

Current expenditures on such long-range projects as these can be reduced by spreading out the workload, but it would be unwise to stop any desirable public-works project. The Bureau attempts instead to limit the new projects undertaken to those that can be completed within a reasonable period covered by the budget forecast. In times of budget deficits, new ones can be postponed—often with less detriment than the current ones can be reduced.

From a budget point of view, considerable information is available for decision-making on these programs. A ratio of anticipated benefits to estimated cost is established for executive review and submission to the Bureau of the Budget. Under Executive Order 9384, the Bureau reviews reports on projects proposed by the Corps of Engineers and the Bureau of Reclamation before they are transmitted to Congress. If Congress authorizes the project, the timing of the construction is determined partly by the urgency of the demand and partly by the over-all economic and fiscal position. However, political influence sometimes outweighs economic value in giving priority for these projects.

The Bureau's workload is affected not only by the number of project reports but also by the growing complexity of water projects serving many purposes, by the conflicting uses of water, and by the increasing public interest in scenic preservation as well as development. The time horizon of up to 100 years used in the planning of water projects, as well as the permanence of concrete structures, requires the weighing of all potential sources of water supply—a task made doubly difficult by the impossibility of accurately forecasting new opportunities that may be developed through research in such fields as desalting and weather modification.

A summary of BOB action on water-project reports during calendar year 1967 gives an idea of the amount of study required and of its unending nature:

Reports	Corps of Engineers	Bureau of Reclamation	Department of Agriculture (Watershed Reports)	Total
Received	60	3	53	116
Cleared	67	3	53	123

Congressmen are vitally interested in water-resources projects. Sometimes projects that have not been requested by the President or recommended by the Secretary of the Army (Corps of Engineers) have been added to the public-works appropriation bill in the closing hours or minutes of a congressional session. Politically, it has not been wise to refuse to proceed with some projects once the funds were appropriated. Today, the pressure upon the President to reduce expenditures, together with the congressional limitations on the total amount of spending, gives the President a much wider latitude in refusing to proceed with projects he considers unnecessary or of low-priority.

Prior to World War II, the costs estimates submitted were inaccurate and the costs-benefit ratios were not scientific. A 1951 study by the Corps of Engineers at the request of the House Appropriations Committee indicated an over-run exceeding 100 per cent of the original estimates on 182 current projects. The Corps explained these over-runs as being 57.7 per cent due to construction price increases, 24.7 per cent to changes in project design, 17.6 per cent to extensions in project scope, 11.6 per cent to changes in local needs and unforeseen conditions, and 5.8 per cent to inadequacies in plans and estimates. As a result of the criticism of the House Committee and the recommendations of the second Hoover Commission task force report on water resources and power, the procedures were improved. Recent analysis has indicated that current estimated costs are much more accurate and sometimes have run below the original estimated cost. The discount rate used to arrive at the cost-benefit ratio, however, is less than the present Treasury rate, which should be used for current estimates.

In appraising the anticipated benefits of a project like a dam, in connection with its authorization, BOB consideration is given to (1) the primary purpose, which might be flood control (how many lives have been lost? what have been the property damage and crop and livestock losses?); (2) the positive benefits that will ensue from power supplied, irrigation, navigation if locks are rebuilt, improved recreational facilities (boating, fishing, swimming, camping); (3) such detriments as the value of homes, factories, forests, and crop lands that will be flooded after the dam is constructed; and (4) other factors such as power needs of the area, both present and prospective, cost-sharing that might be arranged with local interests, and geographic location, especially in view of prospective urban extensions that would make later development impossible.

If the benefits to the community exceed the cost and adverse factors over the estimated life of the development (discounted at the rate of 3¼ per cent to arrive at present value) by a ratio of two to one, the presumption is in favor of scheduling the project as soon as funds can be made available, taking into consideration, of course, the competing projects. If the ratio is one to one or less, the presumption is against approval. In between these two ratios, other factors enter in, such as the length of time required to gain the benefit, the magnitude of the project (most of the desirable large rivershed projects have already been constructed), the importance of the sponsors, and other political aspects. These factors are decided by the President after the Corps of Engineers has completed its survey report and the Bureau of the Budget has submitted its comments. As noted earlier, Congress is very favorably inclined toward these programs, while the Bureau is more selective.

Water-Pollution Control

The federal interest in encouraging and helping the states and municipalities to install adequate waste-treatment facilities and preserve the purity of national water supplies dates from the administrations of Presidents Truman and Eisenhower. Desalting sea water was also started at that time on an experimental basis. Recently, the programs have been accelerated as indicated below:

	1967 Actual	1968 Estimate	1969 Estimate
Program costs funded, saline water conversion	18.5	28.3	32.8
Water-supply and water-pollution control	67.5	106.9	100.4
Total costs funded, construction grants for waste-treatment work	133.9	174.4	242.0

These programs have always been supported by the Bureau, which has tried to encourage local and private interests in progressive approaches to water problems.

Current programs are heavily based on two pieces of legislation passed in the mid-1960's. The Water Quality Act of 1965 required all states to develop water-quality standards and implementation plans for all their interstate and coastal waters. Once these have been approved by the Secretary of the Interior, they will represent a blueprint for future abatement actions. The Clean Water Restoration Act of 1966 authorized $3.4 billion for construction grants for waste treatment facilities and greatly expanded research and development authorizations. The 1969 budget recommended an appropriation of only $225 million as compared with an authorized level of $700 million; however, in 1968 the President also proposed a new long-term debt-financing bill, allowing for a threefold increase in federal support in 1969 alone. This bill has been shelved, but the House of Representatives may increase the appropriation.

The Bureau works with the Department of the Interior to implement the major water pollution control legislation enacted in 1965 and 1966 through review of a large number of special studies made for Congress, such as the economic impact of pollution-control expenditures, manpower needs, and industrial incentives and proposed legislation on such problems as oil spills, acid mine drainage, and vessel pollution. The Bureau also has primary responsibility under Executive Order 11288, issued by President Johnson on July 2, 1966, to review progress of water-pollution abatement at federal facilities.

Tennessee Valley Authority

The Tennessee Valley Authority (TVA) was formed during the Depression under the Tennessee Valley Authority Act of 1933 to undertake unified river-basin development in seven states for navigation, flood control, power production and distribution, fertilizer production, and recreation. It is a corporation wholly owned by the federal government and operated by directors appointed by the President of the United States. Its programs are reviewed by Bureau staff. TVA was a very remarkable undertaking and is the great pride of the states served.

Current appropriations of public funds for TVA supplement proceeds from power operations and borrowings through issuance of revenue bonds against future power revenues, and miscellaneous receipts from fertilizer sales and other nonpower activities. The total fixed assets of TVA as of June 30, 1967, consisted of approximately $2,504 million for the power program and $603 million for nonpower. Of the funds provided, $2,113 million represented non-interest-bearing capital and $100 million interest-bearing capital, both supplied by the federal government, $715 million borrowings from the public, and $179 million accumulated net earnings.

Shortly after General Eisenhower became President, the Budget Bureau was asked to make a study of the operations of the Tennessee Valley Authority. The Bureau was also asked to consider the request of TVA to extend its operations beyond the confines of the Tennessee Valley area—its authorized territory—and a report was submitted by an expert utility engineer. Advocates of more public-power enterprises, both within Congress and outside, received the impression that the Eisenhower Administration was going to limit any further expansion to the area then being served by TVA and might even contemplate a reduction.

A bitter controversy arose. The city of Memphis, Tennessee, which is outside the TVA area, wished to construct a new power plant. Public-power advocates wished to have that work done by TVA. Private companies operating nearby, outside the Tennessee Valley, were anxious to be considered also. Two of the private utility groups, which became known under the names of their heads, Dixon and Yates, submitted a combined bid that to the engineer engaged by the Budget Bureau seemed reasonable. The Memphis authorities, however, decided to go ahead with their own construction, which was done (at a net cost that turned out afterward to be several million dollars greater than the bid by the private group). The Budget Bureau was criticized because Director Roland Hughes favored the outside bid, which he felt was a better one. He also considered that sufficient funds had been advanced already by the federal government either at no interest or at lower rates of interest than had been paid by the Treasury to borrow the funds needed. An arrangement was finally reached whereby the interest rates were increased and TVA was operated efficiently and effectively within the area for which it was organized, enabling it to repay part of the initial loans.

Lands, Wildlife, and Recreational Resources

The management of federal lands raises special budget problems, which are often complicated and require substantial work not directly related to budget outlays on those lands. The Interior Department and the Forest Service of the Department of Agriculture administer the "public domain lands," the national forests, and the outer continental shelf, which contain sizable mineral deposits and timber resources. The Bureau puts substantial staff time into various studies on proposed sales of timber, oil and gas leasing on the outer continental shelf, oil-shale leasing and development, and legislative proposals with respect to public lands and their known or potential mineral values.

The Interior Department's Bureau of Land Management is responsible for the conservation, management, and development of 450 million acres of public lands, over half of which are in Alaska. It also handles leases of grazing lands and mines and minerals belonging to the public on land and under water, including the outer continental shelf. Receipts from leases and timber sales are partly distributed to the states and partly deducted from expenses of operation, including firefighting and construction.

The expenditures cover forestry, range management, fire protection, soil and watershed conservation, and general administration. Most of the receipts for leases are paid over to the states. The obligational authority requested and expenditures have been averaging $50 million a year, divided among forest resources, soil conservation, and recreation.

The Bureau staff has not only reviewed the agency requests for all these programs but has inspected the more important projects and, where applicable, compared the cost with private enterprise operations of a similar character. The main budget problems in this area are the extent of the programs and their timing.

The Bureau of Outdoor Recreation, also under the Department of the Interior, is the center for many activities, including the administration of the Land and Water Conservation Fund from which 50 per cent matching grants can be made to the states for acquiring land and water areas and developing them for recreation purposes. These are reviewed by the Bureau and have contributed to the nation's conservation program.

The National Park Service, one of the best-known and most widely appreciated activities of the federal government, is responsible for the management and protection of 259 park areas comprising 27 million acres. The cost of these activities was about $35 million in 1967 and has increased $5 million a year since; maintenance and rehabilitation of roads, trails, and buildings have averaged about $30 million, construction about $50 million. Most of the Bureau staff assigned to the Park Service budget is acquainted first-hand with its projects.

The Natural Resources Programs Division represents the Bureau in the staff meetings of the Council on Recreation and Natural Beauty (formerly the Recreation Advisory Council) and also handles Bureau liaison with the Citizens' Advisory Committee, both of which were established under their present titles by Executive Order 11278 in May, 1966. The potentials for use of surplus federal lands for recreation are being studied and a proposed program for scenic roads and parkways is being analyzed.

The Commissioner of Fish and Wildlife administers the Bureau of Commercial Fisheries, with expenditures of $22 million to $26 million a year for operations, research, and investigations; subsidy payments to U.S. shipyards for 50 per cent of the cost of constructing fishing vessels; and loans to segments of the fishing industry. He also administers a number of regular programs for wildlife refuges, fish hatcheries, and research with expenditures, in millions, for the past three years budgeted at:

	Operations	Construction
1967	$38	$8
1968	45	9
1969	46	5

Expenditures planned for special programs for migratory birds and federal aid in fish and wildlife restoration were $43 million in 1967, $40 million in 1968, and $48 million in 1969. This includes grants to the states of up to 75 per cent of approved projects.

It is difficult for the Bureau to prevent these and other multiple programs in the natural resources area from growing annually. The Council of Economic Advisers has tacitly accepted gradual inflation in conservation and development funds so long as it does not exceed some guidelines that have been established (but seem to be flexible). The population of the United States is, of course, growing rapidly, as are its demands on land and water supplies.

The numbers of wildlife and fish in American forests, lakes, rivers, and streams are diminishing with the extension of cities and suburbs. The need for conservation has become more important. But Americans have been fortunate in having been able to subsist for so many years on seemingly inexhaustible natural resources; only recently has the serious need for nationwide conservation and resource development policy begun to be fully appreciated. Meanwhile, Congress has demanded cuts in over-all spending to reduce the budget deficit and urged the President to take necessary action, but has nonetheless insisted on raising amounts spent on local natural resources programs of concern to various members' constituents. The President and the Bureau are helpless to do much beyond pointing out the problem of the many competing demands upon the tax dollar and recommending reasonably balanced programs considered to be within the nation's means.

X

Social, Economic,
and Other
Civilian Agency Programs

The program review and related work with the executive agencies whose responsibilities lie outside the areas of national defense and natural resources are handled by the Budget Bureau's Human Resources, Economics, Science and Technology, International, and General Government Management divisions. The Bureau has specialists individually competent in even the most technical aspects of these broad fields.

Health, Labor, and Welfare Agencies

The most important civilian agency in the U.S. Government is undoubtedly the Department of Health, Education, and Welfare, which deals with human resources and how to strengthen them. Its expenditures today are roughly equal to those of the Defense Department, if one excludes the $25-billion military expenditures classified in the 1969 budget as Special Vietnam.

In the Budget Messages of the last three years, funds for labor are combined with health and welfare and education is shown separately, as set forth in Tables 5 and 6. Federal expenditures during the last four years in health, labor, and welfare have increased by $26 billion and are approximately double what they were in fiscal 1965. The greatest part of this increase is in the trust funds, Old Age and Survivors Insurance and Disability (OASI), and so on, but there have also been dozens of new federal programs started during this period.

The Bureau has very little, if any, control over new programs. The work done by the division staffs in this whole area depends on the way the appropriation is to be spent—that is, by established agencies, by new agencies, in grants to states, or for thousands of individual grants like those of the National Institutes of Health (NIH). For new programs, including all of those of the Office of Economic Opportunity (OEO), the only contribution the Bureau staff can make is to review the proposed plans to see how carefully they have been prepared, interview the personnel responsible for preparing and carrying them out, and discuss alternative approaches that should be considered. Only after a program has been operated for several years is any intelligent appraisal of its effectiveness by the Bureau staff practical. Reports of progress made may read well but be without solid support.

In the initial period of formulation of an idea for federal entrance into a new area, the Administration has to decide whether to try to impose a new program on the staff of an existing agency or to form a new agency. A current example is the economic opportunity programs, which were authorized by the Economic Opportunity Act of 1964 (P.L. 88-452, approved August 20, 1964). It was decided to appropriate the funds to the President and to set up the new Office of Economic Opportunity, with $211 million appropriated for the remaining part of fiscal 1965, $1.2 billion in 1966, $1.6 billion in 1967, $1.7 billion in 1968, and $2.1 billion requested for fiscal 1969. With the entirely new programs en-

TABLE 5. HEALTH, LABOR, AND WELFARE EXPENDITURES
AND NET LENDING[a]

Program or Agency	Expenditures and Net Lending			Recommended NOA and LA for 1969[b]
	1967 Actual	1968 Estimate	1969 Estimate	
Expenditures				
Health services and research				
Medical research	$ 1,014	$ 1,065	$ 1,079	$ 1,235
Facilities and medical manpower	445	554	577	694
Organization and delivery of health services	43	111	126	164
Medicare (trust funds)[c]	3,396	5,064	5,785	6,842
Medicaid and other financing	1,366	1,997	2,398	2,425
Direct health care	158	177	194	196
Prevention and control of health problems and other	351	486	521	695
Labor and manpower				
Manpower programs[d]	589	802	926	922
Other[d]	480	524	558	614
Proposed trade adjustment legislation			8	10
Economic opportunity programs				
Work and training programs	737	927	1,003	1,075
Community action programs and other[d]	747	926	994	1,101
Retirement and social insurance (trust funds)				
Old-age, survivors, and disability insurance[c]	21,725	23,918	27,372	31,031
Unemployment insurance	2,189	2,564	2,558	3,557
Civil service retirement and disability	1,965	2,121	2,364	3,740
Railroad retirement[c]	1,315	1,415	1,490	1,905

TABLE 5 *(cont.)*

Program or Agency	Expenditures and Net Lending			Recommended NOA and LA for 1969b
	1967 Actual	1968 Estimate	1969 Estimate	
Other	−77	−72	−78	13
Public assistance and other welfare				
Public assistance (excluding medical assistance)	3,041	3,484	3,605	3,703
Vocational rehabilitation	261	363	434	443
School lunch, special milk, food stamp, and other	522	616	710	719
Proposed food stamp legislation			15	20
Proposed juvenile-delinquency legislation			20	25
Interfund and intragovernmental transactionsc	−694	−641	−711	−711
Applicable receipts from the public	−61	−5	−3	−3
Subtotal expenditures	$39,512	$46,396	$51,945	$60,413
Net lending	$ 572	$ 21	$ −538	$ −538
Total	$40,084	$46,417	$51,407	$59,875

a All figures in millions of dollars.

b Compares with new obligational authority (NOA) and lending authority (LA) for 1967 and 1968, as follows: NOA: 1967, $47,841 million; 1968, $53,131 million. LA: 1967, $570 million; 1968, $18 million.

c Because of their magnitude, interfund and intragovernmental transactions have been deducted from the appropriate figures, as follows (in millions of dollars):

Federal fund contributions to trust funds	*1967*	*1968*	*1969*
Medicare	950	1,280	1,360
OASI			226
Military service credits	122	123	123

d Includes both federal funds and trust funds.

Source: 1969 Budget Message

TABLE 6. EDUCATION EXPENDITURES AND NET LENDING[a]

Program or Agency	Expenditures and Net Lending			Recommended NOA and LA for 1969[b]
	1967 Actual	1968 Estimate	1969 Estimate	
Expenditures				
Elementary and secondary education				
Children from low income families	$1,057	$1,070	$1,073	$1,200
Other education of the disadvantaged	67	70	109	154
Special school projects	75	155	169	219
School books, equipment, counseling, and strengthening state education agencies	213	237	155	121
Assistance to schools in federally impacted areas	447	372	416	410
Other (teacher training)		26	9	
Higher education				
Aid for undergraduate and graduate students	421	597	673	558
Academic facility grants	198	308	213	86
Other aids to higher education	92	153	179	182
Proposed legislation				23
Science education and basic research, National Science Foundation				
Basic research and specialized research facilities	209	226	230	244
Grants for institutional science programs	49	72	78	66
Science education	118	115	120	131
Other science activities	39	43	52	59
Other aids to education				
Training of education manpower	41	13	57	216
Vocational education				
Present program	250	271	247	257
Proposed legislation			7	15
Educational research and development	57	76	99	146

TABLE 6 *(cont.)*

Program or Agency	Expenditures and Net Lending			Recommended NOA and LA for 1969[b]
	1967 Actual	1968 Estimate	1969 Estimate	
Grants for libraries and community services	57	100	141	149
Indian education services	112	116	153	155
Library of Congress and Smithsonian Institution[c]	62	83	98	100
National Foundation on the Arts and Humanities[c]	10	15	23	24
Other present programs	37	55	61	66
Other proposed legislation for public broadcasting			20	20
Applicable receipts from the public	−11	−15	−16	−16
Subtotal expenditures	$3,602	$4,157	$4,364	$4,585
Net lending				
Elementary and secondary education	−2	[d]	1	1
Higher education	447	383	334	686
Subtotal net lending	$ 445	$ 384	$ 335	$ 687
Total	$4,047	$4,541	$4,699	$5,272

[a] All figures in millions of dollars.

[b] Compares with new obligational authority (NOA) and lending authority (LA) for 1967 and 1968, as follows—NOA: 1967, $4,430 million; 1968, $4,673 million. LA: 1967, −$901 million; 1968, −$2,002 million.

[c] Includes both federal funds and trust funds.

[d] Less than $500,000.

Source: 1969 Budget Message.

visaged by this Act, the Bureau accepted the necessity for their direction by the staff of a new agency at the outset at least. As the programs developed, the Bureau recommended that parts be assigned to existing agencies. Grants to carry out the desired work were also made to various public and private organizations, first in the congested urban areas and then throughout the country.

One of the important programs is the development of comprehensive health centers. This was a new idea developed by the Office of Economic Opportunity to include all kinds of counseling, psychiatric and pediatric care, and practically everything furnished by the outpatient ward of a city hospital. Forty-eight of these new centers were started by the OEO in various metropolitan areas around the country. The program is now being expanded and, on the Bureau's recommendation, part of the funds for new centers have been assigned to HEW, which will use OEO models as a prototype. In time, the whole program is to be incorporated into the more permanent organization of the older agency. Although a multiplicity of programs across agency lines is not desirable, any new addition to the load of an established bureaucracy is apt to result in disruption and delay. The Bureau prefers to make haste slowly, to minimize the inevitable initial waste.

Health Programs

The manifold federal activities in health come under the general supervision of an assistant secretary for Health, and most of them are discharged by the Public Health Service headed by the Surgeon General. The Public Health Service has a fine staff with a long record of important and successful programs. For these, the decision of the Bureau staff is generally not whether but how much money can be allocated effectively. The Department's broad health mission is described in the recently enacted Partnership for Health Act as follows:

1. To promote and assure the highest level of health attainable for every person, in an evironment that contributes positively to healthful individual and family living.
2. To develop an effective partnership involving close intergovernmental collaboration, official and voluntary efforts, and participation of individuals and organizations.
3. To assure that federal financial assistance is directed to sup-

porting the marshalling of all national, state, and local health resources.

4. To assure comprehensive health services of high quality for every person, without interference with existing patterns of private professional practice of medicine, dentistry, and related healing arts.

This is developed in a number of ways, such as by grants to states for comprehensive state health planning, project grants for area-wide health planning, project grants for training, studies, and demonstration for comprehensive health planning, formula grants to states for comprehensive public health services, and project grants for health services development.

In the area of health grants for research, scholarships, and other subsidies, the Bureau carefully watches the language of the authorizing legislation as well as the amount of the appropriations. In many cases, the authorized amount is a limit rather than an expected expenditure for that particular program, if sufficient qualified technicians are not available. The staff of the Bureau of the Budget reviews and becomes thoroughly familiar with the purpose of each of these grant programs. It is often impracticable to spend efficiently the increases granted by Congress, particularly since thousands of individual research grants are being made to individual applicants. The work of the Bureau staff is not focused on the individual research grant but rather on the general level of research, on the fields of research to be stressed, and on the opportunities for application of research findings to medical care practices. Grants are also made to schools to support and enlarge faculty, to buy books and develop new curriculums, to modernize laboratories, and to purchase educational aids and equipment. No encouragement has been necessary for the agency staff to embark on new ventures and projects. The main objective of the Bureau has been to control and moderate the increases to obtain an orderly, progressive, and efficient operation.

The socio-economics of health care has been receiving a great deal of attention recently. Expenditures for medical care, including physicians' services, hospitals, and drugs, have been growing at an average rate of about 8 per cent per annum over the last twenty years—more than twice the increase in the cost-of-living index. The Bureau staff has investigated the reason for this rapid growth, which has made the actual cost of the Medicare and Medicaid programs greatly exceed budget estimates and has found that the answer seems to be that a lot of people are seeing doctors and dentists who had never done so before. The nation's medical and dental schools are turning out approximately the same number of graduates. With the demand growing faster than the supply, according to the old economic principle of supply and demand, increases in prices are inevitable. Unfortunately, the "new economics" has found no solution to this one. The Bureau also can and does question the need for government grants that might take the place of personal health expenditures by people able and willing to pay for them. Part of the demand for medical care is determined by the patient, part by the physician, who may suggest hospitalization or require office treatment rather than home care. Also, specialization has added to the problems of the consumer.

The operations of the government and its research grants in biomedicine have made possible the pre-eminent position of the United States in this area. The problem today is not only to cope with the vast new opportunities opening up after each new discovery but to cut back the programs that are no longer essential or even sufficiently important in relation to other opportunities for advancement. It is estimated that the federal government will finance about 65 per cent of the combined business and private investment in all biomedical research, which seems temporarily out of proportion to a proper balance in a free enterprise economy. In a period of budget stringency, it may be necessary to reduce or postpone some of these desirable programs.

Dr. Victor R. Fuchs, assistant director of Research, National Bureau of Economic Research, recently made several constructive suggestions toward better medical care at less cost that appealed to the Budget Bureau. He believes that significant changes will not occur in medical care without changes in the direction of medical education, and that instead of medical schools "we should have schools of health." His objective would be to train personnel and increase knowledge to meet the future health needs of the community at various levels. He also suggests that target rates could be established for each hospital or group of hospitals providing comparable service. Inefficient hospitals would be under strong pressure to bring their costs down while efficient hospitals would be provided educational funds for further improving the range and quality of services offered.

Job Training and Employment

Job training is receiving special attention today and is supported by the Bureau as being more effective than direct aid. Agencies participating in programs directed toward the underprivileged, inadequately trained, or unemployed are numerous, however, and here again the Bureau staff has no control over new manpower programs except as to where the funds are administered. Shall they be appropriated to the OEO or to the Department of Labor? The OEO has certain advantages. It is new and fresh in the field and without preconceived ideas. It is also more flexible. This problem was considered by an interagency group composed of representatives from the Department of Labor, the OEO, and the Budget Bureau, and it was decided to appropriate the funds to the OEO but to delegate part of the operations to Labor as an extension of its previous experience under the Manpower Development and Training Act of 1962. On-the-job training is administered by the Labor Department in cooperation with employers, associations, community and civic groups, and the unions. Job Corps programs are administered by the OEO. The new Concentrated Employment Program in urban areas is administered in part by the OEO in connection with its health and child-care programs and in part by Labor through grants to Community Action programs. Some of these have been very successful and others have flopped. The Bureau does not have any staff in the field to investigate such situations, but there is usually much criticism in the press, and the OEO has both an audit staff and an Office of Research and Evaluation. The Bureau requires a detailed report on each program, which is studied and compared with evaluations by different private groups and foundations working in this field.

The Job Corps reports received by the Bureau show profiles of a variety of young men when they first go in and when they come out with a job or become a public charge. The early reports of the OEO were generally unsatisfactory, but more recently the Bureau is satisfied with the success of the Job Corps graduates over twenty years of age. Many are being accepted, however, at too early an age, and at sixteen or seventeen they are frequently unable to hold a job.

The federal-state employment service system, which includes the U.S. Employment Service of the Department of Labor, is a supplier of basic manpower services with special emphasis on disadvantaged persons, providing them with counseling and special placement efforts. These programs have been productive, and the Bureau has supported efforts in this area as more constructive than welfare payments. Other programs are devoted to youth, schools, and summer work. The estimated numbers of individuals participating in these programs in the past three years are

	1967	1968	1969
Structural training	383,000	492,000	638,000
Youth, school, and			
work experience	670,000	435,000	590,000
Other	9,000	44,000	64,000
Total	1,062,000	971,000	1,292,000

In spite of the various programs already mentioned, pub-lic-assistance grants to the states are still running at a very high figure. This is a real concern to the Bureau. In 1969, financial assistance and social services will be provided to a monthly average of 8.8 million so-called indigent individuals, or more than 4 per cent of the total population, which is greater than the number reported as unemployed and is in addition to 22 million receiving Social Security benefits. The 1969 Budget Annex states that Congress approved an appro-priation for 1968 of $4.1 billion for "grants to states for old age assistance, medical assistance, aid to families with depen-dent children, aid to the blind, aid to the permanently and totally disabled" and that recent program trends indicate that the appropriations for 1968 will be inadequate to meet the federal share of the states' expenditures by an estimated $1.1 billion. This should be studied by a commission of experts. In my opinion, there must be leakage somewhere. In many areas of the country, even the so-called distressed areas, there are often more opportunities for employment than qualified workers available or willing to work, particularly in domestic service and outdoor work. Since the system of taxation known as "transfer payments" represents sums withdrawn from the income of workers and added to the income of others without requiring any constructive effort on the part of the recipients, the job-training programs, scholarships, internships, and other programs requiring self-help as well are preferred by the Bureau as better answers to unemployment problems.

The Presidential Commission on Income Maintenance Programs was appointed in 1968 to review all aspects of existing welfare and related programs, and a bill entitled the Human Investment Act was introduced in the Eighty-ninth and again in the Ninetieth Congress to encourage the private sector of the economy to take a larger share in job training of the underprivileged. This proposed legislation is patterned after the Investment Credit Act, which allows a 7 per cent credit against corporate income taxes for investments in new machinery and would allow a 10 per cent credit for various specified training expenses, such as salaries of participants of on-the-job training programs under the Manpower Development and Training Act or under cooperative educational programs. From a Budget Bureau point of view, such legislation might help to relieve unemployment at less cost than training programs conducted by the federal government.

Since taking office, President Nixon has delivered a number of messages concerning welfare proposals, manpower training, revenue-sharing, and family planning. In cooperation with other agencies, the Budget Bureau has devoted a large amount of time to developing the specific proposals and the clearance of bills already introduced or in preparation. It is hoped that at least some of the recommendations may be enacted next year. From a budgetary point of view, substantial changes and improvements are needed, particularly in population and family planning. The Presidential approach aims at a complete replacement of the present welfare system, a comprehensive new job training and placement program, a revamping of the Office of Economic Opportunity, and a start on the sharing of federal tax revenues with the states.

Social Security and Welfare Activities

The contributions to the trust funds and the benefits from them are all specified in the Old Age and Survivors Insurance and Disability (OASI) legislation. They are handled through the federal OASI trust funds. The Social Security Act provides for payment of monthly benefits financed under contributions made equally by the workers and employers. The taxes on earnings have been increased periodically to cover current payments. Surpluses that accumulated primarily in the early years of the program were invested in government securities and provided a reserve of $26.2 billion by the end of fiscal year 1968. There is no control by the Bureau over these activities, and the only question that has been raised is whether the government's liability should be funded. The Bureau's answer is that substantial reserves are desirable but funding the actuarial liability is impossible. If funded, it would have to be invested in government bonds, which would be extremely deflationary, since the actuarial liability would be approximately equal to, if not greater than, the total national debt. In spite of the framework of the trust funds, it is clear that workers in future years are going to have to pay for the upbringing and education of the younger generation as well as support the older generation substantially out of current earnings (as has always been the case).

Trust funds have also been established for unemployment insurance, civil-service retirement and disability, and railroad retirement. The Budget Bureau's efforts in this respect are to study the legislation and see that the operations are periodically reviewed and checked as to planning and substance. Postauditing is done by the General Accounting Office.

Education

Table 6, referred to earlier, sets forth the expenditures for three years and new obligation authority recommended for 1969 on various educational programs. In the last five years, these expenditures have more than doubled as special attention has been given to improving the quality of education for the disadvantaged, expanding the supply of qualified teachers, and educating the handicapped. An appropriation of $1.2 billion was recommended for fiscal 1969 as was another $1.2 billion for fiscal 1970, to meet "the special educational needs of educationally deprived children." The fiscal year 1970 funds were requested in the 1969 budget in order that the elementary and secondary schools receiving the grants could be notified in advance of the beginning of the academic year as to the amounts they might expect to receive. Most of these grants are absolute, but some are matching. They cover a wide variety of programs with support for remedial teachers, health services, science and language-teaching centers, mobile laboratories, guidance, counseling and testing programs, and textbooks and other instruction materials.

These education programs are especially difficult for the Bureau to evaluate or to control. The staff is alert to what is being said in educational journals and the press generally. There are many seminars on education being held in many parts of the country to which members of the staff are invited. They talk to educators in special areas, with welfare workers, with institutions like the Ford Foundation and the Brookings Institution and others, to check on what the agencies themselves report. There is undoubtedly a wide difference in success between programs, and it takes experience with the results for a period of time to make an adequate evaluation.

For a number of years, special grants have been made to communities that have substantial federal establishments, such as military posts, which are not on the tax rolls. These have been tested and for the most part approved by the Bureau. They are treated in the education budget as special school assistance in lieu of taxation.

Higher-education funds are allotted to colleges and universities for scholarships to needy undergraduate students, work-study grants for students who work part time, and various loan funds. Vocational education programs to train students as semi-skilled or skilled workers are covered by matching grants to the states and aid more than 7 million students. Student-assistance programs are available for higher education in the form of loans and scholarships, which are distributed by the colleges and universities. The individual amounts average $850 per student and it is estimated that 750,000 new loans will be made in 1969. Many of these are repaid and, in budgetary terms, seem to be justified.

Since 1950, very substantial grants and loans have been made to colleges for construction of buildings and other facilities. These are currently being reduced in amount because of budget stringency and emphasis on other educational programs. The Bureau's efforts are primarily directed to seeing that the programs are carried out substantially as authorized and that Congress is made aware of the results so far as it is possible to identify them. Substantial projects for research and training under several different acts are joint efforts of different agencies including the National Science Foundation, the Department of Labor, the OEO, NIH, and others to cover laboratories, research and development centers, improvement in school curricula, and greater attention to "evaluation of the educational process."

Housing and Community Development

Immediately after World War II, the tremendous shortage in private homes and in adequate hospital facilities made it imperative to use all practicable incentives to encourage and supplement private initiative in these areas. Public-housing programs received a great deal of attention for several years and then tapered off as more emphasis was placed on individual units, but attention has been redirected toward these programs as the result of greater recognition of urban needs.

The Federal Housing Administration (FHA) was originally

created by the National Housing Act in 1934 and was brought under the Government Corporation Control Act in 1948. Until the end of 1967, $115.3 billion of insurance had been written, with $55 billion still outstanding. This was encouraged by the Bureau and has been very successful, with income exceeding expenses and losses to date.

The Federal National Mortgage Association (FNMA) buys, sells, and otherwise deals in mortgages insured by the Federal Housing Administration or guaranteed by the Veterans Administration and certain loans insured by the Farmers Home Administration. The corporation also makes short-term loans on the security of such loans and mortgages and sells securities based on its own mortgages set aside for that purpose. Before September 1, 1968, the FNMA's operations had been consolidated in the budget figures because the Secretary of the Treasury held outstanding preferred stock; however, the sales to the public of participation certificates, with mortgages deposited as collateral, were not included with other transactions affecting the national debt. The President's Commission on Budget Concepts recommended that these transactions also be consolidated. Because the sale of participation certificates had substantially increased during fiscal 1968, and was expected to increase in fiscal 1969, it was decided to require the banking institutions dealing with the FNMA through the secondary mortgage market to purchase sufficient stock to make possible the retirement of the preferred stock owned by the Treasury. On September 30, 1968, the $163.8 million of outstanding preferred stock held by the Secretary of the Treasury were retired, and $54 million of retained earnings deemed to have been earned on the government's investment in the secondary market operations were paid over to the Treasury. As a privately owned corporation, the FNMA was deconsolidated as of that date. The result was to exclude its operations from the consolidated budget figures and to exclude the obligations of the FNMA from the national debt figures after the end of the first quarter of fiscal 1969.

Therefore, there has been a large reduction in the direct public debt ($10.9 billion) and an increase in the contingent liability of the federal government as guarantor, resulting from the conversion to complete private ownership of the secondary market operations of the FNMA and also the federal intermediate credit banks and the banks for cooperatives. The estimated new loans net of these institutions, if they were still partly owned and consolidated, would have increased the expenditures under net lending by $1.852 million in fiscal 1969 and $2.230 million in fiscal 1970.

Table 7 covers the budgetary impact of housing and community development. The effects of net lending programs are now shown below the ordinary expenditures without reductions resulting from the sale of participating certificates. The President's Commission on Budget Concepts recommended that provision be made for showing subsidies on loans to the extent that interest rates on Treasury borrowing (or participation certificates) exceed those of the underlying loans. This has not as yet been done. The Independent Offices Appropriation Act of 1967 established a permanent indefinite appropriation to cover such insufficiency. The 1968 Act established an annual definite appropriation that is a much more satisfactory way of budgeting. Unfortunately, the 1969 Budget Message proposed a return to the "permanent indefinite appropriation."

Veterans Administration

Benefits and services to veterans are mounting as a result of the Vietnam war. These services are fixed by law and are handled by the Veterans Administration. In addition to service-connected compensation and non-service-connected pen-

TABLE 7. HOUSING AND COMMUNITY DEVELOPMENT
EXPENDITURES AND NET LENDING[a]

Program or Agency	Expenditures and Net Lending			Recom- mended NOA and LA for 1969[b]
	1967 Actual	1968 Estimate	1969 Estimate	
Expenditures				
Public-housing programs	$ 251	$ 297	$ 350	$ 380
Aids to private housing				
Department of Housing and Urban Development				
Supplements to the private market				
Rent supplement program	1	4	16	17
Other	-17	-21	16	6
Support of the private market: Federal Housing Administration and other[c]	-7	-138	-110	
Federal Savings and Loan Insurance Corporation	-201	-384	-378	
Urban renewal and community facilities				
Model Cities Program	1	25	250	1,000
Aids to improved land use				
Urban renewal	370	499	699	750
Open-space land grants	19	60	60	
Urban planning assistance and other	22	31	46	55
Proposed metropolitan development legislation			3	10
Assistance for public facilities				
Urban mass transportation	42	100	150	190
Basic water and sewer facility grants	6	90	130	150

TABLE 7 *(cont.)*

Program or Agency	Expenditures and Net Lending			Recommended NOA and LA for 1969[b]
	1967 Actual	1968 Estimate	1969 Estimate	
Neighborhood facility grants and other	12	22	39	44
Research and other	32	39	55	75
Proposed legislation			14	30
National Capital region[c]	66	90	104	140
Interfund and intragovernmental transactions	−19	−15	−14	−14
Applicable receipts from the public	d	d	d	
Subtotal expenditures	$ 577	$ 697	$1,429	$2,833
Net lending				
Public-housing programs	14	22	−16	
Aids to private housing Department of Housing and Urban Development				
Supplements to the private market	248	744	456	1,205
Support of the private market[c]	1,269	2,440	809	709
Federal Savings and Loan Insurance Corporation	44	−8	−20	
Urban renewal and community facilities	114	42	61	80
National Capital region	19	16	65	141
Subtotal net lending	$1,708	$3,257	$1,355	$2,135
Total	$2,285	$3,954	$2,784	$4,968

[a] All figures in millions of dollars.

[b] Compares with new obligational authority (NOA) and lending authority (LA) for 1967 and 1968, as follows—NOA: 1967, $1,503 million; 1968, $1,869 million. LA: 1967, $5,421 million; 1968, $2,095 million.

[c] Includes both federal funds and trust funds.

[d] Less than $500,000.

Source: The 1969 Budget Message.

sions, medical care and hospital services are furnished in over 200 Veterans Administration hospitals and clinics across the country.

One of the problems with which the Budget Bureau is concerned has been to see that quality hospital services are available to meet the needs of the veterans on the most efficient basis. Otherwise, the programs are beyond the control of the Bureau. In addition, it has been difficult to effect closure of hospitals no longer needed, because of political pressure brought to bear in spite of budget and agency approval.

Commerce and Transportation

A number of important agencies deal in one way or another with commerce and transportation, two of them being, of course, the departments of Commerce and Transportation. Table 8 shows their principal categories of expenditures and lending. Like the Department of the Treasury, the Department of Commerce, originally established by Congress early in the century to develop foreign and domestic commerce, today directs a great deal of attention to one of the Budget Bureau's primary concerns: our balance-of-payments deficits. Overseas commercial exhibitions are being expanded and more information made available to American manufacturers regarding potential markets abroad. Economic development in depressed areas is also being stressed.

One development of this type in which the Bureau has been particularly interested in a cross-agency program for the Appalachian area. Under the Appalachian Regional Development Act of 1965, funds were appropriated to the President for special programs to promote economic growth in the Appalachian Region. Amendments to the Act in 1967 authorized construction of an Appalachian development highway system with local-access roads. Obligational authority of

TABLE 8. COMMERCE AND TRANSPORTATION EXPENDITURES
AND NET LENDING[a]

Program or Agency	Expenditures and Net Lending			Recommended NOA and LA for 1969[b]
	1967 Actual	1968 Estimate	1969 Estimate	
Expenditures				
Advancement of business				
Export promotion[c]	$ 18	$ 20	$ 29	$ 32
Small-business assistance	75	60	43	13
Physical environment[c]	176	168	177	178
Physical standards	38	31	29	29
Promotion of technology[c]	54	57	59	61
Economic and demographic statistics[c]	32	46	48	50
Federal Deposit Insurance Corporation (trust funds)	−239	−261	−274	
Other aids to business[c]	33	39	40	37
Area and regional development				
Department of Commerce, economic development assistance	52	153	186	229
Appalachia and other[c]	86	159	239	216
Air transportation				
Federal Aviation Administration	883	892	1,228	1,064
Civil Aeronautics Board subsidies	62	58	54	53
Water transportation				
Maritime Administration[c]	302	364	380	482
Coast Guard[c]	497	486	608	559
Other	−7	5	12	5
Ground transportation				
Highways[c]				
Present programs	4,041	4,363	4,340	4,787
Proposed legislation			51	85
Other	10	21	28	21
Postal service	1,141	1,087	767	920
Regulation of business	101	100	107	111

TABLE 8 *(cont.)*

Program or Agency	Expenditures and Net Lending			Recommended NOA and LA for 1969[b]
	1967 Actual	1968 Estimate	1969 Estimate	
Interfund and intragovernmental transactions	−1	−24	−8	−8
Applicable receipts from the public	−47	−132	−149	−149
Subtotal expenditures	$7,308	$7,695	$7,996	$8,776
Net lending				
Advancement of business, small business assistance	101	114	67	150
Area and regional development, Department of Commerce, economic development assistance	29	53	65	88
Other	8	−8	−8	−6
Subtotal net lending	$ 138	$ 158	$ 125	$ 232
Total	$7,446	$7,853	$8,121	$9,008

[a]All figures in millions of dollars.

[b]Compares with new obligational authority (NOA) and lending authority (LA) for 1967 and 1968, as follows—NOA: 1967, $8,653 million; 1968, $9,066 million. LA: 1967, $938 million; 1968, $217 million.

[c]Includes both federal funds and trust funds.

Source: The 1969 Budget Message.

$140.8 million was initially transferred in fiscal 1967 from other accounts and $126.7 million was appropriated in fiscal 1968 and $213.6 million requested for 1969. Additional amounts of $645 million have been authorized by Congress to be appropriated for fiscal years 1970-72. Part of the program relating to land conservation and erosion control is administered by the Department of Agriculture. A loan program is administered by the Secretary of Housing and Urban

Development. The Appalachian Regional Commission has been established as an independent agency to coordinate the local and state projects and accelerate over-all development of Appalachia, including the building of hospitals and regional health diagnostic or treatment centers, as well as programs for sealing abandoned coal mines and reclamation of stripped areas.

This type of regional development has operating advantages and, from a budget point of view, minimizes the danger of duplication of programs. It also raises a larger question as to whether the whole federal departmental and agency structure should be revised instead of expanding the across-agency programs now being authorized.

Two of the best-known agencies of the Department of Commerce—the Bureau of the Census and the Office of Business Economics—are under the policy supervision of the assistant secretary for Economic Affairs. They collect, analyze, and distribute information of great use to business and government. Working closely with the Council of Economic Advisers and the Office of Statistical Policy in the Budget Bureau, these agencies respond to changes in business conditions and continually explore and develop new techniques. The only serious budgetary problems have been in determining the best location for the collection of certain statistical data. Another unit of Commerce, the National Bureau of Standards, is responsible for the basic measurements and standards of physical quantities and conducts research in electronics, polymers, metallurgy, ceramics, and so on. It is also engaged in developing more-effective utilization of the government's automatic-data-processing equipment and systems. The Budget Bureau and the GAO are cooperating in this activity. Still another part of the Department of Commerce, the Maritime Administration, is responsible for managing two very large federal subsidies, of serious concern to the Budget Bureau: the construction differential subsidy (NOA

1969, $119.8 million) and the operating differential subsidy (NOA 1969, $213 million), which provide American shipping with the difference between the cost of construction in the United States and operation under the American flag and the cost in foreign countries. The difference exists largely because American shipping-industry wages are many times those of competitors and because of the demands and frequent strikes over the years by the dominant maritime unions.

The newest department of the federal government is the Department of Transportation, separated from Commerce in 1967. It includes the big three federal administrations—aviation, highways, and railroads—as well as the Coast Guard, with its aids to navigation, marine safety, and law enforcement, which was transferred from the Treasury Department.

The appropriation for the Federal Aviation Administration provides $663 million for the necessary expenses of the FAA, including air-navigation facilities and "carrying out the provisions of the Federal Airport Act; and purchase and repair of skis and snowshoes." The air-traffic-management system includes operation of control towers at 319 major civil airports and 344 flight service stations. The expenditures are indicated in Table 8 and include new facilities and equipment and research and development. The Budget Bureau believes that this is an area that lends itself easily to user charges and considers their application to be desirable. Air transportation has been subsidized from the beginning of the air age, and, with its rapid growth, has tended to supersede railroad passenger travel. Initially, federal expenditures were for building airports, then for enlarging them. Current funding increases are due to the substantial expenditures required for air-traffic control and to the much debated large federal contributions (90 per cent) to research, construction, and flight-testing of a prototype civil supersonic transport, for which $223 million NOA is requested. Subsidy payments by the Civil Aeronautics Board to airlines have been decreasing in recent years. When the research and development expenditures in initiating new programs have been completed, the Bureau encourages the transfer of full responsibility to the private sector as soon as possible through surcharges for use of the facilities.

The largest operations of the Federal Highway Administration are through the federal-aid-to-highways trust funds—started under President Eisenhower in 1956—by which 90 per cent of the costs of the 41,000-mile national system of interstate and defense highways is being financed. Funds are also provided on a fifty-fifty matching basis with the states for primary, secondary, and some urban roads. The Budget Bureau believes that this is a perfect example of good user charges; the financing is provided entirely out of federal taxes on motor fuel, tires, tubes, and other accessories. Federal payments through fiscal 1968 have totaled approximately $37 billion.

The Federal Railroad Administration was established on October 15, 1966, with responsibility for the railroad safety program ($3.8 million NOA requested for 1969), high-speed ground-transportation research and development ($16.2 million NOA for 1969, initially Boston to Washington) and The Alaska Railroad, which is financed out of a revolving-fund balance. The Bureau believes that the decline in passenger travel on U.S. railroads is due to poor service and failure to adopt new and improved facilities and has been constantly consulted in connection with legislation needed to permit new developments.

The Post Office

The U.S. Post Office was established in 1775, one of the initial agencies of the government with a government-protected monopoly. The operations of the post office are supposed to be self-supporting, in accordance with the user-charge principle. However, current postal policy, approved by Congress in 1958 (P.L. 85-426) and again in 1962 (P.L. 87-793), is that postal rates and fees be fixed as required in order to produce the amount of revenue approximately equal to the cost of operations "less the amount determined to be attributable to the performance of public services." This differential is one of the catches. Another difficulty is the determination of the rates to be applied to different classes of service. The Bureau of the Budget has no say as to the rates established under the different classifications of mail that are proposed by the Department and fixed by Congress.

The Postmaster-General and his staff, in my opinion, have consistently tried to make operations more efficient and to introduce labor-saving devices. In this, they have had the encouragement of the Budget Bureau. However, postal appointments throughout the country have a political character, and the postal unions for many years have been strongly entrenched. The Post Office and Civil Service committees of the House and Senate have usually supported their repeated demands for wage increases without approving commensurate rate increases in time to offset resulting deficits. In 1967, Postmaster-General Lawrence F. O'Brien proposed that the Post Office operations be removed from congressional control and that a public corporation be formed, which would be able to borrow money itself and be expected to operate at a profit. A President's Commission on Postal Organization was appointed in 1967 to study this whole question and report to the President. I was asked to testify before the Commission and expressed strong support for Postmaster O'Brien's proposal; I think it is the only way in which postal operations will ever be run efficiently.

Mail-handling is highly labor-intensive. Even today, with the introduction of labor-saving machinery, these handling costs are just under 80 per cent of total costs of operation;

in the 1930's, during the Depression, the lowest rate was 70 per cent. A good deal of overtime work is required, which includes a 10 per cent differential. Insufficient amounts have been spent on research and development, and capital expenditures for the last ten years have averaged only 7 per cent, two-thirds of which is for buildings. The greatest need is for more equipment and cheaper handling, both of which will require substantially increased expenditures for research, development, and procurement.

The bulk-shippers maintain that first-class mail requires regular deliveries and rightly should absorb part of the cost of the other classes; this argument assumes that the postman can carry the other classes in addition to the regular first-class mail on the same delivery and in the same carrier that he regularly uses. The Bureau of the Budget has generally taken the position that it is only fair that each class of mail should carry its full share of the costs. In determining this share, however, more systematic studies should be made to determine the marginal efficiency under the maximum loading a postman can carry in either his pouch or his vehicle. Postal wages have kept step with increases in the private sector, but further and more-detailed study should be given to the wage differentials within the Post Office Department.

These and other matters were covered fully by the report of Frederick R. Kappel, chairman of the President's Commission mentioned above, which was submitted in June, 1968. It made the following recommendations:

1. We recommend that a Postal Corporation owned entirely by the Federal Government be chartered by Congress to operate the postal service of the United States on a self-supporting basis.
The Corporation should be self-supporting because:

Subjecting a business activity to deficit financing stifles management initiative and practically guarantees inefficient operation. The deficit—for the most part a subsidy to the mail system as a whole—is no more justified than partial Treasury support for any other public utility.

2. We recommend that the Corporation take immediate steps to improve the quality and kinds of service offered, the means by which service is provided and the physical conditions under which postal employees work.

3. We recommend that all appointments to, and promotions within, the postal system be made on a non-political basis.

The Commission urges that the Corporation Charter remove residency requirements for postmasters and other personnel and contain a strong provision against any political test or qualification in appointment or promotion, with removal from office specified as the penalty for any Board member, officer or employee found to violate this provision.

4. We recommend that present postal employees be transferred, with their accrued Civil Service benefits, to a new career service within the Postal Corporation.

5. We recommend that the Board of Directors, after hearings by expert Rate Commissioners, establish postal rates, subject to veto by concurrent resolution of the Congress.

The postal service as a whole—not necessarily class by class— should be self-sustaining. Particularly since use of the mails is overwhelmingly commercial in nature, we strongly feel that the users can and should pay the full cost of the postal system.

In a message to Congress, President Nixon supported these recommendations, but the postal unions are opposing them. With the congressional committee divided, it seems doubtful if this important and constructive change will be adopted this year.

Civilian Research and Technology Activities

The National Aeronautics and Space Administration (NASA) has become one of the largest agencies in the United

States for research and development. The most costly phase of its program—the manned lunar flights—is nearing completion as this is written, although budget stringency has caused some delay in the time schedules. The Bureau has consistently pointed out the high cost of the crash aspects of this program, but Congress has generally supported the need for speed in these developments, the cost of which is summarized in Table 9. Crash programs are always much more costly than carefully planned development because initial facilities are soon overtaken by improved techniques, which inevitably result in extensive changes and costly replacements.

TABLE 9. SPACE RESEARCH AND TECHNOLOGY
EXPENDITURES[a]

	1967 Actual	1968 Estimate	1969 Estimate	Recommended NOA for 1969[b]
Manned lunar landing	$3,587	$3,028	$2,571	$2,362
Extended manned flight	62	138	422	463
Space sciences	674	563	498	479
Space applications	122	135	147	148
Space technology	440	420	425	410
Aircraft technology	89	113	120	131
Supporting activities[c]	452	411	394	378
Applicable receipts from the public	−2	−4	−3	−3
Total	$5,423	$4,803	$4,573	$4,369

[a] All figures in millions of dollars.

[b] Compares with new obligational authority (NOA) for 1967 and 1968, as follows: 1967, $4,966 million; 1968, $4,587 million.

[c] Includes both federal funds and trust funds.

Source: The 1969 Budget Message.

In recent years, more and more attention has been given to peaceful applications of atomic energy, although research and development on weapons, underground testing, and naval reactor development (Admiral Hyman Rickover's program) continues.

The Bureau's position throughout the period of intensive research and development by the Atomic Energy Commission (AEC), followed by its period of testing, rapid procurement, and production, under highly classified conditions, has been to balance the needs and potentialities against the resources available. The Bureau staff has become very expert in this whole area, where competition for the dollar is just as keen as it is elsewhere in government. Declassification of discoveries and recent developments by private industry (General Electric, Westinghouse, and others) have enabled the Bureau to begin to balance private-industry development versus further government involvement in an expanding area of great potential industrial opportunity. Table 10 illustrates the breakdown of current programs.

TABLE 10. ATOMIC ENERGY COMMISSION PROGRAM EXPENDITURES[a]

	1967 Actual	1968 Estimate	1969 Estimate
Procurement and production of raw and special nuclear materials	$ 542	$ 491	$ 489
Military applications	849	1,012	1,281
Space applications	159	132	143
Central-station nuclear-power development	127	163	258
Other civilian applications	26	34	32
Basic research in the physical and biomedical sciences	444	421	555
Nuclear science and technology support	139	132	174
General support	131	123	136
Total program funding	$2,417	$2,508	$3,068
Carry-over funds and other adjustments	-218	1	-313
New obligational authority	$2,199	$2,509	$2,755

[a] All figures in millions of dollars.
Source: The 1969 Budget Message.

The National Science Foundation (NSF) is primarily concerned with basic scientific research and with science education at colleges and universities and the improvement of science instruction in secondary schools. Some NSF funds are used in approaches to computer utilization in research and education. Budget recommendations have been carefully prepared and presented.

International Programs

The staff of the Bureau in the International Programs Division is devoting more and more attention to coordinating the activities of the different U.S. Government agencies operating in each country abroad. The head of this division spent a week in India during 1968, reviewing the situation there with a member of his staff, who had been on the scene for several months. State Department representatives today are rightly taking more interest in coordinating country programs, parts of which had been directed independently by other agency representatives who reported directly to their superiors in Washington. It is believed that much more effective operations have been achieved thereby, as well as better over-all control.

Ten years ago, the Budget Bureau was inclined to raise rather than restrict the proposals for overseas representation. But, recently, the State Department seems to have grown more rapidly in numbers than in efficiency, particularly in the Washington area. The Foreign Service supplies most of the personnel representing the United States abroad in embassies and consulates, although the departments of Defense, Commerce, and upward of twenty other agencies also have representatives in many cities. Although the cost of administration of foreign affairs is relatively small compared with the magnitude of U.S. commitments and involvements abroad

TABLE 11. INTERNATIONAL AFFAIRS AND FINANCE
EXPENDITURES AND NET LENDING[a]

Program or Agency	Expenditures and Net Lending			Recommended NOA and LA for 1969[b]
	1967 Actual	1968 Estimate	1969 Estimate	
Expenditures				
Conduct of foreign affairs				
Department of State[c]	$ 321	$ 337	$ 355	$ 350
U.S. Arms Control and Disarmament Agency	10	9	10	10
Tariff Commission	3	4	4	4
Foreign Claims Settlement Commission[c] [d]	21	200	1	1
Department of Justice (trust funds)	2	4	53	
Treasury Department (trust funds)	8	5	6	5
Economic and financial programs				
Agency for International Development				
Development loans	662	625	670	765
Technical cooperation[c]	224	203	216	238
Alliance for Progress	511	465	516	625
Supporting assistance	587	602	621	595
Contingencies and other	334	313	310	280
Applicable receipts from the public[d]	−51	−63	−69	−69
Subtotal Agency for International Development[c] [d]	$2,268	$2,145	$2,264	$2,434
Subtotal, excluding Special Vietnam	($1,844)	($1,687)	($1,784)	($1,954)
International financial institutions				
Present programs	170	223	200	320
Proposed legislation			10	446
Export-Import Bank	−104	−144	−110	
Peace Corps[c] [d]	112	108	110	113

TABLE 11 (cont.)

Program or Agency	Expenditures and Net Lending			Recommended NOA and LA for 1969[b]
	1967 Actual	1968 Estimate	1969 Estimate	
Other[c]	20	21	20	11
Food for Freedom	1,452	1,315	1,444	918
Foreign-information and exchange activities				
United States Information Agency[c d]	185	187	194	179
Department of State and other[c]	59	68	61	54
Applicable receipts from the public[d]	−417	−153	−144	−144
Subtotal expenditures	$4,110	$4,330	$4,478	$4,700
Subtotal expenditures excluding Special Vietnam	($3,687)	($3,872)	($3,998)	($4,220)
Net Lending, economic and financial programs				
Export-Import Bank				
Present programs	540	716	660	608
Proposed legislation			15	
Subtotal net lending	540	716	675	608
Total	$4,650	$5,046	$5,153	$5,308
Total excluding Special Vietnam	($4,227)	($4,588)	($4,673)	($4,828)

[a]All figures in millions of dollars.

[b]Compares with new obligational authority (NOA) and lending authority (LA) for 1967 and 1968, as follows—NOA: 1967, $4,336 million; 1968, $4,402 million. LA: 1967, $779 million; 1968, $865 million.

[c]Includes both federal funds and trust funds.

[d]Relevant "interfund and intragovernmental transactions" and "applicable receipts from the public" have been deducted to arrive at totals.

Source: The 1969 Budget Message.

(see Table 11), the bureau staff still feels that there is too little delegation of power to make decisions in the field and too much official rigidity in following decisions previously made, perhaps years before, in Washington, as well as too much reluctance to accept and propose changes in programs, to develop creative thinking, and to explore new ways of doing things.

Ever since World War II, foreign assistance has been an important part of American foreign policy. It was instrumental in stimulating the rapid revival of Western Europe through the Marshall Plan. The programs now are centered largely in Asia and Latin America.

They include economic, technical, and other assistance, including (under P.L. 480) sale of surplus agricultural commodities for local currencies to be used in turn in support of U.S. aid projects. The Budget Bureau feels that it has been successful in eliminating some wasteful practices from these programs and in restricting them to those generally accepted as productive for long-term, as well as short-term, goals.

The guarantee programs backed by the Foreign Investment Guarantee Fund of the Agency for International Development (AID) are extremely important in encouraging and facilitating U.S. private investment abroad. Specific political guarantees are given against inconvertibility of foreign currency, losses by expropriation or confiscation, and losses due to war, revolution, or insurrection. In addition, "extended risk" guarantees are given for up to 75 per cent of both political and business risks and up to 100 per cent of losses in certain housing projects and investments in credit unions. The Budget Bureau considers this type of subsidy as sound a kind of encouragement as can be given by government. The premiums to date have exceeded expenses and losses by $100 million. Present outstanding guarantees amount to approximately $2 billion.

General Government Management

This Division of the Bureau covers the Department of the Treasury, the General Services Administration (GSA), and agencies responsible for federal judicial functions and such management matters as the Civil Service. What it costs to run the general government, as such, is shown by Table 12.

The Secretary of the Treasury presents his recommendations to the Bureau and justifies them, just as the heads of the other departments do. When cuts have to be made, the Treasury shares in the general belt-tightening. Since the Treasury makes the expenditures, maintains the central accounts of appropriations, receipts, and expenditures, and participates in the joint management-improvement programs with the General Accounting Office (GAO) and the Bureau, the relations of these three agencies are particularly close.

A recent example of the kind of practical interagency study initiated by the Bureau in government management was one completed in May, 1968, of the ports-of-entry inspection activities. In addition to Budget Bureau staff from the General Government Management Division and the Office of Executive Management, the Bureau of Customs of the Treasury Department, the Immigration and Naturalization Service of the Department of Justice, the Agricultural Research Service, and the Department of Health, Education, and Welfare were all represented on the Task Force that made the field trips.

The Task Force visited the facilities at ports of entry accounting for 80 per cent of the 200 million persons entering the United States through all ports of entry in 1968. These were staffed by 3,000 inspectors, representing the four agencies participating in the study. A number of constructive suggestions were made and are being put into effect, the most important being the installation of a one-stop inspection

Table 12. General Government Expenditures
and Net Lending[a]

Program or Agency	Expenditures and Net Lending			Recommended NOA and LA for 1969[b]
	1967 Actual	1968 Estimate	1969 Estimate	
Expenditures				
Legislative functions[c]	$ 167	$ 185	$ 198	$ 196
Judicial functions	87	95	102	102
Executive direction and management	25	31	35	34
Central fiscal operations				
Treasury Department				
Internal Revenue Service	662	688	760	758
Other[c]	253	260	280	264
Other agencies[c]	53	59	63	63
General property and records management				
General Services Administration:				
Public Buildings Service				
Construction, sites, and planning	184	152	106	11
Operation, maintenance, and other[c]	347	367	379	362
Other[c]	88	110	164	114
Central Intelligency Agency building	1	d		
Central personnel management				
Civil Service Commission				
Present programs	129	150	153	153
Proposed legislation			12	20
Department of Labor and other[c]	61	62	53	53
Law enforcement and justice				
Department of Justice:				
Present programs[c]	401	425	458	457
Proposed legislation		10	39	80
Other	25	27	32	33

TABLE 12 *(cont.)*

Program or Agency	Expenditures and Net Lending			Recommended NOA and LA for 1969b
	1967 Actual	1968 Estimate	1969 Estimate	
Other general government				
Territories and				
possessions	157	187	198	184
Treasury—claims	49	8	6	6
Otherc	7	8	1	11
Interfund and intragovernmental				
transactions	−85	−92	−94	−94
Applicable receipts from				
the public	−161	−115	−117	−117
Subtotal				
expenditures	$2,452	$2,618	$2,827	$2,690
Net lending	2	−40	−37	−36
Total	$2,454	$2,578	$2,790	$2,654

aAll figures in millions of dollars.

bCompares with new obligational authority (NOA) and lending authority (LA) for 1967 and 1968, as follows—NOA: 1967, $2,463 million; 1968, $2,548 million. LA: 1967, −$3 million; 1968, −$42 million.

cIncludes both federal funds and trust funds.

dLess than $500,000.

Source: 1969 Budget Message.

system with *selective* baggage examination and greater airline and terminal-operator cooperation. Other suggestions made were that carriers should accept a standard of ten to fifteen minutes for delivery of baggage, pier facilities should be greatly improved and should include better baggage handling, and Customs should facilitate pre-baggage-inspection payment of duty. It was also suggested that, at an appropriate time, the complete responsibility for inspection of passengers and their baggage be assigned to one of the four inspection agencies.

The Internal Revenue Service is the largest unit in the

Treasury, as indicated in Table 12. The volume of business involved in preparing and mailing tax-return forms and then receiving and classifying them is enormous, but the greater part of the cost is in auditing the returns and collecting delinquent accounts. The Bureau's review is based on comparison of unit costs and yield from investigatorial work. For example, the Commissioner may feel that, by increasing the number of auditing staff by 1,000 at an estimated cost of $10 million, the government would recover $25 million in unpaid taxes and perhaps discourage underpayment of taxes. How careful is this estimate and on how much evidence is it founded? How much ill-will may be generated? The point of "diminishing returns" must be carefully watched.

As a matter of fact, one review made by the Bureau indicated that there was a return of about $10 for every $1 spent in auditing. Since the audit covered the most lucrative returns, every increase in staff would be likely to lower the return per $1 spent. There was no indication, however, that they were anywhere near a break-even point.

One of the budget tricks sometimes used by congressmen to bypass the appropriation committees is to authorize certain programs to be financed by borrowing from the Treasury. This practice is opposed by the Bureau. It does not appear in the accounts until the actual loans are made and a Treasury debt is incurred.

Under the Defense Production Act of 1950, designated agencies are authorized, with the President's approval, to expand production of critical materials certified by the Office of Emergency Planning to be essential to the national defense. A revolving fund not exceeding $2.1 billion was authorized to be established by borrowing from the Treasury. This is not good budgeting procedure, but some emergency authorization is undoubtedly necessary to enable immediate action when Congress is not in session.

Funds for both the legislative and judicial branches are

included in the general government budget. Under the Budget and Accounting Act, estimated expenditures and proposed appropriations for these two branches must be included in the Budget without revision. The comptroller-general (head of the GAO) is in a similar position, as responsible and reporting to Congress.

The expenditures of the Department of Justice in 1969 were estimated to increase $62 million over 1968, largely because of a proposed program of federal financial and technical assistance to the state and local governments to help combat crime. Almost half of the total expenditures of the Department of Justice are made by the Federal Bureau of Investigation.

The General Services Administration (GSA) is the largest landlord and the largest lessee in the country, and probably in the non-Communist world. Its largest activity is the rental, operation, protection, and utilization of almost 100 million square feet of government-owned space and 31 million square feet of leased space. Practically all the agencies are involved. Representatives of the Bureau spend considerable time with the GSA in planning better utilization of space, improved up-keep, and disposal of unneeded facilities. The rather run-down condition often associated with government buildings in the past is no longer a characteristic of federal-government space today. The agency's general supply fund stocks "common-use commodities" for issue on a reimbursable basis to government agencies. The volume of business in 1968 and the forecast for 1969 is just over $1 billion dollars. Defense and many of the other large agencies have their own common stocks, but the GSA is considered by the Bureau to be the logical source of supply for all the smaller agencies.

A small start has been made by the GSA in automatic data processing (ADP), but this agency may not be the best choice to manage a governmentwide operation in this technique. The Budget Bureau's deputy director of management in the

General Government Management Division served in the Air Force in data systems and automation before becoming the Budget Bureau's automatic-data-processing chief in 1966. The work of his group consists of providing ADP policy and guidelines to the agencies; reviewing the agency plans and proposals for ADP equipment; assisting agencies in managing their equipment; minimizing equipment incompatibility and helping to develop American standards in ADP hardware and software; and providing training, making special studies, and improving agency efforts in this field.

During 1958 and 1959, the Bureau started a study that formed the basis for its general responsibilities in this field and engaged a consulting organization to survey the personnel problems and training involved in operating ADP installations. A one-day conference was held to acquaint 800 high-level federal executives with the advantages and problems involved, and guidelines were provided. A computer-sharing exchange was started in Philadelphia and later extended nationally by the GSA. Still later, a computer-service center was established at the National Bureau of Standards to serve the Washington area. In July, 1967, a governmentwide information system was set up and a perpetual inventory of government equipment was started, with instructions for computer selection and use.

For more effective leadership in this important area, the Bureau was recently strengthened with additional technical staff. It should be strengthened further. An advanced computer center for general use is urgently needed to prevent a continuation of the unnecessary proliferation of equipment throughout the government.

XI

Bureau Relations with the Executive Circle, Congress, State and Local Governments, and the Public

The Bureau of the Budget has numerous relations within the executive branch at various levels apart from those described in earlier chapters. Similarly, its relations with Congress are more extensive than already indicated, and it has a variety of special relationships with state and local governments, as well as with the American press and the general public.

The Executive Circle

Although he is not a member of the Cabinet, the Director of the Bureau of the Budget is expected to attend the Cabinet meetings, held in the Cabinet room next to the President's office in the White House. Each Cabinet officer has his own chair. The President sits at the middle of the table; the Vice-President sits opposite him, the Budget Director at one end of the table, and the assistant to the President at the other. There is a second tier of seats for any others invited to attend.

President Eisenhower believed in having regular Cabinet

221

meetings to keep him directly in touch with the department heads and their current problems and to keep them in touch with one another and with what was going on in other agencies. He named one of his assistants as Cabinet secretary to jot down notes of what transpired, but no regular minutes were kept. The Budget Director was expected to make a presentation of the budget preview for each new year and, after Congress adjourned, he was also expected to evaluate the effects of congressional action on the President's recommendations in the Budget Message. Frequent presentations were also made on the budgetary aspects of action contemplated in special areas.

Presidents Kennedy and Johnson held fewer Cabinet meetings, usually only to discuss some special situations. Many smaller meetings were held with department heads, and the Budget Director was frequently invited to these. He saw the President frequently, several times a week, sometimes several times a day, to discuss the budgetary situation in general or its impact in special areas under consideration. President Nixon holds Cabinet meetings regularly. He relies on a free exchange of ideas with his advisers as well as careful briefings, before making decisions. As Vice-President, he presided most effectively at regular Cabinet meetings during several illnesses of President Eisenhower.

The National Security Council (NSC)—established by the National Security Act of 1947 and amended in 1949 to advise the President with respect to the integration of domestic, foreign, and military policies relating to the national security —served a very important purpose under President Eisenhower. It met regularly on Thursdays, and the Budget Director (or his deputy) was expected to attend regularly and to be prepared to report when called upon with respect to the impact on the national budget of plans under consideration. Another purpose of the Director's attendance, obviously, was to keep him informed of proposed acts that would have an important budget impact. He was also usually called upon to present a summary of the budget proposals just before the Budget Message was finally approved—with particular reference to the relation of the Defense Department budget to the total. The chairman of the Joint Chiefs of Staff was also expected to attend the Council meetings and frequently one or more of the service chiefs. Others were invited from time to time to join the statutory members, consisting of the President, the Vice-President, the Secretary of State, the Secretary of Defense, the director of the Office of Emergency Planning, and the director of the Central Intelligence Agency (established in 1947 along with the NSC).

Presidents Kennedy and Johnson dispensed with regular Council meetings. The staff under President Johnson was moved to the White House and became a sort of general staff to the President on national security affairs. Walt W. Rostow, assistant to the President for security affairs, acted as Director of the National Security Council and prepared frequent memoranda for the President on current plans and developments. The Budget Director was called upon whenever the budget effects of contemplated actions became important. One of the assistant directors of the Bureau attended the Council's staff-operating meetings three times a week.

Soon after his election, President Nixon indicated that he was going to restore NSC to the important position that it had previously held. He announced that it would meet regularly and that he expected it to formulate alternative plans for defense of the United States and, with the cooperation of the allies, to consider ways to best protect the rights and safety of the non-Communist world. The day after his inauguration, President Nixon called a meeting of the Security Council and said that it would meet twice a week for the next several weeks. Meetings since that time have been held frequently.

The Operations Coordinating Board was established within

the structure of the National Security Council by Executive Order 10700 of February 25, 1957, with staff work provided partly by the Bureau. The NSC Planning Board was formed as the planning agency for policy recommendations to be considered by the Council and representatives of the participating agencies at the assistant-secretary level, including the Budget Bureau. The Planning Board was abolished in 1961, but a smaller group performing the same function was set up by Presidential directive resulting from an action memo of the National Security Council. This was called the Senior Interdepartmental Group (SIG). It was chaired by the undersecretary of state and included the Secretary of Defense, the director of the CIA, with the Agency for International Development and the Bureau also represented.

A smaller inner council met for luncheon with President Johnson every Tuesday. This informal but powerful group was composed of the Secretary of Defense, the Secretary of State, the chairman of the Joint Chiefs of Staff, the director of the CIA and the assistant to the President for security affairs. The Secretary of the Treasury and the director of the U.S. Information Agency were regularly invited, also, and the Director of the Bureau of the Budget attended on occasion.

The Advisory Board on Economic Growth and Stability was established in the Executive Office of the President by the Employment Act of 1946. Meetings during the 1950's were held weekly in the Office of Economic Advisers, presided over by the chairman of the Council. The other official members, when I was in the Budget Bureau, were the Secretary of Health, Education, and Welfare; the undersecretaries of Agriculture, Commerce, Labor, and the Treasury; the deputy undersecretary for economic affairs of the Department of State; A.L. Mills, Jr., a member of the board of governors of the Federal Reserve System; Gabriel Hauge, assistant to the President; and the Budget Director. This board (called the ABEGS) under the chairmanship of Arthur F. Burns, then head of the Council of Economic Advisers, and his successor, Raymond J. Saulnier, was the central clearing agency for current reports on the economic situation in the United States and abroad and the various plans and programs for its improvement. It was an important channel of communication between agencies and the President, to whom weekly reports were rendered about the state of the nation and progress of different measures being used to stabilize the economy.

Under President Johnson, this group was superseded by an active interagency group known as "Troika." The Council of Economic Advisers, Treasury, and the Budget Bureau had representatives at three different levels. The Chairman of the Council presided with the Budget Director and Secretary of the Treasury present at the top-level meeting about once a month. Representatives of the same agencies at the assistant-secretary level met two or three times a month to prepare and discuss the agenda for the top-level meeting. The staff of the three agencies assigned for the purpose met weekly or more often, and the Council was assigned a full-time, sophisticated staff and office space for review of economic data from many sources. The Budget Bureau supplied current budget-data and reports on expenditures.

President Nixon has enlarged this group, which is now known as the "Quadriad." It is primarily responsible for the formulation of suggestions for the Administration's economic and fiscal policy. President Nixon also appointed the Budget Director to two other important bodies. One, a Cabinet committee on economic policy, was set up to assist in the formulation of long-range national economic goals. It consists of the President; the secretaries of the Treasury, Agriculture, Commerce, and Labor; the Budget Director, the Chairman of the Council of Economic Advisers, and Arthur F. Burns, counsellor to the President. The second important new agency to which President Nixon appointed the Budget Director was the Urban Affairs Council established by his first executive order after taking office. Other members are the Vice-President; the Attorney General, Counsellor Burns, and the secretaries of Labor, Transportation, Agriculture, Housing and Urban Development, Commerce, and Health, Education and Welfare, with a top Presidential assistant, Daniel P. Moynihan, as executive secretary.

A multiplicity of organizations each directed toward a specific goal is useful in that expert staff members are assigned by each of the organizations to work together at an assistant-secretary level. They prepare papers in advance and draw up the agenda for meetings to save the time of the principals for discussion of policy. Practically every member of the top staff of the Bureau is assigned to some specific interagency group. This comprises a substantial part of the constructive work being performed by the Bureau, which thus participates in initiating and formulating policy decisions. These may be in many different areas of activity, but all necessarily affect the Budget either directly or indirectly.

The National Advisory Council on International Monetary and Financial Problems was established in 1945 to coordinate the policies and operations of the representatives of the United States on the International Monetary Fund and the International Bank for Reconstruction and Development, the Export-Import Bank of Washington, and all other agencies of the government "to the extent that they make or participate in the making of foreign loans or engage in foreign financial, exchange or monetary transactions." When I was in the Bureau, it was chaired by W. Randolph Burgess, undersecretary of the Treasury Department. It met several times a month and was attended by representatives of the principal agencies affected by changes in the international situation. I found it helpful in keeping informed on current developments and getting to know the reactions of the individuals as well as the agencies affected, both of which were useful in budget preparation, clearing legislation, and management improvement programs. It was superseded by another agency with the same name, the National Advisory Council on International Monetary and Financial Policies, established in 1966 to coordinate the policies and operations of the representatives of the United States on international financial organizations, including the more recently organized Inter-American Development Bank and Asian Development Bank.

After President Kennedy's first announcement of a program to deal with the balance-of-payments problem in February, 1961, a Cabinet committee on balance of payments was appointed, consisting of the secretaries of the Treasury, Defense, and Commerce departments, the undersecretary of the Department of State, the Administrator of AID, the Budget Director, and the chairman of the Council of Economic Advisers. The committee later included the Secretary of Transportation, the undersecretary of Agriculture, the special representative for trade negotiations, the chairman of the Federal Reserve Board of Governors (ex-officio), and a staff member of the National Security Council. The Budget Bureau was asked to prepare a "gold budget" for the committee and the President. An executive committee was established at the assistant-secretary level for the same agencies and an information committee at the staff level chaired by the Commerce representative to prepare projections as needed.

The Secretary of the Treasury holds a biweekly luncheon to discuss fiscal and economic affairs with the full Council of Economic Advisers, the Budget Director, the undersecretaries, and several assistant secretaries of the Treasury Department. The Bureau staff also frequently meets with representatives of the other offices within the Executive Office of the President. In addition, the Office of Economic Opportunity is asked for comments on the proposals of other agencies in their areas, and vice-versa, for the purpose of obtaining better cooperation and avoiding overlapping. The Office of Science and Technology participates in the Budget Director's review of related agencies and also the final meeting with the Secretary of Defense, the Budget Director, and the special assistant to the President for security affairs.

The foregoing description of certain interagency committees is only illustrative of the hundreds of interagency meetings and *ad hoc* groups in which Budget officers and staff are continuously engaged as a part of their regular responsibilities.

The Joint Financial Management Program conducted by the Bureau of the Budget, the Treasury Department, the General Accounting Office, and the Civil Service Commission was discussed at some length in Chapter IV. An important and successful interagency effort, it deserves mention in this chapter as well. In its twentieth annual report, dated December 20, 1968, a significant saving from the increasing use of letters of credit is described:

> The letter-of-credit method of financing Federal programs requiring large advances of cash was introduced in May, 1964, as a result of a Joint Program study. This method of financing provides the means for reducing Federal financing costs by keeping funds in the Treasury until actually needed by recipients. It permits the recipient, as authorized by the program agency, to draw on the Treasury, through the recipient's bank and the Federal Reserve System, when funds are actually needed to cover cash requirements. Withdrawals by letter of credit, since inception of the system, have increased from $1.5 billion in fiscal year 1965 to $18.3 billion in 1968.

Reference has already been made to the two commissions on organization of the executive branch of the government—the first Hoover Commission, established in 1947, and the second Hoover Commission, established in 1953. The Bureau of the Budget was directly concerned with carrying out many of the recommendations of both, which required many conferences with agency heads and members of Congress.

The President's Advisory Commission on Government

Organization—established by Executive Order 10432 of January 24, 1953 "to advise the President, the Assistant to the President, and the Director of the Bureau of the Budget with respect to changes in the organization and activities of the executive branch of the government which, in its opinion, would promote economy and efficiency in the operations of that Branch"—had Nelson A. Rockefeller as chairman. The Bureau worked out the details of many of the proposals presented to the President, which formed the basis for several reorganization plans.

Congressional Relations

Weekly meetings with legislative leaders were considered very important by President Eisenhower, to keep him advised on congressional plans, tactics, and progress and to keep them fully informed of Administration thinking on general policies and particularly on the measures then before Congress. These meetings sometimes were for Republican leaders and committee chairmen of the House and Senate. At other times, they were bipartisan, since the President was particularly anxious to maintain close relations between Congress and the executive branch. The Budget Director was expected to attend the meetings and was occasionally asked to make a presentation on the budgetary impact of a program of interest to one of the committees or in connection with a pending bill. Such meetings were always helpful to the Bureau as well as to Congress. While the viewpoints were frequently different, each member attending knew exactly where the others stood; the discussion was very frank. Similar meetings, without the same formality or regularity, were held under Presidents Kennedy and Johnson, and smaller informal contacts were even more frequent. Today, regular meetings are again being held with the legislative leaders by President Nixon.

The direct access of the Bureau's representatives to Congress is quite limited compared to the access enjoyed by the other executive agencies. The agencies, not the Bureau, present their share of the President's budget requests and are expected to justify it. They appear to defend or oppose substantive measures before the policy committees. The agencies' relationships with Congress are persistent, all-encompassing, and enormously influential. The Bureau does not have this kind of intimate relationship.

Many congressional hearings are attended by the Director and other representatives of the Bureau on invitation. Budget representatives may attend other hearings that have a direct budget impact when they are "open," whether or not they are called upon to testify. There are many daily contacts over the telephone.

Senator Harry Byrd, Sr., was for many years chairman of the Senate Committee on Finance and was also chairman of the Joint Committee on Reduction of Nonessential Federal Expenditures. He held an annual meeting of this Joint Committee, at which he liked to question the Director of the Budget about his activities in reducing nonessential federal expenditures. It also gave the Senator an opportunity to express his own strong views on this subject. He was a constant advocate of cutting or eliminating what he thought were nonessential expenditures and a strong supporter of the Budget Bureau.

For many years, Congressmen Clarence Cannon of Missouri and John Taber of New York were majority and minority leaders of the House Appropriations Committee, according to which Party was in power. Frequent meetings were held with them during the year, and each of them was helpful on certain occasions, difficult on others. They both liked the object classifications in the Budget presentation and objected to the change-over to the project classifications. In fact, when this change-over had become complete they insisted that a separate annex be printed showing objects, as previously prepared, just for their own personal convenience. It always seemed to the Bureau that the number of typewriters in the State Department or the number of automobiles in Defense did not in themselves indicate whether the operations were efficient. However, these congressional leaders used to compare the changes from year to year and would question the agency heads on these details. Being forewarned, the agency representatives were always ready with answers.

Intergovernmental Relations

A joint federal-state-action committee was appointed by President Eisenhower as a result of a suggestion he had made to the governors' conference in July, 1957, proposing closer relations between the federal and state governments. Five members were appointed by the President—the Secretary of the Treasury, who was co-chairman, the Secretary of Labor, the Secretary of Health, Education, and Welfare, the Director of the Budget, and a special assistant to the President. The governors appointed five members: Co-chairman Lane Dwinell of New Hampshire, Victor Anderson of Nebraska, James P. Coleman of Mississippi, Price Daniel of Texas, and George Docking of Kansas. A joint staff was appointed to assist the members and a number of productive meetings were held. This committee recommended that a permanent advisory commission on intergovernmental relations be established, and such a body was created on September 24, 1959. Then the committee did a most unusual thing—it requested the President to dissolve it as a formal body. Before doing so, a final report was submitted and a final resolution passed as follows:

> Whereas it is difficult for the Nation to abandon or for the States to recoup a governmental function once assumed by the Federal Government,
>
> It is the sense of the Joint Federal-State Action Committee that

the States and their political subdivisions should be encouraged to exercise their responsibilities with increased diligence and that the Federal Government, except in serious emergencies, should not enter or assume any new or additional function in fields of traditional State or local activity.

In its final report the committee made a number of telling points, some of which are quoted below:

> In the Committee's view, the best way to avoid an unnecessary concentration of governmental responsibility in Washington is to prevent in advance, whenever possible, the need for "crash" programs involving the national government. In some measure, the present degree of Federal participation in State and local affairs reflects previous failures to anticipate needs. This failure in a sense creates a vacuum into which the Federal Government almost irresistibly moves or is forced.
>
> 1. Careful selectivity is essential in considering any future proposals for Federal stimulative grants;
> 2. Such grants should be made only where a clear-cut national interest exists and where such action encourages State and local authorities to assume or carry out functions for which they are primarily responsible;
> 3. Built-in mechanisms should be included in such grant legislation to prevent continuing operating responsibilities by the Federal Government in spheres properly State and local in scope; and
> 4. In any future stimulative grant program that might be established, the States and localities should have the utmost flexibility and control in the administration of the program and funds, in keeping with the purpose of the Federal legislation.

The stated purpose of the Act of September 24, 1959, which established the permanent Advisory Commission on Intergovernmental Relations, is:

> To bring together representatives of Federal, State, and local govern-

ments for consideration of common problems

To discuss the administration of Federal grant programs and the controls involved in their administration

To make available technical assistance to the executive and legislative branches of the Federal Government in the review of proposed legislation

To discuss emerging public problems that are likely to require intergovernmental cooperation

To recommend the most desirable allocation of governmental functions

To recommend methods of coordinating and simplifying tax laws and practices to achieve a more orderly and less competitive fiscal relationship between the levels of government

To reduce the burden of compliance for taxpayers

To authorize receipt of non-Federal funds.

The Advisory Commission on Intergovernmental Relations has now been in existence for nine years and has made many constructive suggestions. Its ninth annual report, dated January 31, 1968, directed particular attention to urban problems, which are under study by the Bureau and have an important impact on demands made in the federal budget:

> the apparent reason for much of the dissatisfaction of minority groups in the cities was and is rooted in local government structure and fiscal arrangements—including the "white noose" of the suburbs, under-financing of central city schools, inadequate housing, unbalanced patterns of State aid, and repressive restrictions upon the administration of public welfare. These and other sources of unrest stem primarily from State constitutions and statutes and are not directly controllable by Federal law or regulation.

The urban riots of 1967 produced wide disagreement on many points. One point of consensus, however, did emerge—the restoration of vitality in the Nation's urban areas is an assignment surpassing the present capabilities of any one level of government and even of all levels acting collectively. It was increasingly agreed that private enterprise must become more deeply involved in urban problems if these problems are to become manageable and if the metropolitan areas themselves are to remain governable.

It is becoming increasingly apparent that a considerable portion of the "infrastructure" of metropolitan problems is soluble only by State action. Restrictions upon the debt-carrying and taxing capacities of local governments; criteria for annexation of unincorporated areas; standards for the exercise of zoning powers; machinery for adoption and enforcement of building and housing codes; the ease or difficulty with which small suburban communities may be incorporated; the independence or dependence provided in the inherent powers of local governments in metropolitan areas—all of these very crucial determinants of the social, political, and economic fate of central cities is a matter of State constitutions or statute.

These statements are particularly significant because the Advisory Commission is composed of three private citizens, three members of the Senate, three members of the House of Representatives, three officers of the executive branch in the federal government, four governors of states, four mayors, three members of state legislative bodies, and three elected county officials. The federal programs to aid state and local governments have been expanding very rapidly and across agency lines, as indicated in Table 13, which shows the dollar amounts (in millions) of federal grants by Agency.

President Nixon appointed the Director of the Bureau of the Budget, Robert P. Mayo, as one of the three representatives of the Executive Branch on the Advisory Commission, and members of the staff of the Office of Executive Management spend considerable time in work connected with it.

The Operational Coordination staff is in charge of liaison with public interest groups, the Government Organization staff is responsible for improving intergovernmental organization, and the Financial Management staff is concerned with important budget controls at different levels. These projects have top priority under Bureau policy objectives. The President's August 13, 1969, message to Congress, with his revenue- or tax-sharing proposals will have important budget ef-

TABLE 13. FEDERAL GRANTS, BY AGENCY

	1967 Actual	1968 Estimate	1969 Estimate
Executive Office of the President	$ 0.4	$ 0.3	$ a
Funds appropriated to the President			
Economic opportunity programs	1,050.4	1,272.0	$1,426.0
Other (primarily public works acceleration and disaster relief)	74.6	195.9	267.6
Department of Agriculture	989.6	1,227.5	1,346.8
Department of Commerce	79.8	115.3	156.2
Department of Defense			
Military	26.4	27.1	32.5
Civil	14.5	28.2	71.6
Department of Health, Education and Welfare	7,182.0	8,776.2	9,395.4
Department of Housing and Urban Development	707.7	1,103.0	1,713.5
Department of the Interior	274.7	374.4	471.7
Department of Justice	2.6	16.1	50.6
Department of Labor	559.6	629.0	669.3
Department of State	6.6	6.1	5.5
Department of Transportation	4,092.5	4,371.0	4,417.0
Treasury Department	86.8	93.7	96.1
Civil Service Commission			12.0
Veterans Administration	9.9	13.4	14.8
Other independent agencies	23.4	30.8	51.7
National Capital region[b]	58.0	82.0	99.0
Total	$15,239.5	$18,362.3	$20,297.3

[a]Less than $500,000.

[b]Includes federal payments to the District of Columbia of the following amounts: 1967, $58.0 million; 1968, $70.0 million; 1969, $80.2 million.

Source: The 1969 Budget Message.

fects if enacted. The program consists of four major elements:

1. The size of the fund to be shared will be a stated percentage of total personal taxable income to be disbursed annually by the Treasury Department, starting with one-third of 1 per cent for the second half of fiscal year 1971 and increasing to a regular constant figure.

2. The allocation among the fifty states and the District of Colum-

bia will be based on the population adjusted for each state's revenue effort so as to give a bonus incentive for its own tax efforts.

3. Each state will distribute its participation by a prescribed formula among the local governments according to their share of total local government revenue raised in the state, unless some other distribution plan is worked out with its local governments.

4. Administrative requirements will be kept at a minimum.

During 1968, the Commission approved two major policy reports with recommendations for action by federal, state, and local governments: *Urban and Rural America, Policies for Future Growth,* and *Intergovernmental Problems in Medicaid* Two further research studies are now under way, one on state aid to local government and another on state-local responsibilities for labor-management relations in public employment.

Relations with the Press and the Public

The Bureau's mail is voluminous and, as in other agencies, nine of every ten letters contain a request. The Director always tries to explain the budgetary effects of proposals and the fiscal position of the government. Frequently, incoming letters are referred by other agencies and by the White House staff for answer by the Bureau.

The annual budget document itself is cumbersome and extremely difficult to understand. Various means of breaking it up have been tried such as publishing part of it as a "budget in brief" in a separate pamphlet. After Congress had completed action on the appropriation bills, a midyear review used to be published by the end of August in order to give a re-estimate of the then-current fiscal year's figures. Of course, this becomes impossible if Congress stays in session until November or December, but I think it should be done whenever possible. In recent years, special analyses have been published separately. They cover the important programs that cut across a number of government agencies. The 1969 and 1970 booklets include tables and explanations for credit programs, public works, education and training programs, health programs, federal research, and aid programs to state and local governments. These, I think, are helpful in educating the public and explaining their impact on the economy of the country.

The budget itself is now condensed and printed in a reasonably small book of about 500 pages. The detailed schedules and appropriations are included in an appendix that is like a telephone book and runs to 1,100-1,200 pages. The tables and explanations and the legislative language are essential to the congressional committees, even if they are not of much use to the general public.

The Bureau does not hold weekly or monthly press conferences as many other agencies do. At the time of the annual Budget Message, a press conference is held at which the Message is analyzed with charts and a rather detailed presentation covering the most important programs. When I was in the Bureau, all the office and division heads and chief assistants were present at these press conferences, which were attended by nearly a hundred representatives of the press, domestic and foreign. The sessions lasted from two to three hours, and the questions were always intelligent and well-phrased. I liked to make a general statement and call upon the best expert in each particular field to supplement my answers to questions. We seemed to get a pretty good coverage in the press, judging from the clippings collected afterward. Such conferences are a very important way of conveying budget problems to the public.

The Director and his assistants are invited throughout the year to address business association meetings in all sections of the country. They generally try to accept or at least designate someone to attend, because they are anxious to explain the budget impact of the programs demanded by the public.

The Bureau's Advisory Council on Federal Reports was organized in 1942. Its purpose is to advise and help the Bureau's Office of Statistical Policy in simplifying and improving federal questionnaires, reporting procedures, and statistical programs. Five national business organizations are members of the Advisory Council: the American Retail Federation, the American Society of Association Executives, the Chamber of Commerce of the United States, the Financial Executives Institute, and the National Association of Manufacturers. Many other industry groups, such as the Machinery and Allied Products Institute, the National Association of Broadcasters, and the National Small Business Association, are also represented through the American Society of Association Executives.

Many of the executive agencies have their own advisory committees, composed of representatives of business and other groups. The Business Advisory Committee of the Department of Commerce is one of the most useful, since the meetings are well attended by representatives of many important business interests in the country. As Director of the Budget, I was frequently invited to address this group, which gave me a good opportunity to explain informally some of the nation's budgetary problems on which the cooperation of the business community was needed.

In addition to these contacts with the press, the general public, and the special interest groups, the Budget Director and his deputy, like other Presidential appointees, are expected to attend many social functions, both official and unofficial, in Washington. For that matter, all high-ranking representatives of the executive departments and agencies are expected to meet as many people as possible and to explain government views and programs to everyone interested— including diplomats and visitors from other nations. The large "national day" and other receptions at the hundred-odd embassies in the capital, White House dinners and receptions, and other gatherings offer many such opportunities.

Washington social life also serves another useful purpose, which is worth mentioning. Since every official's working day is full of meetings, it is sometimes, for weeks on end, difficult to make appointments to see certain persons. A few minutes' conversation at a party may save an interminable delay in getting some bit of needed information. I found this to be true with Treasury and State Department officials, as well as congressional leaders.

In general, however, social contacts are simply one extension of the kind of communication the Budget Bureau must maintain with all of its publics. What is interesting, in cosmopolitan Washington, is how often the questioner is someone from another nation, curious about the operations of an agency to which there is no parallel in his home government —and very much aware of the Bureau's significance not only in the domestic affairs but also to the world-wide commitments of the United States.

XII

Budget Trends and Opportunities

A substantial part of every Budget Director's time is devoted, not to the Bureau's affairs narrowly conceived, but to participation in conferences on high national policy, both domestic and foreign. Nor is such involvement confined merely to the Director. It is important that key members of the staff and their assistants also concern themselves with the inevitable impact of national policies. Fully as important is the role of the Bureau as a clearinghouse for and coordinator of "the President's program"; far more often than the public realizes, the Bureau is itself a contributor to the formulation of this program.

As an analytical and planning center for policies that are both short and long range, the Bureau of the Budget is concerned with the magnitude of the budget totals, their mixture, and their net result on the peace, security, and well-being of the United States. Today, all these factors are as much affected by what is happening outside the nation's boundaries as within. The trend of budget expenditures since World War II—and especially during the last three years—brings this out clearly.

Recent Figures

Before taking a closer look at recent budget figures and trends, it is interesting to consider the long historic record. For that reason, Table 14, taken from the 1969 Budget Message, and showing the administrative budgets since 1789, is reproduced immediately following, along with Table 15, showing income receipts over the past ten years and estimates for fiscal 1968 and 1969, and Table 16, showing expenditures and net lending for the same period. The first of these tables gives the only statistical information on a reasonable, consistent basis available for the full span of years; the other two show administrative budget figures plus trust funds, on the all-inclusive basis only recently adopted.

TABLE 14. THE "ADMINISTRATION BUDGET" AND PUBLIC DEBT, 1789–1969 (in millions of dollars)

Fiscal Year	Administrative Budget			Public Debt at End of Year
	Re-ceipts	Ex-pen-ditures	Net	
1789-1849	1,160	1,090	+70	63
1850-1899	13,895	14,932	-1,037	1,437
1900	567	521	+46	1,263
1901	588	525	+63	1,222
1902	562	485	+77	1,178
1903	562	517	+45	1,159
1904	541	584	-43	1,136
1905	544	567	-23	1,132
1906	595	570	+25	1 143
1907	666	579	+87	1,147
1908	602	659	-57	1,178
1909	604	694	-89	1,148
1910	676	694	-18	1,147

TABLE 14 *(cont.)*

| Fiscal Year | Administrative Budget | | | Public Debt at End of Year |
	Receipts	Expenditures	Net	
1911	702	691	+11	1,154
1912	693	690	+3	1,194
1913	714	715	*	1,193
1914	725	725	*	1,188
1915	683	746	-63	1,191
1916	762	713	+48	1,225
1917	1,100	1,954	-853	2,976
1918	3,630	12,662	-9,032	12,455
1919	5,085	18,448	-13,363	25,485
1920	6,649	6,357	+291	24,299
1921	5,567	5,058	+509	23,977
1922	4,021	3,285	+736	22,963
1923	3,849	3,137	+713	22,350
1924	3,853	2,890	+963	21,251
1925	3,598	2,881	+717	20,516
1926	3,753	2,888	+865	19,643
1927	3,992	2,837	+1,155	18,512
1928	3,872	2,933	+939	17,604
1929	3,861	3,127	+734	16,931
1930	4,058	3,320	+738	16,185
1931	3,116	3,577	-462	16,801
1932	1,924	4,659	-2,735	19,487
1933	1,997	4,598	-2,602	22,539
1934	3,015	6,645	-3,630	27,734
1935	3,706	6,497	-2,791	32,824
1936	3,997	8,422	-4,425	38,497
1937	4,956	7,733	-2,777	41,089
1938	5,588	6,765	-1,177	42,018
1939	4,979	8,841	-3,862	45,890
1940	5,137	9,055	-3,918	48,497

TABLE 14 *(cont.)*

Fiscal Year	Administrative Budget			Public Debt at End of Year
	Re-ceipts	Ex-pen-ditures	Net	
1941	7,096	13,255	−6,195	55,332
1942	12,547	34,037	−21,490	76,991
1943	21,947	79,368	−57,420	140,796
1944	43,563	94,986	−51,423	202,626
1945	44,362	98,303	−53,941	259,115
1946	39,650	60,326	−20,676	269,898
1947	39,677	38,923	+754	258,376
1948	41,375	32,955	+8,419	252,366
1949	37,663	39,474	−1,811	252,798
1950	36,422	39,544	−3,122	257,377
1951	47,480	43,970	+3,510	255,251
1952	61,287	65,303	−4,017	259,151
1953	64,671	74,120	−9,449	266,123
1954	64,420	67,537	−3,117	271,341
1955	60,209	64,389	−4,180	274,418
1956	67,850	66,224	+1,626	272,825
1957	70,562	68,966	+1,596	270,634
1958	68,550	71,369	−2,819	276,444
1959	67,915	80,342	−12,427	284,817
1960	77,763	76,539	+1,224	286,471
1961	77,659	81,515	−3,856	289,211
1962	81,409	87,787	−6,378	298,645
1963	86,376	92,642	−6,266	306,466
1964	89,459	97,684	−8,226	312,526
1965	93,072	96,507	−3,435	317,864
1966	104,727	106,978	−2,251	320,369
1967	115,849	125,718	−9,869	326,733
1968 est	118,575	137,182	−18,607	351,599
1969 est	135,587	147,363	−11,776	363,540

*Less than $500,000.

Source: The 1969 Budget Message.

TABLE 15. BUDGET RECEIPTS, BY SOURCE, 1958–69
(in millions of dollars)

Description	Actual										Estimate	
	1958	1959	1960	1961	1962	1963	1964	1965	1966	1967	1968	1969
Individual income taxes	34,724	36,719	40,715	41,338	45,571	47,588	48,697	48,792	55,446	61,526	67,700	80,900
Corporation income taxes	20,074	17,309	21,494	20,955	20,523	21,579	23,492	25,461	30,073	33,971	31,300	34,300
Employment taxes	8,624	8,821	11,248	12,679	12,835	14,746	16,959	17,358	20,662	27,823	29,730	34,154
Unemployment insurance	1,924	2,131	2,668	2,904	3,337	4,112	4,045	3,819	3,777	3,652	3,660	3,594
Premiums for insurance and retirement	682	769	768	866	873	944	1,006	1,079	1,126	1,853	2,049	2,275
Excise taxes	10,638	10,578	11,676	11,860	12,534	13,194	13,731	14,570	13,061	13,719	13,848	14,671
Estate and gift taxes	1,393	1,333	1,606	1,896	2,016	2,167	2,394	2,716	3,066	2,978	3,100	3,400
Customs	781	925	1,105	982	1,142	1,206	1,252	1,442	1,767	1,901	2,000	2,070
Other receipts	777	463	1,200	913	825	1,042	1,126	1,617	1,923	2,168	2,443	2,744
Total, budget receipts	79,617	79,048	92,481	94,393	99,656	106,578	112,702	116,855	130,901	149,591	155,830	178,108
MEMORANDUM												
(Excluded above; offset against expenditures)												
Interfund and intragovernmental transactions	4,119	5,330	5,309	6,508	5,654	7,099	6,655	6,761	7,592	6,588	7,415	8,241
Proprietary receipts from the public										4,948	4,430	4,617

Source: The 1969 Budget Message.

TABLE 16. BUDGET OUTLAYS, BY FUNCTION, 1958–69
(in millions of dollars)

Description	Actual										Estimate	
	1958	1959	1960	1961	1962	1963	1964	1965	1966	1967	1968	1969
Expenditures												
National defense	44,461	46,667	45,848	47,532	51,179	52,275	53,682	49,586	56,771	70,095	76,491	79,792
International affairs and finance	2,912	2,790	3,310	3,242	4,034	4,279	4,434	4,196	4,343	4,110	4,330	4,478
Space research and technology	89	145	401	744	1,257	2,252	4,171	5,091	5,932	5,424	4,804	4,574
Agriculture and agricultural resources	2,541	4,718	2,893	2,877	3,491	4,398	4,545	4,032	2,764	3,156	4,412	4,474
Natural resources	1,203	1,233	1,084	1,626	1,736	1,607	2,042	2,140	2,167	2,113	2,416	2,483
Commerce and transportation	2,922	4,367	4,643	4,929	5,193	5,516	6,283	7,043	6,789	7,308	7,695	7,996
Housing and community development	-36	30	21	157	160	193	151	116	442	578	698	1,428
Health, labor, and welfare	15,763	18,019	19,105	22,368	23,963	25,677	27,201	28,143	33,194	39,512	46,396	51,945
Education	375	550	659	740	842	953	1,109	1,309	2,449	3,602	4,157	4,364
Veterans benefits and services	5,076	5,183	5,063	5,392	5,378	5,666	5,552	5,634	5,707	6,366	6,798	7,131
Interest	6,936	7,070	8,299	8,108	8,321	9,215	9,810	10,358	11,285	12,548	13,535	14,400
General government	1,010	1,159	1,332	1,508	1,653	1,799	2,072	2,231	2,316	2,452	2,618	2,827
Special allowances											100	1,950
Undistributed adjustments to amounts above	-2,076	-2,239	-2,272	-2,506	-2,547	-2,666	-2,931	-3,164	-3,421	-4,022	-4,591	-5,049
Total, expenditures	81,177	89,693	90,385	96,717	104,660	111,465	118,122	116,715	130,740	153,238	169,856	182,797
Net Lending												
National defense	1	-12	-7	-41	*	-64	-31	-3	-1	-3	-2	-4
International affairs and finance	433	418	-235	127	528	-95	-283	-21	100	540	716	675
Agriculture and agricultural resources	472	700	457	462	648	731	642	777	911	1,221	899	1,135
Natural resources	3	6	11	18	21	18	23	16	19	19	16	7
Commerce and transportation	56	71	27	74	193	145	139	275	193	138	158	125
Housing and community development	165	1,064	1,078	64	490	-1,012	-301	-147	1,984	1,708	3,257	1,355
Health, labor, and welfare	*	1	*	*	1	1	2	19	32	572	21	-538
Education	165	180	204	201	231	288	225	229	376	445	384	335
Veterans benefits and services	261	245	363	296	248	-146	129	88	214	532	370	211
General government	-12	-14	-15	-3	-8	-11	-1	16	5	2	-40	-37
Total, net lending	1,544	2,659	1,882	1,198	2,351	-145	545	1,249	3,832	5,176	5,779	3,265
Total, expenditures and net lending	82,720	92,352	92,268	97,915	107,011	111,320	118,667	117,966	134,572	158,414	175,635	186,062

*Less than $500,000.
Source: The 1969 Budget Message.

In addition to the very large increases in military and space programs, all kinds of domestic programs have been showing rapid increases in spending. For example, various programs for rehabilitation, work support, and training through institutions and on the job have curved upward in the last six years, as shown in Chart 5.

Chart 5

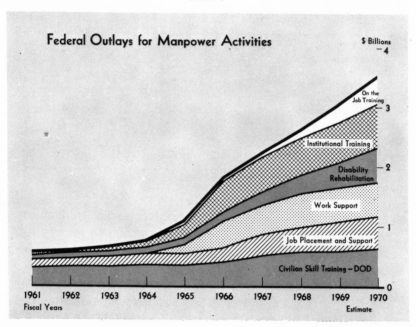

Federal involvement in education, beyond vocational guidance in very moderate grants, is an important development of the last few years. Payments to local educational agencies were first authorized in 1950, but only during the second half of the 1960's have educational programs become a major federal activity, (which, with the rapid increase in costs and a larger percentage of the nation's youth demanding higher education, is likely to increase in the future). During the last six years, according to the BOB "Special Analyses," federal outlays for education have increased in all categories by the following amounts (in millions of dollars):

Education Level	Outlays					
	1964		1968 Actual	1969 Estimate	1970	
	Ac- tual	Per cent			Esti- mate	Per cent
Elementary and secondary	546	17	3,228	3,052	3,358	34
Higher	1,742	56	4,363	4,651	5,030	51
Adult and continuing	108	3	306	336	357	4
Training of public employees	309	10	402	457	494	5
Foreign	169	5	242	290	292	3
Other	246	8	223	257	271	3
Total	3,121	100	8,764	9,043	9,802	100

Source: Special Analyses 1970 Budget Message.

The tremendous expansion of research and development expenditures since World War II has contributed greatly to the growth of industry and the economy generally. According to the BOB "Special Analyses," expenditures in this area by the federal government more than doubled between 1954 and 1960 and again between 1960 and 1969, as indicated (in millions of dollars) below:

Fiscal Year	DOD	NASA[1]	AEC	HEW	NSF	Other	Total
1954	2,487	90	383	63	4	121	3,148
1955	2,630	74	385	70	9	140	3,308
1956	2,639	71	474	86	15	161	3,446
1957	3,371	76	657	144	31	183	4,462
1958	3,664	89	804	180	33	220	4,990
1959	4,183	145	877	253	51	293	5,803
1960	5,654	401	986	324	58	315	7,738

Fiscal Year	DOD	NASA[1]	AEC	HEW	NSF	Other	Total
1961	6,618	744	1,111	374	77	356	9,278
1962	6,812	1,257	1,284	512	105	403	10,373
1963	6,849	2,552	1,335	632	142	478	11,988
1964	7,517	4,171	1,505	793	190	519	14,694
1965	6,728	5,093	1,520	738	192	604	14,875
1966	6,735	5,933	1,462	879	225	768	16,002
1967	7,680	5,426	1,467	1,075	277	917	16,842
1968	8,148	4,724	1,593	1,250	315	835	16,865
1969 estimate	8,036	4,250	1,668	1,181	336	954	16,425
1970 estimate	8,254	3,950	1,721	1,321	348	1,106	16,700

[1]National Advisory Committee for Aeronautics prior to 1958.
Source: Special Analyses 1970 Budget Message.

Federal payments toward medical assistance and health care have grown even more rapidly, particularly through Medicare and Medicaid, as shown in Chart 6.

Chart 6

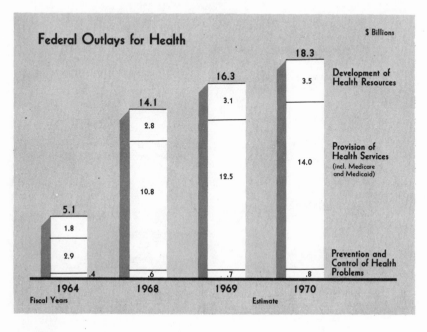

Federal expenditures for public works, after increasing rapidly from 1961 to 1964, tended to even off for the next four years, but the 1970 recommendations, showed a 12 per cent increase.

The largest increases of all have been in grants to state and local governments for federal highways and airport expansion. The over-all needs of the state and local governments are growing as rapidly as those of the federal government, while the yield from property taxation has been approaching its potential limits. Federal aid programs have been growing in importance in categorical grants, allocation of user charges, and block grants. Chart 7 shows the large amounts involved and the rapidly increasing trend.

Chart 7

Federal Aid to State and Local Governments

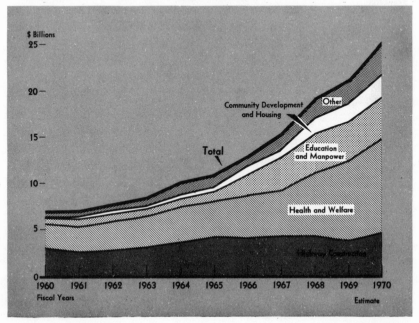

The difficulties experienced by the President and the Budget Bureau in presenting figures for anticipated receipts and disbursements before congressional action are evident from the following table, compiled by the author, showing total receipts and outlays, in billions of dollars, for the three fiscal years 1968, 1969, and 1970:

Fiscal Year		Receipts	Outlays	+Surplus −Deficit
1968	Per original 1968 Budget Message, January 24, 1967. Total cash receipts and payments	168.1	172.4	− 4.3
	As revised in 1969 Budget Message, January 29, 1968	155.8	175.6	−19.8
	Final, as reported in 1970 Budget Message, January 15, 1969	153.7	178.9	−25.2
1969	Per original 1969 Budget Message	178.1	186.1	− 8.0
	As revised in 1970 Budget Message	186.1	183.7	+ 2.4
	As reported in joint statement by Secretary of the Treasury Kennedy and Budget Director Mayo, July 28, 1969	187.8	184.8	+ 3.1
1970	Per original 1970 Budget Message	198.7	195.3	+ 3.4
	As revised in Budget Bureau's "Summer Review," August, 1969	198.8	192.9	+ 5.9

Some of these difficulties have been due to the closest approach to runaway inflation that the nation has ever experienced. The government has been partly responsible. In fiscal 1968, it permitted a $25.2 billion deficit, the largest in history except for three years during World War II. In addition, Congress voted, in early 1969, for large increases in compensation for itself and the upper echelons of government. In these circumstances, neither business nor labor took any steps to support the government's fiscal and monetary restraints. Accountants should take some blame for failing to require changes for price-level adjustment in financial statements by business and government. (The author here includes himself, for comparative figures used in this book.)

The most significant changes in income for fiscal 1968 resulted from the original overestimates caused by the inclusion of the anticipated yield of the surtax that President Johnson had requested on individual and corporate income taxes, for which a bill was not passed until June 2, 1968. They are shown, in billions of dollars, in more detail in the table opposite.

The drop in miscellaneous receipts for fiscal 1968 between the original estimate and the revised estimate is largely the result of reclassification due to the eliminatio of certain receipts arising out of what are called "the proprietary activities of the government," which are now deducted from expenditures of the agencies involved in accordance with the recommendations of the President's Commission on Budget Concepts. The increase in 1968 outlays between the original Budget Message and the revision a year later is correspondingly understated.

The changes in conditions between the dates of the original budget messages, later estimates, and the final figures caused wide variations in both receipts and expenditures. The increase of almost $4 billion in the national defense budget for fiscal 1968 seems to have become apparent only after January of that year. The increase in interest charges, however, was forecast before the end of calendar 1967.

	1968			1969		1970
	Original Estimate	Revised Estimate	Actual	Original Estimate	Revised Estimate	Original Estimate
Individual income taxes	73.2	67.7	68.7	80.9	84.4	90.4
Corporation income taxes	33.9	31.3	28.7	34.3	38.1	37.9
Employment taxes	28.4	29.7	29.2	34.2	34.8	39.9
Excise taxes	13.7	13.8	14.0	14.7	14.8	15.7
Estate and gift taxes and customs	5.2	5.1	5.1	5.4	5.5	5.7
Miscellaneous	13.6	8.2	7.9	8.6	8.4	9.1
Total receipts	168.1	155.8	153.7	178.1	186.1	198.7

The mounting deficit during fiscal 1967 and 1968 caused such serious concern throughout the country that something had to be done in Washington. The result was to force agreement between Congress and the President, in spite of the fact that it was an election year. Congress passed and President Johnson signed a bill on June 29, 1968, that became the Revenue and Expense Act of 1968. This remarkable historical document, cut obligational authority already established by Congress. It provided the 10 per cent surtax on incomes, effective January 1, 1968, for corporations and April 1, 1968, for individuals, which the President had requested earlier, but it also required an accompanying cut in expenditures, which the President described in a prepared statement in part as follows:

This bill deals with expenditures as well as taxes. It requires the President to reduce Federal expenditures by $6 billion from the January budget for the fiscal year 1969. . . . The Congress—as a condition of its approval for the tax bill—has imposed a deep reduction in that budget.

I have accepted this decision of the Congress because the tax bill is so imperative to the economic health of the nation.

It is my belief that in the course of the normal appropriations process Congress will reduce the budget by considerably less than $6 billion. In that event, under the law I sign today, Congress will shift to the President the responsibility for making reductions in programs which the Congress itself is unwilling to do.

This departure from the traditional appropriations process is most unwise. I believe Congress also acted unwisely in the requirement that Federal employment be rolled back to the level of two years ago. This conflicts with the needs of a growing nation for increased and efficient public services.

National Debt and Contingent Liabilities

The amount borrowed from the public as of June 30, 1969, represented by "public debt securities," was $353.7

billion. Agency securities, principally family housing mortgages and participation certificates issued by the government
National Mortgage Association and the Export-Import Bank,
amounted to $14.3 billion, making the total federal securities
issued at that date $368 billion. Of this amount, the $87.7
billion held as investments by government trust funds was
only a relatively small fraction of the actuarial liabilities.

In addition, the contingent liabilities and commitments of
the federal government are more than twice the direct liability. The Federal Deposit Insurance Corporation had
$296.7 billion of insurance in force on December 31, 1968
(the latest available figure), and the Federal Savings and Loan
Insurance Corporation had $132.9 billion insurance in force
at the same date. Although totals mean nothing except as
measures of magnitude, the amount of insurance in force for
all agencies exceeds $600 billion; the government loan and
credit guarantees amount to approximately $100 billion; and
undelivered orders, approximately $75 billion.

Present Portents

Charles L Schultze, former Director of the Budget, in a
chapter entitled "Budget Alternatives After Vietnam" in
Agenda for the Nation, edited by Kermit Gordon (Washington, D.C.: Brookings Institution, in press), discusses the
government receipts that may become available in future
years with the ending of the war in Vietnam, and how they
might be spent. His very able presentation illustrates the
problems involved in forecasting generally, and in the military and several civilian areas specifically. He does not think
that reductions in the military budget will suffice to take care
of needed domestic programs, which must depend on the
expected annual increase in federal receipts from increases in
productivity and the gross national product. This second
source he calls a "fiscal dividend," which I think is a mis-

nomer and has unwise connotations for increased spending, since it is not a dividend in the ordinary sense and should be considered as available for reduction in the national debt as well as "to expand public programs or reduce tax rates."

In my opinion, also, increases in receipts due to increases in trust funds, particularly social security and employment taxes, should not be considered as general funds available for other programs. Social security taxes were planned to increase the trust fund receipts faster than current benefit payments would be increased so as to be able to build up some reserve toward the tremendous actuarial liability that is being created—which is, or will shortly be, larger than the amount of the national debt. In addition, I think that congressional action and current programs already have built in large increases for urban rehabilitation, subsidized housing, and aids to education—elementary, high school, college, and technical —that will absorb a large part of the gains from increased productivity and the gross national product so that the "surplus" available for a wide variety of other domestic and foreign needs will be small indeed.

However, with these reservations, I think Schultze's conclusions are sufficiently important to warrant summarizing here. He believes that several major facts stand out from an examination of the budget situation following cessation of hostilities in Vietnam:

1. The fiscal dividend during fiscal 1970 and 1971 will be relatively small. Expiration of the temporary surtax, large built-in increases in federal civilian expenditures, the probability of increasing non-Vietnam military outlays, and sharp increases in social security benefits will largely offset the growth in federal revenues and the budgetary savings from a cessation of the war.

2. In the subsequent three years, the annual fiscal dividend will increase rapidly, amounting to almost $40 billion by fiscal 1974.

3. Large claims will be made on the fiscal dividend for expanding high-priority social programs and launching new program initiatives.

4. Three major sets of policy decisions could expand the fiscal dividend substantially: First, a re-examination of U.S. strategic weapons policy and overseas commitments could reduce non-Vietnam military spending; second, some part of the rapid increase in payroll tax revenues could be captured for the fiscal dividend rather than being used in toto to raise social security benefits; and third, a rigorous screening of existing federal programs could produce significant budgetary savings.

Schultze testified to much the same effect before the Sub-committee on Economy in Government of the Joint Economic Committee of the Congress on June 3, 1969 and was questioned closely by Senator William Proxmire. In these hearings on "The Military Budget and National Priorities," Schultze also said that BOB officials during the Johnson Administration had taken a hard look at the cost-effectiveness of weapons systems but had not questioned the need for such systems. Present Budget Director Mayo, in subsequent testimony before the same subcommittee on June 12, said that President Nixon had changed procedures to give the Bureau as much opportunity to challenge Defense Department spending as the spending of any of the civilian agencies.

Budget Director Mayo also submitted a formal statement for the Proxmire hearings, in which he said:

In our economic planning for the period following the end of Vietnam hostilities, we expect to obtain greater resources for the Federal sector from two sources. One source involves the growth dividend that will be derived from the additional tax revenues yielded by an expanding economy. The other involves the so-called peace dividend that will be derived from reduced spending in Southeast Asia. It is generally accepted that the annual growth dividend will amount to about $15 billion by fiscal year 1972, which would be beyond the period of the elimination of the surcharge. However, at least half of that amount will have to be used to finance the built-in expenditure increases in existing programs referred to earlier. Thus, in each year in the future no more than half of the growth dividend will be available for program expansion or tax reduction.

As a result, it is clear that the extent to which we redirect funds from Southeast Asia will largely determine our ability to:

—expand existing civilian programs,

—introduce new civilian programs,

—reduce taxes,

—share revenues with State and local governments, and

—restore non-Vietnam national security programs to appropriate levels (in real terms).

Early in his Administration, President Nixon directed that a thorough review be made of all Federal programs—military as well as non-military. The first phase of the review was concluded when revised budget estimates for fiscal year 1970 were published in mid-April. As indicated earlier, we are continuing to evaluate those estimates. In establishing priorities for the fiscal 1971 budget, we are taking a hard look at the military budget and its relationship to other national priorities, with a heavy reliance on continuing program evaluation. . . .

The magnitude of the Defense budget is largely a function of the existing and potential threats to the Nation and its international commitments. To be sure, alternative budgets are possible, given these commitments; it is possible to procure more or less forces, depending on the assessment of risks, strengths of allies, and the number and kind of contingencies we want to face. Also, as this Committee has stressed, the level of the Defense budget depends on the efficiency and management control we exert in acquiring equipment and supplies. But, while we will—as we must—insist upon efficient procurement to reduce costs, considerably lower defense costs will be obtained only if we reduce our international commitments significantly. Such a decision can be made only by the President, with the consent of the Congress.

Director Mayo included with his testimony a table, reproduced here as Table 17, which illustrated very clearly the recent changes in kinds of U.S. spending.

TABLE 17. CHANGING COMPOSITION OF FEDERAL BUDGET OUTLAYS, 1959–69 (fiscal years)

Functional Categories	Outlays (in billions of dollars)			Percentage Distribution			Change: 1959 to 1969 (in billions of dollars)
	1959	1964	1969	1959	1964	1969	
National defense							
DOD, military	41.5	49.6	77.8	45.0	41.8	41.9	36.3
Military assistance program (MAP)	2.2	1.2	0.6	2.4	1.0	0.3	-1.6
Subtotal, military and MAP	43.7	50.8	78.4	47.4	42.8	42.2	34.7
(Support of Southeast Asia operations	(−)	(−)	(28.8)	(−)	(−)	(15.5)	(28.8)
Other	2.9	2.8	2.6	3.2	2.4	1.4	-.3
Subtotal, national defense	46.6	53.6	81.0	50.6	45.2	43.6	34.4
Civilian programs							
International affairs and finance	3.3	4.1	4.0	3.5	3.5	2.1	0.7
Space	.1	4.2	4.2	0.2	3.5	2.3	4.1
Agriculture and natural resources	6.6	7.2	9.0	7.1	6.0	4.9	2.4
Human resources programs	19.6	28.4	58.1	21.3	24.0	31.3	38.5
Veterans	5.4	5.7	7.7	5.9	4.8	4.2	2.3
Other civilian programs	5.6	8.5	11.0	6.1	7.2	5.9	5.4

TABLE 17 *(cont.)*

Functional Categories	Outlays (in billions of dollars)			Percentage Distribution			Change: 1959 to 1969 (in billions of dollars)
	1959	1964	1969	1959	1964	1969	
Subtotal, civilian programs	40.6	58.1	94.1	44.1	49.0	50.7	53.4
Interest	7.1	9.8	15.6	7.7	8.3	8.4	8.5
Undistributed intra-governmental transactions	-2.2	-2.9	-5.1	-2.4	-2.5	-2.8	-2.9
Total	92.1	118.6	185.6	100.0	100.0	100.0	93.5

Note: Detail will not necessarily add to totals because of rounding.

Future Hopes

A study of the foregoing material makes it possible to forecast some trends for government receipts and expenditures during the 1970's. The tremendous growth experienced by the American economy and that of the whole free world during the 1960's will undoubtedly continue (preferably at a reduced pace). If the United States can check inflation or limit it to something like 2 per cent a year, which is the announced policy of the present Administration and the Federal Reserve Board, we can expect to avoid a big bust and the recession that would inevitably follow unbridled inflation. In any case, the gross national product will reach $1 trillion during fiscal 1971. Total budget receipts under present laws should reach $200 billion in fiscal 1971. Barring a world conflagration, the feeling of the country is such that it is unlikely that the national defense figure will exceed $80 billion. The resources becoming available in the years ahead should allow an increasingly effective attack on domestic problems.

It is not within the scope of this book to forecast the budget situation for the 1970's, but it is clear that it will offer great opportunities for progress and tax reduction at the same time, particularly if the nation's leaders and its citizenry use imagination and courage in tackling social and international problems. It is to these considerations I now turn. The United States at the present time must have, it seems to me, three basic goals:

1. The attainment of world stability without major wars, if not world peace
2. Control of inflation, certainly of the galloping kind, within the United States, and a more stable international currency
3. The reduction of domestic disorders, particularly interracial problems and the crime wave, with greater progress in urban rehabilitation

These are all of serious moment to the Bureau of the Budget, and a great deal of time and attention has been directed to developing plans toward their achievement. Some measure of success will mean a tremendous opportunity to reduce taxes and reallocate the resources that will become available in the future to more productive areas. This in turn will produce cumulative gains all along the line.

As a former Director of the Bureau of the Budget, may I, in conclusion, permit myself the luxury of indicating my purely personal judgment with reference to certain issues of the first magnitude that are already confronting the nation, and which the Bureau must make objects of its concern. Most of them are relevant to one or more of the three goals noted above.

I would give first priority to ways and means of strengthening and eventually uniting the North Atlantic community, with some open-end arrangement for other nations to join later. The history of the successes and missed opportunities in the area need not be repeated here. We are clearly at a watershed in these matters—with the Soviet aggression in Czechoslovakia and her strong presence in the Middle East. Although negotiations with the Soviet Union must continue at every level, experience has shown that we have had more success in reaching agreement with the Russians after each new achievement toward strengthening our allied position. Within the Atlantic Community, therefore, quiet exploration of areas of agreement, meetings of parliamentarians, summit conferences could and should be visualized as leading up to that "moment of truth" at which time we must seriously consider possible over-all constitutional arrangements.

Success in this proposal would accomplish more budgetary aims than anything else in sight, including a more stable international monetary system and correction of our balance-of-payment deficit. The Bureau of the Budget is and must be concerned with broad long-range proposals of this character if we are ever to obtain a proper mix in our budgetary expenditures within an appropriate proportion of our gross national product.

Population control through some kind of planned parenthood is another important budget objective both at home and abroad. Many of our foreign and domestic aid projects fail to accomplish their objective of raising the standard of living because of the too rapid increase in the number of recipients. Increasing food production will not suffice. The Foreign Assistance Act of 1967 for the first time included specific reference to "Programs Relating to Population Growth":

Sec. 291 General Provisions (a) It is the sense of the Congress that, while every nation is and should be free to determine its own policies and procedures with respect to problems of population growth and family planning within its own boundaries, nevertheless, voluntary family planning programs to provide individual couples with the knowledge and medical facilities to plan their family size in accordance with their own moral convictions and the latest medical information, can make a substantial contribution to improve health, family stability, greater individual opportunity, economic development, a sufficiency of food, and a higher standard of living.

Recent AID programs supported by the Bureau have authorized birth control information and appliances as an important part of the programs.

Another area for major change—this purely domestic—is surely a better coordination in fiscal policy between Congress and the executive branch of government. Control of inflation is certainly dependent upon coordinated leadership of the federal government. Our successive budget deficits have had a cumulative effect on prices and wage increases. These cannot be controlled without a more moderate and steady increase in desirable programs, even if this also moderates the rate of economic growth. President Nixon has indicated his determination to tackle this program. The events during the past two years have indicated the importance of steady growth rather than erratic ups and downs in the available funds. The lack of the essential cooperation between Congress and the executive branch resulted in failure to check the inflation at a sufficiently early date to be able to slow down the so-called over-heated economy by budget restraint, by the postponement of some new programs, the reduction of less important programs, and also by earlier tax increases. Some better instrumentality for arriving at a more prompt consensus and for more finely honed tools is imperative. The classical antagonism between the executive branch and Congress is outdated. The pressure on the Bureau of the Budget during the past two years has been extremely intense. All of the agency proposals have been scanned and rescanned for cuts and eliminations, and the results anticipated have not been obtained because of the reluctance of Congress and the President to specify the cuts and take responsibility for them.

Tax policy and administration come under the Treasury, but the Bureau of the Budget has more interest than most other agencies in the determination of the level and the means for raising the necessary revenues. Various proposals have been studied by the Bureau that would allow greater flexibility to meet economic changes between the date of the budget preparation and the date the need develops. Congress has been reluctant to grant the executive branch the initiative to raise or lower taxes even with the increasing emphasis on the importance of maintaining a high level of employment and reducing inflationary threats to a minimum. The Bureau believes that further study should be given to alternative plans that would allow more flexibility to meet sudden changes in conditions. A joint committee on taxation, something like the present congressional Committee on Internal Revenue Taxation but including representatives of the Treasury, the Bureau, and the Council of Economic Advisers, might be a useful agency to meet this objective. It might be expanded further at a later date to include representatives of state and local governments when plans are under consideration to substitute transfer of revenues rather than categorical or block grants in aid. A modification of this would be for the Congressional Joint Economic Committee, the Appropriation Committees, and the General Accounting Office to appoint representatives and staff to meet with representatives of the Council of Economic Advisers, the Treasury, and the Bureau of the Budget to exchange views about future programs and future budgets. This could prove to be very beneficial in cooperative planning on a continuing, not a spasmodic basis. If useful, this might even be extended to include representatives of the Department of State and the Senate Committee on Foreign Relations in a similar cooperative venture with Defense and the Senate Committee on Military Affairs. The Bureau of the Budget would, I am sure, be glad to suggest or furnish staff to assist in inaugurating some such joint planning efforts.

I would also urge that the creation of two new offices to relieve the President from some of his impossible burden be considered. All recent Presidents in some fashion or other have sought better over-all coordination in fields of foreign affairs and domestic administration.

Most parliamentary governments have a head-of-state, either a monarch or a president and, in addition, both a prime minister or first minister of the government and a foreign secretary or foreign minister. It would further our good relations with other nations and relieve the burdens upon the President and the Secretary of State, if a new office of prime minister or first minister were to be established. This would enable the Secretary of State to give more of his attention to the operating problems of the Department, to appointments, and to promotions. There is a general feeling outside of government that more leadership and less staff work inside the State Department is desirable. A reorganization plan was prepared in the Bureau some years ago to make this effective, and in addition to create a second vice-president, which would be an appointive post. The Vice-President of the United States, as President of the Senate, is required to give a considerable part of his time to congressional matters and is also expected to represent the President on important occasions in this country and abroad. Most industrial concerns have found it necessary to create an executive vice-president to look after the many departmental problems that require the full time of a principal executive officer. Such an appointive officer would become an important member of the Cabinet and would be the responsible head, under the President, for the actual operations of the government.

Our domestic problems are being tackled with earnestness

and vigor. More attention is being paid to underlying causes. The Bureau, most of the other agencies of government, and civil organizations are working on their solution. To lessen crime by dropouts, to end student disorders, for the education and training of our youth and the bridging of the so-called generation gap, and to ease racial friction, few things would be more helpful than some type of universal training. Several proposals have been studied by the Bureau. Any one of them would undoubtedly require several billion dollars a year at the outset, but it would result in much greater savings than that in the end. One of the better plans calls for every boy and girl upon reaching the age of eighteen or graduating from high school, whichever comes first, to give eighteen months of service to the country. This would offer an important new outlook and training to our young people, who would be used in areas where their capabilities lie. Those who so elected would be trained in a branch of defense. Others would go into the vital outdoor work required in forestry conservation, the development of national parks, and the building and landscaping of highways. Still others might work in the ghettoes and in such necessary public services as the post office. They would receive instruction and practice in how to live within a community, while the time spent, budgetwise, would more than pay for itself in that needed work would be done at a minimum pay scale and certain costs of welfare and crime prevention would be materially lessened. The great advantage of this plan, in my opinion, would be the broad opportunity it provides for training in the obligations and responsibilites that go with freedom. The recent demonstrations and the many applications for service in the Peace Corps indicate the great moral compulsions among young people, which need direction.

The advent of a new Administration always presents special opportunities for review, analysis, and improvements. Some of the situations that have been criticized may already have been corrected before this book is published, and some of the suggestions already adopted. There will be plenty of opportunity for further improvements, however, because this is an era of rapid change and the Bureau of the Budget is at the center of the federal establishment.

The Bureau and its Director are, or should be, the right arm of the President in coordinating and developing the over-all structure and policy of this, the most powerful government in the world. This is the measure of their importance—and their responsibility.

Appendix A

Careers in the
Bureau of the Budget

Broad-gauged-program analysts comprise the majority of the Budget Bureau's professional staff. Numerically, it is a small staff—about 360 professional and 180 support personnel. Their work relates figures with philosophy, aligns needs and resources, weighs choices, and develops priorities. Public service at this level is much more than a vocation. It is a unique privilege and a formidable challenge.

Requirements and Opportunities

Recruitment by the Bureau of the Budget is designed to attract outstanding young people for full careers in the federal service—people who are willing to learn and apply new techniques and procedures of management analysis, whether it be in program-planning-budgeting, work measurement, operations research, industrial engineering, or cost analysis. Graduate training in economics, political science, public administration, business administration, mathematics, science, or the law will prepare applicants for most positions. For all positions, major emphasis is placed on the candidate's demonstrated ability to analyze problems, to organize his findings, to communicate effectively both orally and in writing, and to work constructively with others.

A new staff member is usually assigned to one of six program divisions (Economics, Science, and Technology; General Government Management; Human Resources; International; Natural Resources; National

Security) or one of the functional offices (Budget Review, Legislative Reference, Executive Management, Program Evaluation, Statistical Policy). All positions are in Washington, D.C. A moderate amount of travel is involved in most assignments.

All candidates must pass a civil-service examination. For most candidates, this is the management-intern option of the Federal Service Entrance Examination. Applicants who are completing requirements for a Ph.D. or who have professional work experience may be able to apply through higher level examinations. They should consult Bureau representatives with regard to the appropriate avenues.

Opportunities for advancement are excellent. The Bureau's goal is the development of well-rounded career executives. Careful selection is only the initial step toward this objective. Newly appointed staff members usually work with a senior staff member in a team relationship, and they develop on the job. Responsibilities increase as rapidly as staff members can assume them. Rotation and transfer between organizational units and program areas are supplemented, when appropriate, by formal training.

Salaries and Job Satisfaction

Salaries are, by statute, comparable with those offered in private industry and by academic institutions. All Bureau employees enjoy the government's liberal leave and holiday policies. In addition, the government pays a large part of the cost for group life insurance, health insurance, and retirement.

A staff member of the Bureau of the Budget is granted the privilege —and accepts the responsibility—of serving the people of the United States by helping the President discharge his duties. The Bureau exists solely for that purpose. While pay is not the prime consideration to professional workers, federal-salary scales allow a satisfactory standard of living. More important, the staff member's assistance in solving some issue of public policy or in the successful carrying out of major government programs may make a distinct contribution to the nation that cannot be measured in material terms.

Summer and Temporary Employment

The Bureau usually appoints a limited number of outstanding graduate students each summer to work with regular staff members. Eligibility on an appropriate civil-service examination and interest in a long-range career with the Bureau of the Budget are important factors in selection. Throughout the year, there are also often temporary assignments available during periods of especially heavy work load.

Where to Get Additional Information

(1) Personnel Officer, Executive Office of the President, Bureau of the Budget, Washington, D.C. 20503—for additional information on the Bureau of the Budget, and its activities and to make application.

(2) School placement office—for additional material on the Bureau of the Budget and the federal Civil Service Commission and to make an appointment with visiting representatives of the Bureau.

(3) Offices of the U.S. Civil Service Commission—for material on Civil Service examinations that may not be available in school placement offices.

Appendix B

Selections from Principal Laws
Relating to the
Bureau of the Budget

Budget and Accounting Act of 1921
(31 U.S.C. 1), as Amended

SEC. 201. (a) The President shall transmit to Congress during the first fifteen days of each regular session, the Budget, which shall set forth his Budget message, summary data and text, and supporting detail. The Budget shall set forth in such form and detail as the President may determine—

(1) functions and activities of the Government;

(2) at such times as may be practicable, information on program costs and accomplishments;

(3) any other desirable classifications of data;

(4) a reconciliation of the summary data on expenditures with proposed appropriations;

(5) estimated expenditures and proposed appropriations necessary in his judgment for the support of the Government for the ensuing fiscal year, except that estimated expenditures and proposed appropriations for such year for the legislative branch of the Government and the Supreme Court of the United States shall be transmitted to the President on or before October 15 of each year, and shall be included by him in the Budget without revision;

(6) estimated receipts of the Government during the ensuing fiscal year, under (1) laws existing at the time the Budget is transmitted and

also (2) under the revenue proposals, if any, contained in the Budget;

(7) actual appropriations, expenditures, and receipts of the Government during the last completed fiscal year;

(8) estimated expenditures and receipts, and actual or proposed appropriations of the Government during the fiscal year in progress;

(9) balanced statements of (1) the condition of the Treasury at the end of the last completed fiscal year, (2) the estimated condition of the Treasury at the end of the fiscal year in progress, and (3) the estimated condition of the Treasury at the end of the ensuing fiscal year if the financial proposals contained in the Budget are adopted;

(10) all essential facts regarding the bonded and other indebtedness of the Government; and

(11) such other financial statements and data as in his opinion are necessary or desirable in order to make known in all practicable detail the financial condition of the Government. (31 U.S.C. 11)

SEC. 202. (a) If the estimated receipts for the ensuing fiscal year contained in the Budget, on the basis of laws existing at the time the Budget is transmitted, plus the estimated amounts in the Treasury at the close of the fiscal year in progress, available for expenditure in the ensuing fiscal year are less than the estimated expenditures for the ensuing fiscal year contained in the Budget, the President in the Budget shall make recommendations to Congress for new taxes, loans, or other appropriate action to meet the estimated deficiency.

(b) If the aggregate of such estimated receipts and such estimated amounts in the Treasury is greater than such estimated expenditures for the ensuing fiscal year, he shall make such recommendations as in his opinion the public interests require. (31 U.S.C. 13)

SEC. 203. (a) The President from time to time may transmit to Congress such proposed supplemental or deficiency appropriations as in his judgment (1) are necessary on account of laws enacted after the transmission of the Budget, or (2) are otherwise in the public interest. He shall accompany such proposals with a statement of the reasons therefor, including the reasons for their omission from the Budget.

(b) Whenever such proposed supplemental or deficiency appropriations reach an aggregate which, if they had been contained in the Budget, would have required the President to make a recommendation under subsection (a) of section 202, he shall thereupon make such recommendation. (31 U.S.C. 14)

SEC. 204. (a) Except as otherwise provided in this Act, the contents, order, and arrangement of the proposed appropriations and the statements of expenditures and estimated expenditures contained in the Budget or transmitted under section 203, and the notes and other data submitted therewith, shall conform to requirements prescribed by the President.

(b) The Budget, and statements furnished with any proposed supplemental or deficiency appropriations, shall be accompanied by information as to personal services and other objects of expenditure in the same manner and form as in the Budget for the fiscal year 1950: *Provided,* That this requirement may be waived or modified, either generally or in specific cases, by joint action of the committees of Congress having jurisdiction over appropriation: *And provided further,* That nothing in this Act shall be construed to limit the authority of committees of Congress to request and receive such information in such form as they may desire in consideration of and action upon budget estimates. (31 U.S.C. 581)

SEC. 205. Whenever any basic change is made in the form of the Budget, the President, in addition to the Budget, shall transmit to Congress such explanatory notes and tables as may be necessary to show where the various items embraced in the Budget of the prior year are contained in the new Budget. (31 U.S.C. 581a)

SEC. 206. No estimate or request for an appropriation and no request for an increase in an item of any such estimate or request, and no recommendation as to how the revenue needs of the Government should be met, shall be submitted to Congress or any committee thereof by any officer or employee of any department or establishment, unless at the request of either House of Congress. (31 U.S.C. 15)

SEC. 207. There is created in the Executive Office of the President a bureau to be known as the Bureau of the Budget. There shall be in the bureau a Director and a Deputy Director, who shall be appointed by the President. The deputy director shall perform such duties as the director may designate, and during the absence or incapacity of the director or during a vacancy in the office of director he shall act as director. The Bureau, under such rules and regulations as the President may prescribe, shall prepare the Budget, and any proposed supplemental or deficiency appropriations, and to this end shall have authority to assemble, correlate, revise, reduce, or increase the requests for appropriations of the several departments or establishments. (31 U.S.C. 16)

SEC. 208. The Director, under such rules and regulations as the President may prescribe, shall appoint attorneys and other employees and shall make expenditures for rent in the District of Columbia, printing, binding, telegrams, telephone service, law books, books of reference, periodicals, stationery, furniture, office equipment, other supplies, and necessary expenses of the office, within the appropriations made therefor. (31 U.S.C. 17)

SEC. 209. The Bureau, when directed by the President, shall make a detailed study of the departments and establishments for the purpose of enabling the President to determine what changes (with a view of securing greater economy and efficiency in the conduct of the public service) should be made in (1) the existing organization, activities, and methods of business of such departments or establishments, (2) the appropriations therefor, (3) the assignment of particular activities to particular services, or (4) the regrouping of services. The results of such study shall be embodied in a report or reports to the President, who may transmit to Congress such report or reports or any part thereof with his recommendations on the matters covered thereby. (31 U.S.C. 18)

The President, through the Director of the Bureau of the Budget, is authorized and directed to evaluate and develop improved plans for the organization, coordination, and management of the executive branch of the Government with a view to efficient and economical service. (31 U.S.C. 18a)

The President, through the Director of the Bureau of the Budget, is authorized and directed to develop programs and to issue regulations and orders for the improved gathering, compiling, analyzing, publishing, and disseminating of statistical information for any purpose by the various agencies in the executive branch of the Government. Such regulations and orders shall be adhered to by such agencies. (31 U.S.C. 18b)

Note. The two immediately preceding paragraphs were enacted as sections 104 and 103 of the Budget and Accounting Procedures Act of 1950, 64 Stat. 834, and were not specifically designated as amendments to the Budget and Accounting Act, 1921. They are included here as codified in the U.S. Code.

SEC. 212. The Bureau shall, at the request of any committee of either House of Congress having jurisdiction over revenue or appropriations, furnish the committee such aid and information as it may request. (31 U.S.C. 20)

SEC. 213. Under such regulations as the President may prescribe (1) every department and establishment shall furnish to the Bureau such information as the Bureau may from time to time require, and (2) the Director and the Deputy Director, or any employee of the Bureau when duly authorized, shall, for the purpose of securing such information, have access to, and the right to examine, any books, documents, papers, or records of any such department or establishment. (31 U.S.C. 21)

SEC. 214. The head of each department and establishment shall prepare or cause to be prepared in each year his requests for regular, supplemental, or deficiency appropriations. (31 U.S.C. 22)

SEC. 215. The head of each department and establishment shall submit his requests for appropriations to the Bureau on or before a date which the President shall determine. In case of his failure to do so, the President shall cause such requests to be prepared as are necessary to enable him to include such requests with the Budget in respect to the work of such department or establishment. (31 U.S.C. 23)

SEC. 216. (a) Requests for regular, supplemental, or deficiency appropriations which are submitted to the Bureau by the head of any department or establishment shall be prepared and submitted as the President may determine in accordance with the provisions of section 201.

(b) The requests of the departments and establishments for appropriations shall, in such manner and at such time as may be determined by the President, be developed from cost-based budgets.

(c) For purposes of administration and operation, such cost-based budgets shall be used by all departments and establishments and their subordinate units. Administrative subdivisions of appropriations or funds shall be made on the basis of such cost-based budgets. (31 U.S.C. 24; 70 Stat. 782)

Government Corporation Control Act of 1945, as Amended

SEC. 102. Each wholly owned Government corporation shall cause to be prepared annually a business-type budget which shall be submitted to the Bureau of the Budget, under such rules and regulations as the President may establish as to the date of submission, the form and content, the classifications of data, and the manner in which such budget program shall be prepared and presented. The budget program shall be a business-type budget, or plan of operations, with due allowance given to the need for flexibility, including provision for emergencies and contingencies, in order that the corporation may properly carry out its activities as authorized by law. The budget program shall contain estimates of the financial condition and operations of the corporation for the current and ensuing years and the actual condition and results of operation for the last completed fiscal year. Such budget program shall include a statement of financial condition, a statement of income and expense, an analysis of surplus or deficit, a statement of sources and application of funds, and such other supplementary statements and information as are necessary or desirable to make known the financial condition and operations of the corporation. Such statements shall include estimates of operations by major types of activities, together with estimates of administrative expenses, estimates of borrowings, and estimates of the amount of Government capital funds which shall be returned to the Treasury during the fiscal year or the appropriations required to provide for the restoration of capital impairments. (31 U.S.C. 847)

SEC. 103. The budget programs of the corporations as modified, amended, or revised by the President shall be transmitted to the Congress as a part of the annual Budget required by the Budget and Accounting Act, 1921. Amendments to the annual budget programs may be submitted from time to time.

Budget programs shall be submitted for all wholly owned Government corporations covering operations for the fiscal year commencing July 1, 1946, and each fiscal year thereafter. (31 U.S.C. 848)

SEC. 104. The Budget programs transmitted by the President to the Congress shall be considered and legislation shall be enacted making necessary appropriations, as may be authorized by law, making available for expenditure for operating and administrative expenses such corporate funds or other financial resources or limiting the use thereof as the Congress may determine and providing for repayment of capital funds and the payment of dividends. The provisions of this section shall not be construed as preventing Government corporations from carrying out and financing their activities as authorized by existing law, nor as affecting the provisions of section 26 of the Tennessee Valley Authority Act, as amended. The provisions of this section shall not be construed as affecting the existing authority of any Government corporation to make contracts or other commitments without reference to fiscal year limitations. (31 U.S.C. 849)

SEC. 107. Whenever it is deemed by the Director of the Bureau of the Budget, with the approval of the President, to be practicable and in the public interest that any wholly owned Government corporation be treated with respect to its appropriations, expenditures, receipts, accounting, and other fiscal matters as if it were a Government agency other than a corporation, the Director shall include in connection with the budget program of such corporation in the Budget a recommendation to that effect. If the Congress approves such recommendation in connection with the budget program for any fiscal year, such corporation, with respect to subsequent fiscal years, shall be regarded as an establishment other than a corporation for the purposes of the Budget and Accounting Act, 1921, and other provisions of law relating to appropriations, expenditures, receipts, accounts, and other fiscal matters, and shall not be subject to the provisions of this Act other than this section. The corporate entity shall not be affected by this section. (31 U.S.C. 852)

Budget and Accounting Procedures Act of 1950

SEC. 103. The President, through the Director of the Bureau of the Budget, is authorized and directed to develop programs and to issue regulations and orders for the improved gathering, compiling, analyzing, publishing, and disseminating of statistical information for any purpose by the various agencies in the executive branch of the Government. Such regulations and orders shall be adhered to by such agencies. (31 U.S.C. 18b)

SEC. 104. The President, through the Director of the Bureau of the Budget, is authorized and directed to evaluate and develop improved plans for the organization, coordination, and management of the executive branch of the Government with a view to efficient and economical service. (31 U.S.C. 18a)

SEC. 106. The head of each executive agency shall, in consultation with the Director of the Bureau of the Budget, take whatever action may be necessary to achieve, insofar as is possible, (1) consistency in accounting and budget classifications, (2) synchronization between accounting and budget classifications and organizational structure, and (3) support of the budget justifications by information on performance and program costs by organizational units. (70 Stat. 782; 31 U.S.C. 18c)

SEC. 110. This part may be cited as the "Accounting and Auditing Act of 1950."

SEC. 111. It is the policy of the Congress in enacting this part that—

(a) The accounting of the Government provide full disclosure of the results of financial operations, adequate financial information needed in the management of operations and the formulation and execution of the Budget, and effective control over income, expenditures, funds, property, and other assets.

(b) Full consideration be given to the needs and responsibilities of both the legislative and executive branches in the establishment of accounting and reporting systems and requirements.

(c) The maintenance of accounting systems and the producing of financial reports with respect to the operations of executive agencies, including central facilities for bringing together and disclosing information on the results of the financial operations of the Government as a whole, be the responsibility of the executive branch.

(d) The auditing for the Government, conducted by the Comptroller General of the United States as an agent of the Congress be directed at determining the extent to which accounting and related financial reporting fulfill the purposes specified, financial transactions have been consummated in accordance with laws, regulations, or other legal requirements, and adequate internal financial control over operations is exercised, and afford an effective basis for the settlement of accounts of accountable officers.

(e) Emphasis be placed on effecting orderly improvements resulting in simplified and more effective accounting, financial reporting, budgeting, and auditing requirements and procedures and on the elimination of those which involve duplication or which do not serve a purpose commensurate with the costs involved.

(f) The Comptroller General of the United States, the Secretary of the Treasury, and the Director of the Bureau of the Budget conduct a continuous program for the improvement of accounting and financial reporting in the Government. (31 U.S.C. 65)

SEC. 112. (a) The Comptroller General of the United States, after consulting the Secretary of the Treasury and the Director of the Bureau of the Budget concerning their accounting, financial reporting, and budgetary needs, and considering the needs of the other executive agencies, shall prescribe the principles, standards, and related requirements for accounting to be observed by each executive agency, including requirements for suitable integration between the accounting processes of each executive agency and the accounting of the Treasury Department. Requirements prescribed by the Comptroller General shall be designed to permit the executive agencies to carry out their responsibilities under section 113 of this part, while providing a basis for integrated accounting for the Government, full disclosure of the results of the financial operations of each executive agency and the Government as a whole, and financial information and control necessary to enable the Congress and the President to discharge their respective responsibilities. The Comptroller General shall continue to exercise the authority vested in him by section 205 (b) of the Federal Property and Administrative Services Act of 1949 (63 Stat. 389) and, to the extent he deems necessary, the authority vested in him by section 309 of the Budget and Accounting Act, 1921 (42 Stat. 25). Any such exercise of authority shall be consistent with the provisions of this Section.

(b) The General Accounting Office shall cooperate with the executive agencies in the development of their accounting systems, including the Treasury Department, in the development and establishment of the system of central accounting and reporting required by section 114 of this part. Such accounting systems shall be approved by the Comptroller General when deemed by him to be adequate and in conformity with the principles, standards, and related requirements prescribed by him.

(c) The General Accounting Office shall from time to time review the accounting systems of the executive agencies. The results of such reviews shall be available to the heads of the executive agencies concerned, to the Secretary of the Treasury, and to the Director of the Bureau of the Budget, and the Comptroller General shall make such reports thereon to the Congress as he deems proper. (31 U.S.C. 66)

SEC. 113. (a) The head of each executive agency shall establish and maintain systems of accounting and internal control designed to provide—

(1) full disclosure of the financial results of the agency's activities;

(2) adequate financial information needed for the agency's management purposes;

(3) effective control over and accountability for all funds, property, and other assets for which the agency is responsible, including appropriate internal audit;

(4) reliable accounting results to serve as the basis for preparation and support of the agency's budget requests, for controlling the execution of its budget, and for providing financial information required by

the Bureau of the Budget under section 213 of the Budget and Accounting Act, 1921 (42 Stat. 23);

(5) suitable integration of the accounting of the agency with the accounting of the Treasury Department in connection with the central accounting and reporting responsibilities imposed on the Secretary of the Treasury by section 114 of this part.

(b) The accounting systems of executive agencies shall conform to the principles, standards, and related requirements prescribed by the Comptroller General pursuant to section 112(a) of this part.

(c) As soon as practicable after the date of enactment of this subsection, the head of each executive agency shall, in accordance with principles and standards prescribed by the Comptroller General, cause the accounts of such agency to be maintained on an accrual basis to show the resources, liabilities, and costs of operations of such agency with a view to facilitating the preparation of cost-based budgets as required by section 216 of the Budget and Accounting Act, 1921, as amended. The accounting system required by this subsection shall include adequate monetary property accounting records as an integral part of the system. (31 U.S.C. 66a; 70 Stat. 783)

SEC. 114.   (a) The Secretary of the Treasury shall prepare such reports for the information of the President, the Congress, and the public as will present the results of the financial operations of the Government: *Provided,* That there shall be included such financial data as the Director of the Bureau of the Budget may require in connection with the preparation of the Budget or for other purposes of the Bureau. Each executive agency shall furnish the Secretary of the Treasury such reports and information relating to its financial condition and operations as the Secretary, by rules and regulations, may require for the effective performance of his responsibilities under this section.

(b) The Secretary of the Treasury is authorized to establish the facilities necessary to produce the financial reports required by subsection a of this section. The Secretary is further authorized to reorganize the accounting functions and install, revise, or eliminate accounting procedures and financial reports of the Treasury Department in order to develop effective and coordinated systems of accounting and financial reporting in the several bureaus and offices of the Department with such concentration of accounting and reporting as is necessary to accomplish integration of accounting results for the activities of the Department and provide the operating center for the consolidation of accounting results of other executive agencies with those of the Department. The authority vested in and the duties imposed upon the Department by sections 10, 15, and 22 of Act entitled "An Act making appropriations for the legislative, executive, and judicial branches of the Government for the fiscal year ending June thirtieth, eighteen hundred and ninety-five, and for other purposes", approved July 31, 1894 (28 Stat. 162, 208-210), may be exercised and performed by the Secretary of the Treasury as a part of his broader authority and duties under this section and in such a manner as to provide a unified system of central accounting and reporting on the most efficient and useful basis.

The Anti-Deficiency Act, Section 3679 of the Revised Statutes

(a) No officer or employee of the United States shall make or authorize an expenditure from or create or authorize an obligation under any appropriation or fund in excess of the amount available therein; nor shall any such officer or employee involve the Government in any contract or other obligation, for the payment of money for any purpose, in advance of appropriations made for such purpose, unless such contract or obligation is authorized by law.

(b) No officer or employee of the United States shall accept voluntary service for the United States or employ personal service in excess of that authorized by law, except in cases of emergency involving the safety of human life or the protection of property.

(c) (1) Except as otherwise provided in this section, all appropriations or funds available for obligation for a definite period of time shall be so apportioned as to prevent obligation or expenditure thereof in a manner which would indicate a necessity for deficiency or supplemental appropriations for such period; and all appropriations or funds not limited to a definite period of time, and all authorizations to create obligations by contract in advance of appropriations, shall be so apportioned as to achieve the most effective and economical use thereof. As used hereafter in this section, the term "appropriation" means appropriations, funds and authorizations to create obligations by contract in advance of appropriations.

(2) In apportioning any appropriation, reserves may be established to provide for contingencies, or to effect savings whenever savings are made possible by or through changes in requirements, greater efficiency of operations, or other developments subsequent to the date on which such appropriation was made available. Whenever it is determined by an

officer designated in subsection (d) of this section to make apportion-ments and reapportionments that any amount so reserved will not be required to carry out the purposes of the appropriation concerned, he shall recommend the rescission of such amount in the manner provided in the Budget and Accounting Act, 1921, for estimates of appropria-tions.

(3) Any appropriation subject to apportionment shall be distributed by months, calendar quarters, operating seasons, or other time periods, or by activities, functions, projects, or objects, or by a combination thereof, as may be deemed appropriate by the officers designated in subsection (d) of this section to make apportionments and reapportion-ments. Except as otherwise specified by the officer making the appor-tionment, amounts so apportioned shall remain available for obligation, in accordance with the terms of the appropriation, on a cumulative basis unless reapportioned.

(4) Apportionments shall be reviewed at least four times each year by the officers designated in subsection (d) of this section to make apportionments and reapportionments, and such reapportionments made or such reserves established, modified, or released as may be necessary to further the effective use of the appropriation concerned, in accordance with the purposes stated in Paragraph 1 of this subsection.

(d) (1) Any appropriation available to the legislative branch, the judiciary, or the District of Columbia, which is required to be appor-tioned under subsection (c) of this section, shall be apportioned or reap-portioned in writing by the officer having administrative control of such appropriation. Each such appropriation shall be apportioned not later than thirty days before the beginning of the fiscal year for which the appropriation is available, or not more than thirty days after ap-proval of the Act by which the appropriation is made available, which-ever is later.

(2) Any appropriation available to an agency, which is required to be apportioned under subsection (c) of this section, shall be appor-tioned or reapportioned in writing by the Director of the Bureau of the Budget. The head of each agency to which any such appropriation is available shall submit to the Bureau of the Budget information, in such form and manner and at such time or times as the Director may pre-scribe, as may be required for the apportionment of such appropriation. Such information shall be submitted not later than forty days before the beginning of any fiscal year for which the appropriation is available, or not more than fifteen days after approval of the Act by which such appropriation is made available, whichever is later. The Director of the

Bureau of the Budget shall apportion each such appropriation and shall notify the agency concerned of his action not later than twenty days before the beginning of the fiscal year for which the appropriation is available, or not more than thirty days after the approval of the Act by which such appropriation is made available, whichever is later. When used in this section, the term "agency" means any executive department, agency, commission, authority, administration, board, or other independent establishment in the executive branch of the Government, including any corporation wholly or partly owned by the United States which is an instrumentality of the United States. Nothing in this subsection shall be so construed as to interfere with the initiation, operation, and administration of agricultural price support programs and no funds (other than funds for administrative expenses) available for price support, surplus removal, and available under Section 32 of the Act of August 24, 1935, as amended (7 U.S.C. 612 (c)). with respect to agricultural commodities shall be subject to apportionment pursuant to this section. The provisions of this section shall not apply to any corporation which obtains funds for making loans, other than paid in capital funds, without legal liability on the part of the United States.

(e) (1) No apportionment or reapportionment, or request therefor by the head of an agency, which, in the judgment of the officer making or the agency head requesting such apportionment or reapportionment, would indicate a necessity for a deficiency or supplemental estimate shall be made except upon a determination by such officer or agency head, as the case may be, that such action is required because of (A) any laws enacted subsequent to the transmission to the Congress of the estimates for an appropriation which require expenditures beyond administrative control; or (B) emergencies involving the safety of human life, the protection of property, or the immediate welfare of individuals in cases where an appropriation has been made to enable the United States to make payment of, or contributions toward, sums which are required to be paid to individuals either in specific amounts fixed by law or in accordance with formulae prescribed by law.

(2) In each case of an apportionment or a reapportionment which, in the judgment of the officer making such apportionment or reapportionment, would indicate a necessity for a deficiency or supplemental estimate, such officer shall immediately submit a detailed report of the facts of the case to the Congress. In transmitting any deficiency or supplemental estimates required on account of any such apportionment or reapportionment, reference shall be made to such report.

Appendix C

Executive Orders and Bureau of the Budget Circular A-11

Executive Order 8248—Establishing the Divisions of the Executive Office of the President and Defining Their Functions and Duties

By virtue of the authority vested in me by the Constitution and Statutes, and in order to effectuate the purposes of the Reorganization Act of 1939. Public No. 19 Seventy-Sixth Congress, approved April 3, 1939, and of Reorganization Plans Nos. I and II submitted to the Congress by the President and made effective as of July 1, 1939 by Public Resolution No. 2 Seventy-Sixth Congress, approved June 7, 1939 by organizing the Executive Office of the President with functions and duties so prescribed and responsibilities so fixed that the President will have adequate machinery for the administrative management of the Executive branch of the Government, it is hereby ordered as follows:

I

There shall be within the Executive Office of the President the following principal divisions, namely: (1) The White House Office, (2) the Bureau of the Budget, (3) the National Resources Planning Board, (4) the Liaison Office for Personnel Management, (5) the Office of Government Reports, and (6) in the event of a national emergency, or threat of a national emergency, such office for emergency management as the President shall determine.

II

The functions and duties of the divisions of the Executive Office of the President are hereby defined as follows:

1. The White House Office. In general, to serve the President in an intimate capacity in the performance of the many detailed activities incident to his immediate office. To that end, The White House Office shall be composed of the following principal subdivisions, with particular functions and duties as indicated.

(a) The Secretaries to the President. To facilitate and maintain quick and easy communication with the Congress, the individual members of Congress, the heads of executive departments and agencies, the press, the radio, and the general public.

(b) The Executive Clerk. To provide for the orderly handling of documents and correspondence within the White House Office, and to organize and supervise all clerical services and procedure relating thereto.

(c) The Administrative Assistants to the President. To assist the President in such matters as he may direct, and at the specific request of the President, to get information and to condense and summarize it for his use. These Administrative Assistants shall be personal aides to the President and shall have no authority over anyone in any department or agency, including the Executive Office of the President, other than the personnel assigned to their immediate offices. In no event shall the Administrative Assistants be interposed between the President and any one of the divisions in the Executive Office of the President.

2. The Bureau of the Budget (a) To assist the President in the preparation of the Budget and the formulation of the fiscal program of the Government.

(b) To supervise and control the administration of the Budget.

(c) To conduct research in the development of improved plans of administrative management, and to advise the executive departments and agencies of the Government with respect to improved administrative organization and practice.

(d) To aid the President to bring about more efficient and economical conduct of Government service.

(e) To assist the President by clearing and coordinating departmental advice on proposed legislation and by making recommendations as to Presidential action on legislative enactments, in accordance with past practice.

(f) To assist in the consideration and clearance and, where necessary, in the preparation of proposed Executive orders and proclamations, in accordance with the provisions of Executive Order No. 7298 of February 18, 1936.

(g) To plan and promote the improvement, development and coordination of Federal and other statistical services.

(h) To keep the President informed of the progress of activities by agencies of the Government with respect to work proposed, work actually initiated, and work completed, together with the relative timing of work between the several agencies of the Government; all to the end that the work programs of the several agencies of the Executive branch of the Government may be coordinated and that the monies appropriated by the Congress may be expended in the most economical manner possible with the least possible overlapping and duplication of effort.

3. The National Resources Planning Board.

(a) To survey, collect data on, and analyze problems pertaining to national resources, both natural and human, and to recommend, to President and the Congress long-time plans and programs for the wise use and fullest development of such resources.

(b) To consult with Federal, regional, state, local, and private agencies in developing orderly programs of public works and to list for the President and the Congress all proposed public works in the order of their relative importance with respect to (1) the greatest good to the greatest number of people, (2) the emergency necessities of the Nation, and (3) the social, economic, and cultural advancement of the people of the United States.

(c) To inform the President of the general trend of economic conditions and to recommend measures leading to their improvement of stabilization.

(d) To act as a clearing house and means of coordination for planning activities, linking together various levels and fields of planning.

4. The Liaison Office for Personnel Management. In accordance with the statement of purpose made in the Message to Congress of April 25, 1939, accompanying Reorganization Plan No. I, one of the Administrative Assistants to the President, authorized in the Reorganization

Act of 1939, shall be designated by the President as Liaison Officer for Personnel Management and shall be in charge of the Liaison Office for Personnel Management. The functions of this office shall be:

(a) To assist the President in the better execution of the duties imposed upon him by the Provisions of the Constitution and the laws with respect to personnel management, especially the Civil Service Act of 1883, as amended, and the rules promulgated by the President under authority of that Act.

(b) To assist the President in maintaining closer contact with all agencies dealing with personnel matters insofar as they affect or tend to determine the personnel management policies of the Executive branch of the Government.

5. The Office of Government Reports.

(a) To provide a central clearing house through which individual citizens, organizations of citizens, state or local governmental bodies, and, where appropriate, agencies of the Federal Government, may transmit inquiries and complaints and receive advice and information.

(b) To assist the President in dealing with special problems requiring the clearance of information between the Federal Government and state and local governments and private institutions.

(c) To collect and distribute information concerning the purposes and activities of executive departments and agencies for the use of the Congress, administrative officials, and the public.

(d) To keep the President currently informed of the opinions, desires, and complaints of citizens and groups of citizens and of state and local governments with respect to the work of Federal agencies.

(e) To report to the President on the basis of the information it has obtained possible ways and means for reducing the cost of the operation of Government.

III

The Bureau of the Budget, the National Resources Planning Board, and the Liaison Office for Personnel Management shall constitute the three principal management arms of the Government for the (1) preparation and administration of the Budget and improvement of administrative management and organization. (2) planning for conservation and utilization of the resources of the Nation, and (3) coordination of the administration of personnel, none of which belongs in any department but which are necessary for the over-all management of the Executive branch of the Government, so that the President will be enabled the better to carry out his Constitutional duties of informing the Congress with respect to the state of the Union, of recommending appropriate and expedient measures, and of seeing that the laws are faithfully executed.

IV

To facilitate the orderly transaction of business within each of the five divisions herein defined and to clarify the relations of these divisions with each other and with the President, I direct that the Bureau of the Budget, the National Resources Planning Board, the Liaison Office for Personnel Management, and the Office of Government Reports shall respectively prepare regulations for the governance of their internal organizations and procedures. Such regulations shall be in effect when approved by the President and shall remain in force until changed by new regulations approved by him. The President will prescribe regulations governing the conduct of the business of the division of The White House Office.

V

The Director of the Bureau of the Budget shall prepare a consolidated budget for the Executive Office of the President for submission by the President to the Congress. Annually, pursuant to the regular request issued by the Bureau of the Budget, each division of the Executive Office of the President shall prepare and submit to the Bureau estimates of proposed appropriations for the succeeding fiscal year. The form of the estimates and the manner of their consideration for incorporation in the Budget shall be the same as prescribed for other Executive departments and agencies.

The Bureau of the Budget shall like-wise perform with respect to the several divisions of the Executive Office of the President such functions and duties relating to supplemental estimates, apportionments, and budget administration as are exercised by it for other agencies of the Federal Government.

VI

Space already has been assigned in the State, War and Navy Building, adjacent to The White House, sufficient to accommodate the Bureau of the Budget with its various divisions (including the Central Statistical

Board), the central office of the National Resources Planning Board, the Liaison Office for Personnel Management and the Administrative Assistants to the President, and although for the time being, a considerable portion of the work of the National Resources Planning Board and all of that of the Office of Government Reports will have to be conducted in other quarters, if and when the Congress makes provision for the Housing of the Department of State in a building appropriate to its function and dignity and provision is made for the other agencies now accommodated in the State, War and Navy Building, it then will be possible to bring into this building, close to The White House, all of the personnel of the Executive Office of the President except The White House Office.

This Order shall take effect on September 11th 1939.

FRANKLIN D. ROOSEVELT

The White House
September 8th, 1939
(No. 8248)

Executive Order 9384—Submission of Reports to Facilitate Budgeting Activities of the Federal Government

By virtue of the authority vested in me as President of the United States, and particularly by the Budget and Accounting Act, 1921, as amended (Title 31, U.S. code, Secs. 1-24), it is hereby ordered as follows:

1. In order to facilitate budgeting activities, all departments and establishments of the Executive Branch of the Federal Government, now or hereafter authorized by law to plan, propose, undertake, or aid public works and improvement projects financed in whole or in part by the Federal Government, shall prepare and keep up-to-date, by means of at least an annual revision, carefully planned and realistic long-range programs of such projects (all such programs being hereinafter referred to as "advance programs").

2. (a) Whenever any estimate of appropriation is submitted to the Bureau of the Budget (hereinafter referred to as the "Bureau") by such departments and establishments for the carrying out of any public works and improvement project or projects whether by contract, force account. Government plant and hired labor, or other similar procedure, or for the financing of any such project or projects whether by grants—

in-aid, loans, or other forms of financial assistance or for examinations, surveys, investigations, plans and specifications, or other planning activities, whether preliminary or detailed, for any such project or projects (all such survey and planning activities being hereinafter referred to as "plan preparation"), the advance program or programs relating to the proposed work or expenditure shall be submitted to the Bureau as an integral part of the justification of the estimates presented.

(b) All such departments and establishments shall submit to the Bureau at the earliest possible date estimates of such supplemental appropriations for the fiscal years 1944 and 1945 as are necessary to provide plan preparation for those public works and improvement projects proposed for undertaking during the first three years of their advanced programs. Thereafter, in order that plans for these public works and improvement projects will always be available in advance, all such departments and establishments shall prepare and submit to the Bureau during each fiscal year estimates of such appropriations as may be necessary to provide plan preparation for those projects proposed for undertaking during the succeeding three fiscal years of their advance programs. All such estimates shall be accompanied by recommendations as to the additional legislation, or amendments to existing legislation, that may be necessary to bring projects in their advance programs to an appropriate state of readiness for prompt undertaking when and where needed.

3. The Director of the Bureau, upon the basis of the estimates and advance programs submitted in accordance with the provisions of paragraph 2 of this order, shall report to the President from time to time, but not less than once a year, consolidated estimates and advance programs in the form of an over-all advance program for the Executive Branch of the Government.

4. Before any department or establishment shall submit to the Congress, or to any committee or member thereof, a report relating to, or affecting in whole or in part, its advance programs, or the public works and improvement projects comprising such programs, or the results of any plan preparation for such programs or projects, such report shall be submitted to the Bureau for advice as to its relationship to the program of the President. When such report is thereafter submitted to the Congress, or to any committee or member thereof, it shall include a statement of the advice received from the Bureau.

5. The data and reports required by this order, and such other data, reports, and information as may from time to time be requested by the Bureau concerning advance programs, or the status of any public works

and improvement projects included therein, or the results or status of any plan preparation for such programs or projects, shall be submitted to the Bureau in such form and manner as the Director of the Bureau shall prescribe. The Director of the Bureau shall from time to time issue such regulations as he deems necessary to effectuate this order, and his determinations with respect to the scope and application of this order shall be controlling.

6. The term "departments and establishments" as used in this Executive Order shall be deemed to include any executive department, independent commission, board, bureau, office, agency, regulatory commission or board, Government-owned or controlled corporation, or other establishment of the Government, and the municipal government of the District of Columbia, but shall not include the legislative or judicial branches of the Government.

7. Executive Order No. 8455, dated June 26, 1940, is hereby revoked.

FRANKLIN D. ROOSEVELT

The White House,
October 4, 1943.

Bureau of the Budget Circular A-11

This circular contains the basic instructions by the Director of the Bureau of Budget to the Heads of Executive Departments for the preparation and submission of annual budget estimates. It is revised annually and the instructions for the preparation of the budget requests for fiscal year 1971, dated June 23, 1969 contain some 100 pages of detailed requirements, and another 100 pages of appendixes and exhibits. The transmittal memorandum and the essential general instructions are reproduced hereafter:

Transmittal memorandum A-11

*Statement of General Policies—*Sections 13-1 to 13-8 inclusive

*Summary Statements Required—*Sections 22.1 to 22.3 inclusive

*Analysis and Justification of Programs—*Sections 24.1 to 24.6 inclusive

Transmittal Memorandum No. 33

TO THE HEADS OF EXECUTIVE DEPARTMENTS AND ESTABLISHMENTS SUBJECT: Preparation and submission of annual budget estimates

Transmitted herewith are revised instructions relating to the annual budget process. The general requirements and policies remain almost unchanged. A number of changes are made in the form of the detailed material, however—in part to simplify the tasks of your budget staffs and in part to make the products more usable in our processes.

These revised instructions include the data requirements for special analyses which were set forth last year in Bureau of the Budget Bulletins Nos. 69-3, 69-5, and 69-10. The relevant sections and references are identified in the attached section-by-section analysis, which highlights the significant changes in Circular No. A-11.

A primary objective of this revision is to increase the development of summary data through improved computer utilization, with a corresponding reduction in requirements for detailed schedules. Another change of significance involves the deletion of comparative transfers from the budget schedules. (An effective comparison of program trends can be made by means of a footnote following the financing schedule without distorting the accounting data shown in the past year column of the schedule.)

The Supplementary Source Document (Standard Form 307) has been revised to include all data required for compilation of the tabular analysis of budget authority and outlays. This change is made to facilitate mechanical development of the data and thus eventually to eliminate the regular submission of the detailed schedules for this table. Instead, agencies will be requested, whenever feasible, to correct a machine listing at a later date. For this year, however, as a transitional expedient, the instructions do provide for the preparation and submission of these detailed schedules when specifically requested by the Bureau of the Budget.

Closer coordination of the program and financing schedules with related appropriation text has been accomplished by requiring the schedules to include the gross amount appropriated (including amounts to liquidate contract authority). A deduct entry for the appropriation to liquidate contract authority has been added to permit calculation of the amount of budget authority enacted or requested.

Special pay rates for experts and consultants may be requested, when justified, at rates not to exceed the daily pay of GS-18.

The submission of a summary statement of agency totals from the program and financing schedules is no longer required. This data is now compiled mechanically from the individual schedules. Interfund and intragovernmental payments need no longer be reported. These payments will be coordinated with the receiving agency, however, to insure accurary in the reporting of receipts.

Data to be reported for various special analyses with respect to poverty income level will be related to guidelines specified for government-wide use by the Bureau of the Budget in a forthcoming release under Circular No. A-46. To simplify further the reporting of special analysis data, the last digit has been dropped from the character classification code. The corresponding data used for the special analysis on research and development will be summarized from the special schedules submitted for that analysis (Exhibits 44A and 44B).

As a matter of convenience to agencies, Appendix C has been expanded to list all credit programs which have been identified to date (including those in the expenditure account) which are to be included in the special analysis of Federal credit programs. In addition, the source category of receipts in Appendix D has been revised to facilitate machine compilation of summary tables.

Bureau of the Budget staff will be glad to assist in interpreting the requirements of this Circular. We welcome such opportunities to cooperate with your budget staff on problems of mutual interest.

ROBERT P. MAYO
Director

General Policies

13.1 Basis for program proposals.

Estimates should reflect the considered judgment of the agency head with respect to the scope, content, level, speed and quality of programs that he proposes be carried out in the budget year, consistent with the fiscal policies of the President.

Program decisions reflected in the estimates should be based upon:

(*a*) Consideration of the broad goals and specific program objectives to be achieved over a period of the next several years, and the extent to which action in the budget year is required for such achievement. Where there is flexibility as to the goals and objectives, the budget request should reflect an appropriate choice among practicable alternatives.

(*b*) The selection of the best alternative methods for accomplishing desired goals and objectives. The choice of alternatives should include consideration of both ongoing programs and new program proposals, their relative effectiveness and efficiency and their acceptability to the public.

(*c*) Reasonably accurate forecasting of the work output expected, expressed in suitable measures, and taking account of measured experience of the past.

(*d*) Appropriate use of work output measures—past, present and future—to show progress toward goals and objectives, and to relate such progress (along with contributions of the private sector and State and local governments) to the appropriate measures of need.

In those agencies where there is an integrated planning-programming-budgeting system, the program proposals should be based upon the agency head's evaluation of the issues that have been identified and studied, utilizing the systems analysis and program analysis capabilities of the agency, and the further advice, if any, received through the year from the Bureau of the Budget as a result of its further consideration and analysis of draft Program Memoranda, Special Analytic Studies, and other documents submitted from time to time.

13.2 Coverage and content of budget year estimates.

Appropriation requests and detailed schedules for the budget year will conform to known policies of the President with respect to the specific programs and estimates involved. All estimates must be completely justified with respect to program objectives and plans and the proposed financing (section 24.3).

Estimates shall be based upon the most economical and efficient manner of carrying on the work of each agency. For this purpose, unit cost information should be developed wherever feasible to permit effective assessment of performance and provide a sound basis for projection of future requirements (see section 24.4). Intensive efforts must be made continuously to see that maximum value is obtained for each dollar of Government cost (see Bureau of the Budget Circular No. A-44).

The regular annual estimates shall be complete as to anticipated requirements for continuing activities being carried on at the date of the budget submission, including those for which additional authorizing legislation is required for the budget year. The estimates must cover all authorized activities that are proposed to be carried on in the budget year, as well as the funds necessary to meet specific financial liabilities imposed by law. No supplemental estimate of appropriation or upward amendment of the estimates will be considered later unless it is due to (*a*) circumstances not foreseeable at the time the annual estimates are submitted or (*b*) subsequent action by Congress.

If, in addition to the regular appropriation requests, it appears probable that proposals for *new legislation* may require a further budget request or result in a change in receipts or outlays, a tentative forecast of the supplemental estimate will be set forth separately (sections 22.4, 24.6, 32.7 and 36.1). Such proposed supplementals must be consistent with items appearing in the agency's legislative program required by Bureau of the Budget Circular No. A-19.

Appropriation estimates for special foreign currency programs may be submitted for financing with foreign currencies which are excess to the normal requirements of the United States. Projects to be proposed should be of a quality justifiable for inclusion in the agency's regular dollar budget, but they may be of lower priority than projects included in the dollar estimates (section 27.1).

Estimates for programs which affect the balance of international payments will be based on policies included in Bureau of the Budget Circular No. A-58 on international transactions.

Requests for major procurement programs will provide for full financing of the entire cost. Except for reclamation, rivers and harbors, and flood control projects, requests for construction programs will provide for full financing of the complete cost of construction. Estimates shall not be submitted for construction funds for major construction projects unless planning will have reached a point by the end of the current year that would assure that the agency could award a contract for construction during the budget year.

13.3. Estimates relating to numbers of personnel.

Estimates for the budget year should reflect the most efficient utilization of manpower (see Bureau of the Budget Circular No. A-64). To the maximum extent possible, the estimates are to represent agency plans covering both manpower inputs and work outputs required for implementing program objectives and exercising appropriate managerial control.

Estimates of manpower requirements for measurable workloads should be based on forecasts of workload and manpower productivity wherever feasible (see section 24.4). Statistical standards may be used in the development of productivity trends and to express the relationship between workload indicators and manpower requirements.

The estimates for staffing requirements will assume that improvements in skills, organization, procedures, and supervision will steadily increase employee productivity and at the same time maintain adequate quality. Where automatic data processing equipment is installed, special gains in employee productivity will ordinarily be budgeted after the first year.

Personnel currently authorized will be utilized to the maximum extent in staffing new programs and expansions in existing programs, and a reduced number of personnel should generally be planned where the workload is stable. Estimates of staffing requirements for on-going as well as new programs will be based upon quantitative forecasts of workload for each program, together with adequate substantive data for converting workload to required personnel. Increases in staffing will be approved only when it is demonstrated that essential functions cannot be performed with existing employees.

Estimated requirements for executive direction and administrative services will be held to minimum levels consistent with responsible and effective program management.

Contracts with firms, institutions, or persons will not be used for the purpose of reducing or holding down Government employment when such employment would be more efficient and effective in accomplishing the desired work.

13.4. Estimates of personnel compensation and allowances.

Estimates for personnel compensation and allowances will be prepared on the following bases:

(*a*) Estimates will generally be based on a 40-hour workweek and a total of 52 workweeks, plus the extra days, if any, for those positions where the administrative workweek results in 1 or 2 extra days occurring in the year. The estimates will not include increases over amounts for the preceding year for premium pay, except for extension of the regular workweek that must be specifically and fully justified. Overtime and other premium pay should be estimated as accurately as possible, even though additional costs (other than for extension of the regular workweek) must be absorbed.

(*b*) Estimates will be based on compensation scales in effect on September 15 of the current year, except that provision may be made for (1) any increases to become effective before the end of the budget year specifically provided by laws already enacted, and (2) additional wage-board increases expected to be granted during the remainder of the current fiscal year.

(*c*) Estimates will not provide for prospective upward reclassification of positions subject to the Classification Act, except where a predetermined plan for grade adjustments has already been approved by the Civil Service Commission and the need for funds is firmly established. For purposes of this Circular, such plans include (1) new or revised classification standards, (2) new or revised training agreements, and (3) other upgradings where significant numbers of positions are reclassified for the same reason. The cost of upgrading should generally be offset by savings due to greater productivity and efficiency.

(*d*) The estimates will provide increases to cover within-grade salary advancements only on a basis consistent with recent experience, and will take account of savings in pay above minimum of the grades when such action will be consistent with recent experience. The cost of such advancements should often be offset by savings due to greater productivity and efficiency.

(*e*) Positions vacant at the end of the year and each new position for the budget year will be included at the entrance salary for the position involved.

(*f*) Increases in average compensation for the budget year from all causes, other than changes in pay scales, should be no more than 1% unless a greater increase is specifically justified.

(*g*) Full consideration will be given to savings in personnel costs due to delay in filling vacant positions, leave without pay, lag in recruitment for new positions, filling vacancies at lower rates of pay, part-year employment, and similar factors, as well as to the offset to savings caused by terminal leave payments.

(*h*) Positions above grade GS-15 will be reflected in the schedules only to the extent that positions have been allocated (by the Civil Service Commission or other allocating authority) to those grades or are specifically authorized in substantive law.

(*i*) Authority to pay special rates for experts and consultants may be requested only when the agency demonstrates that the type and caliber of services required cannot be obtained at the maximum rate payable for GS-15 under the Classification Act. When such authority is justified, it may not exceed the daily rate payable for GS-18.

(*j*) Estimates for employees' uniform allowances will be based on policies set forth in Bureau of the Budget Circular No. A-30.

(*k*) Estimates for severance pay will be on a pay-period-by-pay-period basis, notwithstanding the fact that a liability arises at the time of an employee's separation.

13.5. Estimates relating to other objects of expenditure.

(*a*) It will be assumed that, on the average, the general level of prices will be the same during the budget year as at the time the estimates are prepared, except where increases will result directly from laws already enacted (such as increases in FICA tax rates effective at future dates).

(*b*) When an agency provides hospital care on a reimbursable basis, the estimates of reimbursements and other income from charges for such care shall be based on such per diem rates as may be established by the Bureau of the Budget for the particular class of patient and type of care involved, unless different rates or charges are established by or pursuant to a specific requirement of law.

(c) The estimates should not include amounts for additional motor vehicles or replacement of motor vehicles in cities in which the General Services Administration has established motor pools or expects to establish such pools in the current or budget years, except for vehicles which are exempt from inclusion in the pools.

(d) Provision may be made in the estimates for replacement of motor vehicles and other equipment covered by General Services Administration replacement standards in accordance with those standards. Estimates will be based on price limitations in effect for the current year, less estimated exchange or sales allowances for vehicles to be replaced. The need for the projected fleet of automobiles and trucks, whether it involves additions, replacement or retention of present vehicles, must be fully justified (section 27.3).

(e) Provision may be made in the estimates for motor vehicles, where appropriate, for the additional cost of equipment necessary for police-type law enforcement purposes. The need for the additional cost must be fully justified by the use to which the vehicle is put.

(f) When the estimates include funds for the procurement of motor vehicles classed as medium sedans, heavy sedans, or limousines, the need must be justified and the appropriation language must include an identification of the type of vehicle to be provided. Proposed purchases of such vehicles must not increase the number to be operated beyond the limitations established under Bureau of the Budget Circular No. A-22.

(g) Estimates for design and construction of Federal public buildings will include amounts required for incorporation of fallout shelter in those cases where such shelter is required under Department of Defense policy and will indicate the results of consultation with Department of Defense thereon.

(h) Estimates for the design and construction of Federal facilities and buildings will provide for the installation of water pollution control and treatment systems, in accordance with Executive Order No. 11258, Bureau of the Budget Circular No. A-81, and any related instructions.

(i) Estimates for the design and construction of Federal facilities and buildings will provide for the installation of air pollution control systems, in accordance with Executive Order No. 11282, Bureau of the Budget Circular No. A-78, and any related instructions.

(j) As required by Executive Order No. 11296, estimates for the construction of buildings, structures, roads, or other facilities, whether financed directly by Federal funds or through grant, loan, or mortgage insurance programs, should be based upon land utilization plans that preclude the uneconomic, hazardous, or unnecessary use of flood plains.

(*k*) The estimates will include amounts billed by the Employees Compensation Fund for payments made by that fund during the past fiscal year.

(*l*) Agency estimates for current appropriations will include amounts required for the rental of additional space through the first full year of occupancy. The General Services Administration will be reimbursed for rental of space initially occupied for part of a fiscal year (and on a continuing basis for space occupied by activities financed by revolving funds, trust funds, and permanent appropriations). Amounts for the first *full* fiscal year's rental (including space occupied on July 1 of the year concerned) will be transferred (as an appropriation adjustment) to the General Services Administration in that year, and rentals in subsequent years will be financed by the General Services Administration.

(*m*) The estimates will not include amounts for payment of tort claims, except where there is a substantial volume of claims presented regularly.

(*n*) Estimates for travel will reflect application of the policy on the use of less than first class accommodations for air travel set forth in the Standardized Government Travel Regulations (Bureau of the Budget Circular No. A-7).

(*o*) Estimates for construction of family housing and provision of furnishings in personnel quarters should be based on policies contained in Bureau of the Budget Circulars Nos. A-18 and A-15, respectively.

(*p*) Estimates for the acquisition of automatic data processing equipment must be consistent with policies set forth in Bureau of the Budget Circular No. A-54.

(*q*) Estimates for starting commercial or industrial type activities to produce goods or services for Government use will be consistent with the policies set forth in Bureau of Budget Circular No. A-76.

13.6. Estimates of receipts and reimbursements.

The estimates of receipts and reimbursements shall include anticipated collections under proposed legislation, separately identified, as well as under existing legislation.

Estimates of collections resulting from charges for Government services and property should be based on policies set forth in Bureau of the Budget Circulars Nos. A-25 and A-45, where applicable.

13.7. Estimates of outlays.

The method of estimating outlays will be explained, including derivation of the distribution of outlays shown on the supplementary source document (sections 41.1-41.6).

In estimating outlays from appropriations and other authorizations, full account should be taken of time lags between the incurring of obligations and the receipt of goods and services, and the further lags between the receipt of goods and services and the issuance of checks in payment therefor. In estimating outlays generally, the experience of the preceding 5 years may be taken as a guide.

In estimating outlays chargeable to pay increase supplementals it will be assumed that the supplemental will be expended in the same proportion between the current and budget years as other pay. The portion of the pay increase that is earned in the current year but paid in the budget year will be reported as a budget-year expenditure; the remainder will be reported as a current year expenditure.

13.8. Significance of allowances.

When the President has considered the estimates for the executive branch and made his determinations thereon, each agency will be notified. The nature and amounts of the President's determinations are confidential, not to be released until the budget is transmitted to Congress.

Presidential "allowances" with respect to budget year estimates (other than forecasts of supplemental items) represent the sums that he is recommending to the Congress. The President's determinations, both in total and in detail, become the "proposed appropriations" as that term is used in the statute, and must be so justified by the respective agencies (see Bureau of the Budget Circular No. A-10).

Agencies will be notified, at the time Presidential determinations on budget year estimates are made known, of the amount of any current year supplemental estimates to be included for printing in the budget. The forecasts of supplemental items included in the budget are not commitments as to the amounts to be formally recommended to Congress later. The need for each supplemental will be reviewed again when the estimate is formally submitted by the agency, and the amount required will be redetermined at that time.

Upon receipt by an agency of the President's determinations, the agency head will immediately exercise his judgment as to the best and most appropriate distribution of those amounts that have been left flexible for his consideration. Budget submissions will be revised promptly to bring these them into accord with the action of the President, and to reflect the best judgment of the agency head within the allowances received from the Bureau of the Budget.

Summary Statements

22.1. Summary and highlight memorandum.

A summary and highlight memorandum (which may be in the form of a transmittal letter) will lead off the budget submission of each agency. This narrative will summarize, usually in one to five pages, the principal highlights of the agency's budget. It will identify the broad policies proposed, the objectives and program plans on which the estimates are based, and the total amounts requested to carry forward those policies.

22.2. Multi-year program and financial plans.

Agencies operating under a planning-programming-budgeting system will submit with their estimates a comprehensive multi-year Program and Financial Plan (PFP) which presents in tabular form a complete and authoritative summary of agency programs in terms of outputs and costs. The PFP will reflect the agency head's recommendations with respect to the budget and related programs and plans. As a minimum, it will show the 3 years covered by the budget and the 4 succeeding years. Data beyond the budget year are primarily to show the future implications of prior decisions, and program add-ons justified in the budget submission. The PFP will not forecast future decisions, but should show mandatory or built-in changes in levels of output and cost under decisions made in the budget and prior years. Decisions to phase out or reduce programs in future years should also be reflected.

Data in the PFP will be arranged by program structure. The first table should display outputs and costs by program element. While outputs (that is, end products or services produced) are usually easier to measure and to forecast than accomplishments (results in terms of basic goals and missions), increasing emphasis should be given to use of accomplishment measures. In some cases, it may be necessary to have two or three measures of output for a program element. The second table of the PFP should present a summary of costs by program category and subcategory; and budget authority for the budget year. As a general rule, the cost concepts reflected in the PFP should be the same as those used by the agency in preparing its program and financing schedules (section 32.3). Where there is a significant difference between the total systems cost and the cost funded by the responsible agency (because some costs are funded by other agencies, other units of Government, or the private sector) additional lines should be added, with the figures in parentheses, to show the costs that are funded from other sources. Where a significant portion of the agency's costs for any program is met from earmarked receipts, as in the case of public enterprise funds, the table should reflect both the total costs and the resources applied to offset them. Agency formats may be substituted for these requirements if they satisfy budget review needs. The agency should consult with the Bureau of the Budget concerning such substitutions and the details of the display in difficult and unusual cases.

For agencies not utilizing a full PPB system, a similar but simplified multi-year presentation of program and financial data should be included, so far as feasible. Quantitative indicators of output and costs should be presented, using such categories as seem appropriate for analysis.

22.3. "Bridge" to appropriation structure.

Agency Program and Financial Plans will include a "bridge" or "crosswalk" between the agency appropriation accounts and the PPB structure.

This crosswalk will be made by a separate table accompanying the program and financing schedule for *each* appropriation and fund account (exhibit 22A). This table will cover the 3 years reflected in the budget and will distribute the total budget authority and total outlays in the account among applicable PPB categories and subcategories. The PPB categories and subcategories should be denoted in the table by numeric codes, the first two digits representing categories and the third and fourth digits the subcategories. The totals in the table for each appropriation should agree with the comparable amount on the program and financing schedule (sections 32.4-32.5) and on the analysis of budget authority and outlays (section 22.4). The total for each program category should agree with the amount shown on the analysis of changes in program requirements (section 24.2).

Each agency should also provide a summary table showing agency totals by program category and subcategory, with adjusting entries necessary to reconcile these amounts to the agency totals of budget authority and outlays, respectively. The gross total (prior to the adjustments) will equal the sum of the amounts shown on the tables for each appropriation account. This table should be prepared in the format illustrated in exhibit 22A, and identified as "Agency summary" in the heading. This summary table will also be adjusted to accord with the final budget determinations and resubmitted informally within 5 working days after submission of all other budget material for the printer, or as soon as practicable thereafter.

The Program and Financial Plan will also contain a summary table reconciling the financial data in the PFP to the agency appropriation structure, when requested by the Bureau of the Budget. The summary reconciliation (exhibit 22B) will list appropriation accounts for each organization in regular budget order and will normally present data only for PPB categories, but will show subcategories where necessary for clarity or when requested by the Bureau of the Budget. Separate tables will be prepared to cover each of the three years included in the budget.

While exhibit 22B shows the program structure listed across the top and the appropriation structure listed in the stub column, this should be reversed if there are more program categories than appropriations. Appropriations and funds should be listed in the sequence in which they appear in the budget, with separate headings for Federal funds and trust funds. Subtotals should be included for Federal funds and for trust funds; total budget authority and outlays should be shown for both categories and appropriations and funds. Adjusting entries for netting of intrabudgetary transactions and proprietary receipts for the agency as a whole should be shown following the trust fund entries. The totals for each appropriation should agree with the comparable amount on the program and financing schedule and on the analysis of budget authority and outlays (section 22.4). The total for each program category should agree with the amount shown on the analysis of changes in program requirements (section 24.2).

In preparing this material, agencies should consult freely with representatives of the Bureau of the Budget.

— Analysis and Justification of Programs

24.1. Program Memoranda.

Agencies operating under a planning-programming-budgeting (PPB) system will submit with their annual budget estimates Program Memoranda (PM's) and Special Analytic Studies (SAS's) for major program issues. The PM's for issues requiring decision in the budget year will present comparisons of the cost and effectiveness of alternatives for resolving those issues in relation to objectives, recommendations on programs to be carried out, and the reasons for those decisions.

Program Memoranda will refer to, and may summarize the findings of, supporting Special Analytic Studies. If no such studies were made, the PM will indicate whatever basis exists for the choice among the alternatives.

24.2. Analysis of changes in program requirements.

The justification of each PPB program category estimate will begin with a statement relating the estimate to current year programs. This statement will follow the form of exhibit 24, unless a different analysis is required by Bureau of the Budget representatives. Smaller agencies will prepare a similar statement for the agency as a whole.

The first section of the statement will contain a comparison of budget authority and outlays for the program category (for smaller agencies, agency totals) for 19PY−4 and 19PY actual, and 19CY and 19BY estimated.

The analysis of changes in budget authority will begin with the amount for the current year, as enacted. The gross amount of estimated savings in the current year due to cost reductions (to be specifically identified and cross referenced to the September report under Bureau of the Budget Circular No. A-44), program deferrals, etc., will be listed and deducted from the gross amount of anticipated supplemental requirements (each will be briefly identified) in arriving at the amount of anticipated supplementals proposed for separate transmittal. Major current reductions will be shown separately; the remainder will be lumped together as "other savings." The current estimate, computed from the amount enacted, plus any net supplementals proposed for separate transmittal, will serve as the base amount in estimating budget year requirements.

An analysis of changes in budget authority from the current year to the budget year will follow. Larger items should be identified in sufficient detail to be related to the appropriation or bureau involved.

Decreases will be listed under the following headings:

Automatic (nonpolicy).—Decreases in workload and nonrecurring items from the previous year, including full amounts provided for construction, major equipment purchases, etc.

Management improvements.—Cost reduction savings, increased productivity, organizational improvements, etc. Cost reduction savings will be shown as separate line items, cross referenced to and reconcilable with the September cost reduction report.

Program decreases.—Reductions in the quality or quantity of program activities.

Financing changes.—Activities to be financed by another agency or program in the succeeding year.

Increases will be listed under the following headings:

Administration commitments.—Program increases to which the President has publicly and specifically committed the Administration.

Automatic (nonpolicy).—Increased pay costs, other mandatory costs, and workload increases over which the agency has no control under existing law and policy. Exclude annualization costs of activities begun or expanded in the current year over which the agency exercises control; these will be included under "Program increases."

Program increases.—All discretionary program increases. Identify applicable PM's and/or proposed legislation, if any.

Financing changes.—Activities financed by another agency or program in the preceding year.

Where a new program operates on a part year basis in either the current or budget year or when an increase in level is applicable to only part of a year, the amount required for operation for a full year should be shown as a parenthetical entry in the stub column.

The total line will equal the agency's request for budget authority for the budget year. It will be followed by a distribution by appropriation or fund account.

24.3. Additional justification of programs and financing.

A written justification will be provided for each budget submission. Where there are Program Memoranda and Special Analytic Studies (section 24.1), the justification will supplement them. Where there are no Program Memoranda, the justification will include material of the type described in section 24.1 to the extent practicable.

Agencies are encouraged to consult with Bureau of the Budget representatives in the development of program proposals, justification material and exhibits, not specifically provided herein, in order to adequately present the programs and financial requirements. To the maximum extent possible, such justification should represent summaries of operational plans covering both the inputs and outputs required for implementing program objectives and exercising managerial control at agency levels.

To be useful, a written justification must be understood by all reviewers. Agencies should consider the fact that the period available for budget review is short, and the time available does not permit exhaustive study of a mass of text to sift out the essential elements of the case for the proposed estimate. All major issues should be covered, but in concise, specific language.

The Program Memoranda, Special Analytic Studies, and additional narrative justification together (or the justification alone, in the case of smaller agencies) should, to the maximum extent possible and particularly in the case of new programs, cover the following subjects:

(a) The objectives of the program. A precise statement of the objectives of each program, directed to the budget year, but covering future year implications if significant, and specifically covering the:

(1) *Statutory authority,* including description of any new legislative authorization required.

(2) *National problem* to which the program is directed and an indication of how the program helps solve the problem.

(3) *Magnitude of need,* including estimates of the total requirements to meet the problem and for the specific portion of the problem to which the program is directed. The economic, social and other characteristics of the problem should be stated, together with an analysis of the extent to which the need is met by the current program. If either the present program coverage or the magnitude of need are expected to change significantly within the next 5 years, additional data should be supplied.

(4) *Reasons for Federal action,* explaining any enlarged or proposed new Federal action in terms of the unavailability or unwillingness of State, local, or private interests to resolve this problem.

(5) *Program benefits,* describing what specific benefits accrue to identifiable groups, institutions, or areas, etc., the nature and extent of those benefits, and the advantage to the nation.

The narrative should include such additional detailed information (not available in the Program Memoranda or Special Analytic Studies) as may be necessary to provide adequate explanation.

(b) Proposed plans for achieving the objectives. The methods chosen to achieve the objectives, and the reasons for choosing them, should be clearly explained. The explanation should cover:

(1) *Alternatives* considered, their relative benefits and costs, and reasons for selecting the recommended program level.

(2) *Effectiveness* of the present program or expected effectiveness of the proposed increase or new program. This should include

identification of past or on-going analysis of performance/effectiveness and cost/effectiveness, and their specific findings. If cost/effectiveness measures are not available, or such analysis is not under way, this should be explicitly stated, and the reasons therefor. Comparisons with returns from related on-going programs should also be included.

(3) *Relationship* of the program (especially if it is new or enlarged) to other programs, including proposed measures to improve coordination and increase flexibility of action.

(4) *Constraints* on the program other than funds, e.g., limitations of manpower, facilities, or existing organizational, institutional, procedural, or other factors. Identify any special geographic implications.

(c) Derivation of requested appropriation. A conversion of the proposed plan for achievement of the recommended objectives into appropriations is required. Budget authority will be distributed to applicable appropriations on the "Analysis of changes in program requirements" as shown in exhibit 24. The justification should cover the following:

(1) *Outputs or workloads and costs,* showing for the 3 years covered in the budget the outputs or performance measures, cost per unit of output, and total costs. If possible, factors such as production per employee, or ultimate effectiveness measures should be included. As a minimum requirement for measurable work, standards based on statistical procedures will be used to develop productivity trends and to express the relationship between workload and manpower requirements.

(2) *Basis for distribution of funds* (i.e., formulas or principles for allocation, matching, award of loans, grants, or contracts, etc.) and data on resulting geographic distribution (e.g., State, etc.) with identification of any issues.

The narrative justification for new activities to begin in the budget year should also contain an estimate of the amount required in the succeeding year to continue the activity at the level to be reached at the end of the budget year. The amount estimated to be required in the succeeding year for compensation of personnel should also be indicated, computed on the basis of the employment level in effect at the end of the budget year.

For smaller agencies, the justification for an appropriation or fund will be organized in the sequence of the schedule of program and financing, and, for individual activities, will be on the same basis as that schedule. For each activity where practicable, a subsidiary breakdown should set forth personnel compensation, other current expenses, and capital outlay. Where budget activities and organization units do not coincide there shall be included (a) a cross-classifying table which will show organizational totals and how they are distributed by activities, (b) an explanation of the basis for distributing such charges, and (c) such additional explanation as may be needed to justify the size and financial requirements of each organization unit.

24.4. Use of work measurement, unit costs, and productivity indexes.

Work measurement, unit costs, and productivity indexes should be used to the maximum extent practicable in justifying staffing requirements for measurable workload. The agency should be prepared, upon request, to submit detailed analyses of workload, manpower, and productivity trends in support of budget estimates.

Properly developed work measurement procedures should be used to produce estimates of the man-hours per unit of workload, such as the man-hours per claim adjudicated, man-hours per man maintained in the field, man-hours per infested acre of pest control, etc., depending on the agency. These estimates should represent an acceptable level of performance based on current realistic time standards. If the agency does not have a work measurement system that provides this type of information, the use of statistical techniques based on historical manpower input and work outputs may be used.

Unit costs relate the volume of work to the funds required to produce the work. Unit costs may include, in addition to personnel costs, the costs of supplies, travel, equipment, etc. Thus, unit costs reflect the ratio of personnel, materials, travel and other costs to the output produced, and will be stated in the dollars (or cents) required to produce a unit of work. When unit costs include personnel costs, work measurement should be used to support the acceptability of this component.

Productivity indexes are based on the ratio of total output to resource input. Output measure is based on the volume of product or services produced for use outside the organization, with due allowance for differences in the nature of individual products or services. Measure of input may be based on the amount of manpower alone, on manpower costs, or on a more comprehensive measure of resource inputs which includes nonlabor costs.

Whenever any trends in the actual years are reversed in the estimate years, the justification shall deal with the reasons therefor. Changes in unit cost or productivity attributable to the cost reduction program will be separately identified.

Agencies are to extend the use of work measurement and unit cost analysis to both common service activities and program activities. Usually, productivity indexes are based on organization-wide totals of both outputs and inputs, thus already covering both direct and indirect costs. The Bureau of the Budget will, to the extent possible, assist agencies in the establishment or improvement of work measurement and productivity analysis systems.

24.5. Use of tables, charts, and graphs.

The *presentation* of data is important because much of the effort which has gone into the collection and compilation of the data will be lost if it is not presented clearly and effectively. Tables, charts, graphs, maps, and other visual aids can frequently be designed to replace lengthy textual explanations.

Such material should be included, however, only when it will assist the presentation of the justification. Tables, charts, and graphs should be coordinated with the text, and so arranged as to emphasize the most significant facts and relationships.

24.6. Explanations relating to supplemental estimates.

When the need for a supplemental appropriation is forecast in accordance with sections 11.6 and 13.2, a separate justification will be required. The justification will set forth fully the need for the additional appropriations, the reasons for their omission from the regular estimates of the year concerned, and the reasons why it is considered essential that the additional appropriation be granted during the year instead of obtaining the money in a regular appropriation the following year. The explanation of the forecast submitted at this time will not supplant the justification of the supplemental estimate itself when it is formally submitted later.

For anticipated supplementals in the current year to meet the cost of pay increases, the justification should identify, for each appropriation or fund, the total cost of the pay increases and the amount which is being absorbed, and explain any difference from information submitted with the apportionment request for the current year.

Appendix D

Directors of the Bureau
of the
Budget, 1921 - 69

	Term Began	*Term Ended*
Charles G. Dawes	June 23, 1921	June 30, 1922
Herbert M. Lord	July 1, 1922	May 31, 1929
J. Clawson Roop	Aug. 15, 1929	Mar. 3, 1933
Lewis W. Douglas	Mar. 7, 1933	Aug. 31, 1934
Daniel W. Bell	Sept. 1, 1934	Apr. 14, 1939
Harold D. Smith	Apr. 15, 1939	June 19, 1946
James E. Webb	July 31, 1946	Jan. 27, 1949
Frank Pace	Feb. 1, 1949	Apr. 12, 1950
Frederick J. Lawton	Apr. 13, 1950	Jan. 21, 1953
Joseph M. Dodge	Jan. 22, 1953	Apr. 15, 1954
Rowland R. Hughes	Apr. 16, 1954	Apr. 1, 1956
Percival F. Brundage	Apr. 2, 1956	Mar. 17, 1958
Maurice H. Stans	Mar. 18, 1958	Jan. 20, 1961
David E. Bell	Jan. 21, 1961	Dec. 20, 1962
Kermit Gordon	Dec. 28, 1962	June 1, 1965
Charles L. Schultze	June 1, 1965	Jan. 29, 1968
Charles J. Zwick	Jan. 29, 1968	Jan. 20, 1969
Robert P. Mayo	Jan. 21, 1969	

Bibliography

Books

AGGER, EUGENE E. *The Budget in the American Commonwealth.* New York: Columbia University Press, 1907.

BARTELT, EDWARD F. *Accounting Procedures of the United States Government.* Chicago: Public Administration Service, 1940.

BROWNE, VINCENT J. *The Control of the Public Budget.* Washington, D.C.: Public Affairs Press, 1949.

BRYCE, JAMES B. *The American Commonwealth.* rev. ed. New York: Macmillan, 1922.

BUCK, ARTHUR E. *The Budget in Governments of Today.* New York: Macmillan, 1934.

————. *Public Budgeting.* New York: Harper & Bros., 1929.

BULLOCK, CHARLES. *The Finances of the United States from 1775 to 1789, with Especial Reference to the Budget.* Madison: The University of Wisconsin, 1895.

BURNS, ARTHUR E., and WATSON, DONALD S. *Government Spending and Economic Expansion.* Washington, D.C.: American Council on Public Affairs, 1940.

BURNS, ARTHUR F. *The Frontiers of Economic Knowledge.* Princeton, N.J.: Princeton University Press, 1954.

BURNS, ARTHUR F., and MITCHELL, WESLEY C. *Measuring Business Cycles.* New York: National Bureau of Economic Research, 1946.

CLEVELAND, FREDERICK A., and BUCK, ARTHUR E. *The Budget and Responsible Government.* New York: Macmillan, 1920.

COLLINS, CHARLES W. *The National Budget System.* New York: Macmillan, 1917.

DAWES, CHARLES G. *The First Year of the Budget of the United States.* New York: Harper & Bros., 1923.

EMMERICH, HERBERT D. *Essays on Federal Reorganization.* University: University of Alabama Press, 1950.

FABRICANT, SOLOMON. *Capital Consumption and Adjustment.* New York: National Bureau of Economic Research, 1938.

FITZPATRICK, EDWARD A. *Budget Making in a Democracy.* New York: Macmillan, 1918.

FRIEDMAN, MILTON and SCHWARTZ, ANNA JACOBSON. *A Monetary History of the United States, 1867–1960.* Princeton, N.J.: Princeton University Press, 1963.

GALBRAITH, JOHN KENNETH. *The New Industrial State.* Boston: Houghton Mifflin, 1967.

GOLDSMITH, RAYMOND W. *The National Wealth of the United States in the Postwar Period.* Princeton, N.J.: Princeton University Press, 1962.

GORDON, KERMIT. *Reflections on Spending.* Public Policy, vol. 15. Cambridge, Mass.: Harvard University Graduate School of Public Administration, 1966.

————, ed. *Agenda for the Nation.* Washington, D.C.: Brookings Institution, 1968.

GRIFFITH, ERNEST S. *Congress: Its Contemporary Role.* 4th ed. New York: New York University Press, 1967.

GROVES, HAROLD M. *Financing Government.* New York: Henry Holt, 1939.

HANSEN, ALVIN H. *Fiscal Policy and Business Cycles.* New York: W. W. Norton, 1941.

KEYNES, JOHN MAYNARD. *The General Theory of Employment, Interest and Money.* London: Macmillan, 1936.

KUZNETS, SIMON. *National Income and Its Composition, 1919–1938.* New York: National Bureau of Economic Research, 1941.

LANDIS, JAMES M. *The Administrative Process.* Storrs lectures on jurisprudence, Yale School of Law, 1938. New Haven, Conn.: Yale University Press, 1938.

LARY, HAL B. *Problems of the United States as World Trader and Banker.* New York: National Bureau of Economic Research, 1963.

LEWIS, VERNE B. *Budgetary Administration in the U.S. Department of Agriculture.* Chicago: Public Administration Service, 1941.

LEWIS, WILFRED, JR. *Budget Concepts for Economic Analysis.* Reprinted from the staff papers of the U.S. President's Commission on Budget Concepts. Washington, D.C.: Brookings Institution, 1968.

LOWRIE, SELDEN G. *The Budget*. Madison, Wisc.: Democrat Printing Co., 1912.

MAASS, ARTHUR. *In Accord with the Program of the President?* Public Policy, vol. 4. Cambridge, Mass.: Harvard University Graduate School of Public Administration, 1953.

MARSHALL, ALFRED. *Principles of Economics*. 9th ed. New York: Macmillan, 1961.

MITCHELL, WESLEY C. *Business Cycles: The Problem and Its Setting*. New York: National Bureau of Economic Research, 1927.

National Bureau of Economic Research. *The Price Statistics of the Federal Government: Review, Appraisal, and Recommendations*. General Series, no. 73. New York: The Bureau, 1961.

————. *Toward Improved Social and Economic Measurement*. Annual Report. New York: The Bureau, 1968.

NAYLOR, ESTILL E. *The Federal Budget System in Operation*. Washington, D.C.: Hayworth, 1941.

OTT, DAVID J., and ATTIAT, F. *Federal Budget Policy*. Washington, D.C.: Brookings Institution, 1965.

POWELL, FRED W., comp. *Control of Federal Expenditures: A Documentary History, 1775–1894*. Washington, D.C.: Brookings Institution, 1939.

SAULNIER, RAYMOND J.; HALCROW, HAROLD G.; and JACOBY, NEIL H. *Federal Lending and Loan Insurance*. Princeton, N. J.: Princeton University Press, 1958.

SCHULTZE, CHARLES L. *The Politics and Economics of Public Spending*. Washington, D.C.: Brookings Institution, 1968.

SECKLER-HUDSON, CATHERYN, ed. *Budgeting: An Instrument of Planning and Management*. Washington, D.C.: American University, 1944.

SELKO, DANIEL T. *The Federal Financial System*. Washington, D.C.: Brookings Institution, 1940.

SMITH, HAROLD. *The Management of Your Government*. New York: McGraw-Hill, 1945.

Symposium on the Federal Budget in a Dynamic Economy, Washington D. C., 1968. New York: American Bankers Association, 1968.

WEIDENBAUM, MURRAY L. *Federal Budgeting*. Washington, D.C.: American Enterprise Institute for Public Policy Research, 1964.

WILDAVSKY, AARON. *The Politics of the Budgetary Process*. Boston: Little Brown, 1964.

WILLOUGHBY, W. F. *The Movement for Budgetary Reform in the States*. New York: Appleton, 1918.

————. *The National Budget System*. Baltimore: The Johns Hopkins Press, 1927.

———. *The Problem of a National Budget.* New York: Appleton, 1918.

WILMERDING, LUCIUS. *The Spending Power: A History of the Efforts of Congress to Control Expenditures.* New Haven, Conn.: Yale University Press, 1943.

Articles

ALEXANDER, CHARLES B. "The Need for a Budget System in the United States." *Annals of the American Academy of Political and Social Science,* July, 1918, pp. 144–48.

BUCK, ARTHUR E. "The Development of the Budget Idea in the United States." *Annals of the American Academy of Political and Social Science,* May, 1924, pp. 31–39.

BURKHEAD, JESSE V. "Federal Budgetary Developments: 1947–48." *Public Administration Review,* Autumn, 1948, pp. 267–74.

CHASE, STUART. "Behind the Budget." *Atlantic Monthly,* September, 1939, pp. 312–26.

CLEVELAND, FREDERICK A. "Evolution of the Budget Idea in the United States." *Annals of the American Academy of Political and Social Science,* November, 1915, pp. 15–35.

COMPTON, KARL T. "Long-Range Budgeting of Public Capital Expenditures." *Annals of the American Academy of Political and Social Science,* July, 1932, pp. 127–32.

ENSLEY, GROVER W. "A Budget for the Nation." *Social Research,* September, 1943, pp. 280–300.

FAIRCHILD, FRED R. "The United States Budget in the Past Decade." *Proceedings of the Academy of Political Science,* January, 1938, pp. 35–48.

FORD, HENRY JONES. "Budget Making and the Work of Government." *Annals of the American Academy of Political and Social Science,* November, 1915, pp. 1–14.

FUCHS, VICTOR R. "Medical Costs: Why They Are What They Are." *Modern Hospital,* September, 1967, pp. 104–11.

HOLCOMBE, ARTHUR N. "Over-all Financial Planning Through the Bureau of the Budget." *Public Administration Review,* Spring, 1941, pp. 225–30.

JONES, J. WELDON. "The Execution of the Federal Budget." *Accounting Review,* April, 1942, pp. 88–94.

KEY, V. O., JR. "The Lack of a Budgetary Theory." *American Political Science Review,* December, 1940, pp. 1137–44.

MACMAHON, ARTHUR W. "Congressional Oversight of Administration: The Power of the Purse." *Political Science Quarterly,* June and September, 1943, pp. 161–90, 380–414.

MARX, FRITZ MORSETIN. "The Bureau of the Budget: Its Evolution and Present Role." *American Political Science Review*, August and October, 1945, pp. 653–84, 869–98.

NEUSTADT, RICHARD. "Presidency and Legislation." *American Political Science Review*, September, 1954, pp. 641–71.

PEARSON, NORMAN M. "The Budget Bureau: From Routine Business to General Staff." *Public Administration Review*, Spring, 1943, pp. 126–49.

RENICK, E. I. "The Control of National Expenditures." *Political Science Quarterly*, June, 1891, pp. 248-82.

SEIDEMANN, HENRY P. "The Preparation of the National Budget." *Annals of the American Academy of Political Social Science*, May, 1924, pp. 40–50.

SUNDELSON, J. WILNER. "Budgetary Principles." *Political Science Quarterly*, June, 1935, pp. 236–63.

THOMPSON, M. H. "The Control of National Expenditures: A Different View." *Political Science Quarterly*, September, 1892, pp. 468–82.

WALLACE, ROBERT ASH. "Congressional Control of the Budget." *Midwest Journal of Political Science*, May, 1959, pp. 151–67.

WILKIE, HORACE W. "Legal Basis for Increased Activities of the Federal Budget Bureau." *George Washington Law Review*, April, 1943, pp. 265–301.

WILSON, WOODROW. "The Study of Administration." *Political Science Quarterly*, June, 1887, pp. 197–222.

Government Documents

The Budget Appendix. Washington, D.C.: Government Printing Office, annual.

The Budget of the United States Govenment. Washington D.C.: Government Printing Office, annual.

CANNON, JOSEPH G. *The National Budget*. House Document 264. Washington, D.C.: Government Printing Office, 1919.

The Federal Budget in Brief. Washington, D. C.: Government Printing Office, annual.

Joint Financial Management Improvement Program. *Annual Report*. Washington, D.C.: Government Printing Office, annual.

National Bureau of Economic Research. *The National Economic Accounts of the United States: Review, Appraisal, and Recommendations*. Hearings of the Joint Economic Committee of the U. S. Congress. 85th Cong. 1st Sess. Washington, D.C.: Government Printing Office, 1957.

SCHULTZ, CHARLES L. *Recent Inflation in the United States*. Joint Economic Committee of the U. S. Congress, study paper no. 1. Washington, D.C.: Government Printing Office, 1959.

Special Analyses, Budget of the United States. Washington, D.C.: Government Printing Office, annual.

TAFT, WILLIAM HOWARD. *Message of the President of the United States on Economy and Efficiency in the Government Service*. 62d Cong. 2d Sess. Washington, D.C.: Government Printing Office, 1912.

U.S. Advisory Commission on Intergovernmental Relations. *Annual Report*. Washington, D.C.: Government Printing Office, annual.

U.S. Bureau of the Budget. *Statistical Reporter*. Washington, D.C.: Government Printing Office, monthly.

U.S. Commission on Organization of the Executive Branch of the Government (1947–49). *Budgeting and Accounting*. Washington, D.C.: Government Printing Office, 1949.

U.S. Commission on Organization of the Executive Branch of the Government (1953–55). *Budgeting and Accounting*. Washington, D.C.: Government Printing Office, 1955.

U.S. Congress. Joint Economic Committee. *Federal Expenditure Policy for Economic Growth and Stability*. Papers submitted by panelists appearing before the Subcommittee on Fiscal Policy. 85th Cong. 1st Sess. Washington, D.C.: Government Printing Office, 1957.

U.S. Congress. Joint Economic Committee. *The National Economic Accounts of the United States*. Hearings. 85th Cong. 1st Sess. Washington, D.C.: Government Printing Office, 1957.

U.S. Congress. Senate Committee on Government Operations. *Organizing for National Security*. Hearings before the Subcommittee on National Policy Machinery. 3 volumes. Washington, D.C.: Government Printing Office, 1961.

U.S. President's Commission on Budget Concepts. *Report of the President's Commission on Budget Concepts*. Washington, D.C.: Government Printing Office, 1967.

U.S. President's Commission on Economy and Efficiency. *Report of the Committee on Economy and Efficiency*. Washington, D.C.: Government Printing Office, 1912.

U.S. President's Commission on Postal Organization. *Towards Postal Excellence*. Washington, D.C.: Government Printing Office, 1968.

Index

321

PRAEGER LIBRARY OF U.S. GOVERNMENT DEPARTMENTS AND AGENCIES

DATE DUE

GAYLORD			PRINTED IN U.S.A.